William Faubion's

You are invited to the Best Choices on the Oregon Coast

# Books®

Published in the U.S.A.

For additional copies, write or call:
Apple Press Publishing
211 Oregon Pioneer Building
Portland, Oregon 97204-2672
(503) 243-1377

Apple Press Publishing "Best Choices Series"

SERIES #1: Best Choices in the Rural North Willamette Valley: 1985

SERIES #2: Best Choices on the Oregon Coast: 1986

SERIES #3: Best Choices Off Oregon's Interstate: 1986

SERIES #4: Best Choices in Central/Eastern Oregon: 1987

SERIES #5: Best Choices in Portland and the Tri-County Area: 1987.

Apple Press Publishing
Series #2
You are invited to the
Best Choices on the Oregon Coast

Copyright©1986 by Apple Press Publishing

All rights reserved. No part of this book may be reproduced in any form or by any electronic means, including information storage and retrieval systems, without permission in writing from the author, except by a reviewer who may quote brief passages in a review.

Library of Congress Catalog Card Number: 86-70781
ISBN: 0-9615833-1-2   First Edition 1986

To Shirley Saunders, a life-long Oregon resident who is the state's best cook and most supportive person. Her thousands of fine meals and never-ending patience are greatly appreciated by her son, the author.

Oregon's Coast

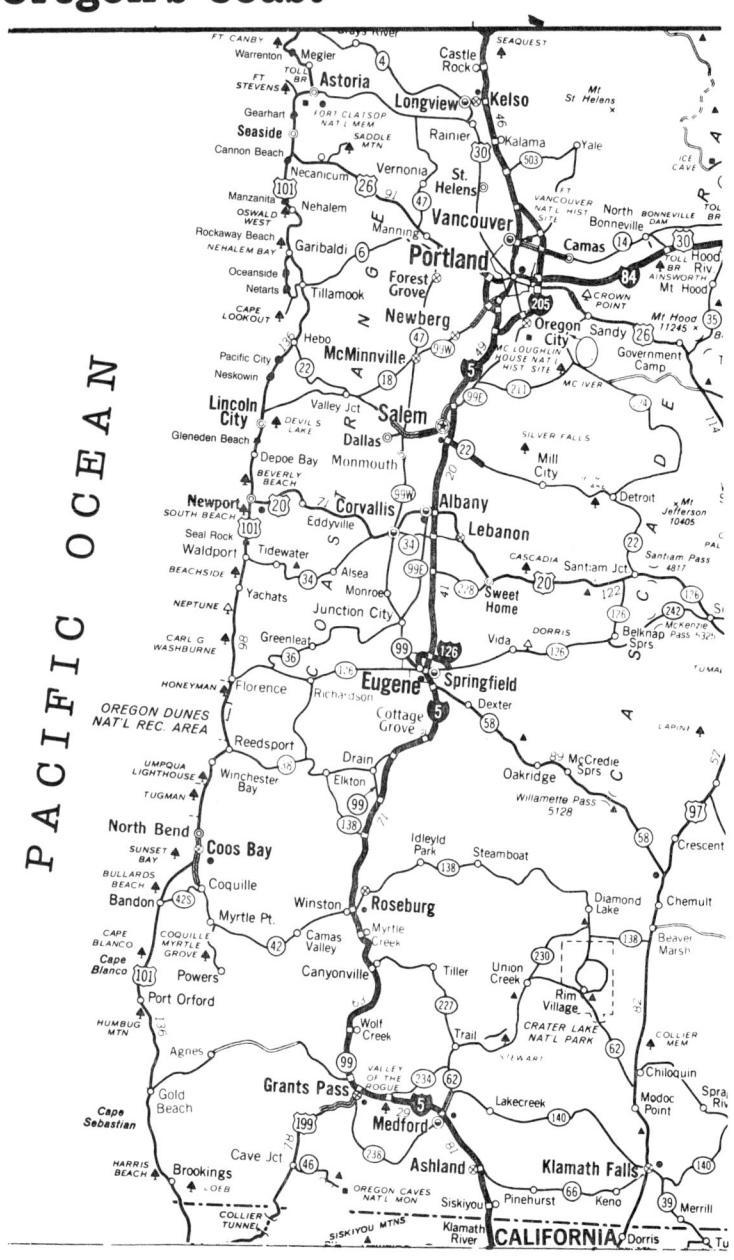

FOREWORD

Traveling the entire length of the Oregon Coast has to be one of the best experiences of my life. At each turn of Coast Highway 101, there for my discovery was another picturesque bay, a desolate beach or a quaint fishing village. There is something for everyone, from barren sand dunes to lush green forests, turbulent rivers to calm lagoons, and sophisticated art galleries to sand sculpture contests.

During the six months spent on the Oregon Coast in writing, I gained a new feeling of passion for the entire 300 miles. I started in Astoria on the northern coast where it looked to me as the city of San Francisco must have appeared to travelers 75 to 100 years ago, with Victorians dotting the steep hills, big ships docked at ports along the waterfront and a large fishing fleet poised to catch the sea's bounty. Travel 300 plus miles south to Brookings and you are in the Banana Belt of Oregon where flowers bloom all year, the famous fragrant lilies are grown and salmon fishing abounds. The temperature rarely gets below 50 degrees or over 75 degrees, with an average of 65 for the year.

Astoria to the north and Brookings to the south — and what's in between is truly impressive. Over twenty rivers filled with salmon, steelhead and trout, the most famous being the beautiful Rogue River. Other fantastic places include the Oregon Dunes National Recreation Area, Depoe Bay, Yaquina Bay, Siletz Bay, Tillamook Bay and Nehalam Bay with their oyster farms, boat rental businesses and charter fishing boats. The coast is a paradise for good food, casual fun and exciting shopping sprees. Some of the best gift shops in the country are found on the Oregon Coast, offering their unique wares. There are wine tasting rooms, apparel shops, art galleries and fun attractions. You can go down to Sea Lion Caves or up the the top of a lighthouse. I have personally visited every place in this book, so the accuracy of what is written should help you find just what you are looking for.

With a project this large, there are always many people to thank. I never could have completed this book on time without the help of my wife, Cindy Tilley Faubion, who had to raise our children almost alone during the long months I was traveling and writing. To Shirley and Bill Saunders, my mother and stepfather, who visited and helped write about some of the places in the book. To my mother-in-law, Ida Tilley, who assisted in writing and helped prevent my wife from being completely alone while I was traveling. Thanks also to Cindy Leavell, who entered the entire book on computer and would be considered an asset to anyone.

There were several contributing writers. John Harkins is a free-lance writer who makes his home on Sardine Creek near the Rogue River. He enjoys whitewater kayaking, downhill skiing and camping with his wife, Jenny, and their two children. He writes both fiction and nonfiction, and particularly enjoys research, especially for travel books.

Gary Cordova loves western sunshine, the open spaces of New Mexico, the Oregon and Maine coastlines, the Colorado Rockies, loud laughter and quiet smiles, poetry and short stories, holding hands with someone special on lazy days, people — young and old, his own secret recipe of lentil soup, and other places, events and things too numerous to mention. He was born in northern California, moved to New Mexico, and ended up in Colorado where he graduated from college while having fun and enjoying the beautiful country. The lure of more beautiful country brought Gary to Oregon where he pretends to be a freelance writer of poetry and fiction, and enjoys the interesting people in Ashland.

Toni Thomas loves God, people, sunshine, ocean sunsets, sand castles, holding hands and scribbling poetry in the woods. Toni has many vague past life experiences. She has done international advertising for Sheraton Hotels world headquarters in Boston, studied humanities and life in the British Isles for five years, backpacked her way across Europe, Turkey, Egypt, Israel and the U.S. She tells us she has attempted to "mustify the study of man" as part of her climb through a graduate degree in Counseling Psychology. She lives in Ashland and is smitten with Oregon's natural beauty, the kindness, and genuine goodhearted people she meets everywhere. She loves living and often grows goosebumps at the sheer wonder and beauty of life.

This book will help guide you through one of America's most beautiful places, 300 miles of the Oregon Coast's most pristine forests, its rocky shorelines, the sandy beaches, and the best reataurants, galleries, shops and accommodations. Spend a weekend or spend a year and you can still never get enough of the tranquility, the people you meet or the places you see. Come to the Oreogn Coast where your visit is truly appreciated. Thanks!

HOW TO USE THIS BOOK

No matter where you are headed on the Oregon Coast, I hope this book will make it more enjoyable. The book is set up on a county by county, city by city basis, starting with Clatsop County and the city of Astoria to the north, and following Oregon's Coastal Highway 101 south to Curry County and the cities of Brookings/Harbor which are just minutes from the California border. The chapters explain something about each city and its attractions, events, accommodations, shops and restaurants.

If you are interested in just one city, look it up in the county's chapter with easy reference in the Table of Contents. If you would like to have a day of adventure and good food, try our self-guided tours listed at the end of the city. I've tried to make your day complete with breakfast at a "best choice" rstaurant right down to a sunset stroll on a local beach.

As you read about the best choices, you will often find the message "See special invitation in Appendix" at the end of the copy. Turn to the back of the book to find the invitations listed city by city as they are in each chapter. The invitations are real! The merchants are inviting you to save at their establishments. Each invitation is for money off or a free gift with purchase. So, use your scissors and cut out your invitations to the best choices on the Oregon Coast. Remember, not *every* best choice was found because of the time allowed, so if you find one you like that is not listed, please write to us so we can include it in a future edition.

TABLE OF CONTENTS

Map of Oregon's Coast iv
Foreword v
How To Use This Book vii

Chapter One — Clatsop County
    About Clatsop County 1
    Clatsop County Parks 1
  Astoria
      About Astoria 2
      Accommodation List 3
      Map of Astoria 4
      Attractions 5
      Bakery 7
      Children's Apparel/Gifts 8
      Crafts/Gifts 9
      Events 9
      Museums 10
      Parks 11
      Restaurant/Deli/Gifts 12
      Restaurant/Gifts 13
      Seafood/Gifts 13
      Winery 14
      Women's Apparel 15
      Astoria Tour 16
  Gearhart
      Accommodations 17
  Seaside
      About Seaside 17
      Map of Gearhart/Seaside 18
      Accommodations 19
      Additional Accommodations 20
      Antiques and Collectibles 21
      Art Gallery 22
      Art Studio 22
      Attractions 23
      Bakery 25
      Bed and Breakfast Inn 25
      Candy 26
      Chocolates 27
      Christmas/Gifts 28
      Collectibles 29
      Department Store 30
      Events 31

    Gallery.. 33
    Gifts.. 34
    Golf 36
    Nursery and Gifts.............................. 36
    Restaurants.................................... 37
    Sporting Goods and Gifts 41
    Seaside Tour 42
Cannon Beach
    About Cannon Beach 43
    Map of Cannon Beach............................ 44
    Accommodations 46
    Additional Accommodations 45
    Antiques 46
    Candy 47
    Events 47
    Gallery/Gifts 48
    Gifts.. 49
    Gifts/Toys/Cards/Apparel 50
    Restaurants.................................... 50
    Seafood 53
    Stained Glass.................................. 53
    Theater 54
    Toy Shop 55
    Wine Shop 55
    Cannon Beach Tour.............................. 56

Chapter Two — Tillamook County
  About Tillamook County 57
  Attractions 58
Manzanita
    Accommodations 61
    Beaches 61
Nehalem
    About Nehalem 61
    Parks 61
    Map of Manzanita/Nehalem/Rockaway 62
Rockaway Beach
    About Rockaway Beach........................... 63
    Accommodation List 64
    Antiques 64
    Bed and Breakfast.............................. 65
    Gifts.. 65
    Kites 66
    Restaurants.................................... 67
    Women's Apparel................................ 67

Garibaldi
  Map of Garibaldi 68
  Bakery 68
  Events 69
  Gifts 69
  Restaurants 70
Tillamook
  Map of Tillamook 71
  Accommodations 71
  Cheese/Gifts 71
  Cheese/Restaurant/Gifts 72
  Gifts 73
  Gifts/Sporting Goods 74
  Restaurants 75
Netarts
  Accommodations 77
Oceanside
  Map of Netarts/Oceanside 77
  Accommodations 77
Pacific City
  About Pacific City 78
  Accommodations 78
Neskowin
  Accommodations 78
  Map of Neskowin/Pacific City 79
  Tillamook County Tour 80
Chapter Three — Lincoln County
  About Lincoln County 81
  Attractions 82
  Events 82
Lincoln City
  About Lincoln City 84
  Map of Lincoln City 85
  Accommodations 86
  Additional Accommodations 87
  Antiques/Gifts 87
  Art Gallery 88
  Art Gallery/Gifts 89
  Attractions 90
  Events 90
  Gifts 91
  Golf 94
  Leather 95
  Museum 96

    Restaurants 97
    Wine Tasting/Gifts 99
    Lincoln City Tour 100

Gleneden Beach
    Accommodations 101
    Additional Accommodations 102
    Gourmet Coffee 102
    Kitchen Gifts 103
    Restaurants 104
    Toys 105

Depoe Bay
    Map of Depoe Bay/Gleneden Beach 106
    About Depoe Bay 107
    Accommodations 108
    Additional Accommodations 108
    Attractions 108
    Charter Fishing 109
    Events 110
    Quality Seafood 110
    Restaurant/Accommodations 111
    Restaurant/Lounge 112

Newport
    About Newport 113
    Map of Newport 114
    Accommodations 115
    Additional Accommodations 116
    Art Gallery 117
    Attractions 119
    Bakery 124
    Charter Fishing 125
    Gifts 125
    Golf 126
    Oyster Farm 127
    Parks 128
    Restaurants 129
    Fresh Seafood/Deli 131
    Women's Apparel 132
    Yarn/Gifts 134
    Newport Tour 135

Seal Rock
    Map of Seal Rock 136
    Attractions 136
    Gifts 137

Waldport
    Map of Waldport 137
    About Waldport 137

    Accommodations 138
    Antiques/Gifts 139
    Events 139
    Parks 140
    Restaurants 141
    Rock Shop 141
    Seafood 142
  Yachats
    Map of Yachats 143
    About Yachats 143
    Accommodations 143
    Crafts/Gifts 147
    Events 147
    Myrtlewood Factory/Gifts 148
    Natural Wonders 148
    Restaurants 149
    South Lincoln County Tour 151

Chapter Four — Lane County
  About Lane County and Florence 153
    Map of Florence 154
    Accommodations 155
    Additional Accommodations 156
    Events 161
    Gifts 162
    Golf 163
    Ice Cream 164
    Myrtlewood Factory/Gifts 165
    Parks 166
    Restaurants 167
    Sporting Goods 169
    Florence Tour 170

Chapter Five — Douglas County
  About Reedsport/Winchester Bay 171
  Attractions 172
  Events 173
  Reedsport
    Map of Reedsport 173
    Accommodations 173
    Attractions 173
    Gifts 174
    Golf 174
    Restaurants 175
  Winchester Bay
    Map of Winchester Bay 177
    Attractions 177

Fresh Seafood/Cannery 178
Restaurants 179
Douglas County Tour 180

Chapter Six — Coos County
About Coos County/The Bay Area 181
Attractions 182
Events 184
Museums 185
Parks 186
Tourist Information Centers 187
Lakeside
  Map of Lakeside 188
  Attractions 188
North Bend
  About North Bend 188
  Antiques 189
  Art Gallery 190
  Crafts/Gifts 191
  Gifts 191
  Golf 192
  Restaurants 193
Coos Bay
  Map of Coos Bay 195
  Accommodations 195
  Art Gallery 197
  Clocks/Antiques 197
  Myrtlewood Factory/Gifts 198
  Restaurants 199
  Scuba/Skiing 201
  Seafoods 202
  Sporting Goods 202
  Toys/Gifts 203
  Bay Area Tour 204
Charleston
  Map of Charleston 205
  Oyster Farm 205
  Restaurant 206
Bandon
  Map of Bandon 207
  About Bandon 207
  Accommodations 209
  Attractions 210
  Books/Science Exhibit 214
  Candy/Gifts 215
  Cheese/Gifts 216

    Crafts/Gifts 217
    Events 217
    Gifts.. 219
    Museum 220
    Pizza 221
    Restaurants.................................. 221
    Seafood 224
    Women's Apparel.............................. 225
    Yarn/Gifts 225
    Bandon Tour 227
Chapter Seven — Curry County
  Port Orford
    Map of Port Orford 229
    Accommodations 229
    Art Gallery 230
    Attractions 231
    Gifts.. 232
    Restaurants.................................. 234
  Gold Beach
    Map of Gold Beach 235
    About Gold Beach 235
    Accommodations 237
    Attractions 238
    Bakery....................................... 241
    Gifts.. 241
    Resort 242
    Restaurants.................................. 243
    Gold Beach Tour 244
  Brookings/Harbor
    Map of Brookings/Harbor 245
    About Brookings/Harbor 245
    Attractions 246
    Bed and Breakfast............................ 247
    Boat and Fishing Outfitters 249
    Events 249
    Fishing Guide Service 251
    Gifts.. 251
    Parks 254
    Restaurants.................................. 256
    Restaurant/Bakery............................ 257
    Sporting Goods 258
    Brookings Tour 259
Appendix — Invitations 261

Chapter One

CLATSOP COUNTY

ABOUT CLATSOP COUNTY

"Deep in history" is a motto used often in describing the historical significance of this region of the Pacific Northwest. In fact, early events seeded far reaching effects in terms of Oregon becoming a part of the United States rather than being a foreign power possession. Although British and Spanish explorers set sail on the waters of the Oregon and Washington coastline in search of the fabled Northwest Passage, the Columbia River was not actually discovered until 1792. That year Captain Robert Grey of Boston entered the river and named it after his ship, the *Columbia*. Then in 1804, President Jefferson commissioned Lewis and Clark to head an expedition across the plains and western mountains to the Pacific Ocean. Lewis and Clark explored the lower region of the Columbia and set up camp at Fort Clatsop near Astoria during the winter of 1805-1806.

CLATSOP COUNTY PARKS

CULLABY LAKE COUNTY PARK

Highway 101 between Seaside and Astoria. Spread over 180 acres, the park offers picnic tables, fire pits, water and toilets. No overnight camping permitted. The lake is a favorite for fishing, swimming and water skiing. Four boat launching ramps are available.

ECOLA STATE PARK

Located between Tillamook Head and Chapman Point, the park spreads over more than 1100 acres including six miles of gorgeous shore frontage. Complete picnic facilities available and there are eight trail outlooks within the park offering breathtaking views as surf laps the coastline. The park is known for its colorful array of foliage and abundant wildlife.

FORT STEVENS STATE PARK

Just 13 miles west of Astoria on Route 101, this is one of the state's largest parks with 602 campsites and most modern facilities; extensive nature trails, bike paths, ocean beach areas noted for surf fishing and clamming. There are picnic tables, water, comfort stations, stoves and fireplaces. Good lake swimming and fishing. Open year 'round.

OSWALD WEST STATE PARK

Ten miles south of Cannon Beach on Highway 101 provides 21 large tent sites available to guests for a period of up to one week at nominal charges. Numerous trails lead off to the breathtaking viewpoints; picnic tables, electric stoves, comfort stations and water available. Park is noted for excellent stream and ocean fishing.

SADDLE MOUNTAIN STATE PARK

Off U.S. 26 about eight miles northeast of Necanicum Junction. Six campsites with picnic tables available. Climb to the top of the mountain for some very outstanding ocean views.

YOUNG'S RIVER FALLS COUNTY PARK

Fifteen miles south of Astoria on Loop Road; ten acre park with picnic tables, fire pits and drinking water. No overnight camping; lots of fishing, hiking and swimming for daytime visitors to enjoy.

ASTORIA

ABOUT ASTORIA

Fort Astoria, the first permanent American settlement on the Pacific Coast, was erected in 1811 by traders of the Pacific Fur Company. In the War of 1812, this fort passed into the hands of the British. In 1818, Fort Astoria was finally restored to the American flagship. The following decades brought many intrepid adventurers to the shores of the Columbia River. Astoria swelled with the likes of fur traders, explorers, homesteading pioneers and missionary settlers. Much of the colorful history of the county is exquisitely illustrated on the pictorial murals which adorn the exterior of the Astoria Column. Take a trip up to Coxcomb Hill to enjoy the historical embellishments on the column. If you wondered how Clatsop County received its name, it is a lasting tribute to the Clatsop Indians who, with many other Chinook tribes, made their home in Oregon. Lewis and Clark mentioned the tribe in their journals and lent their name to the expedition's winter encampment, Fort Clatsop.

CHAMBER OF COMMERCE

Here is a group of friendly people ready to welcome you and help handle your visitor needs while you are in Astoria. The Chamber has maps, accommodation listings, information on attractions, dining, camping and picnic areas, plus an update of special, upcoming events in the Astoria area. Call the Chamber at 325-6311 or stop by personally and get a good dose of community helpfulness. The office is located at the port docks in Astoria.

ACCOMMODATION LIST

CREST MOTEL
5366 Leif Erickson Dr.
Astoria, Oregon
503-325-3141

Jacuzzi, whirlpool, phones, coffee, HBO, radio, river view.

RIVERSHORE MOTEL
59 W. Marine Drive
Astoria, Oregon
503-325-2921

Forty-three units, kitchens, phones, movie channel.

ROSEBRIAR BED AND BREAKFAST
636 14th at Franklin
Astoria, Oregon
503-325-7427

Breakfast, eight units.

THUNDERBIRD/RED LION MOTOR INN
400 Industry (at Astoria Harbor)
Astoria, Oregon

124 units, restaurant, lounge, air conditioning, phones, TV, view of harbor.

4 Clatsop County

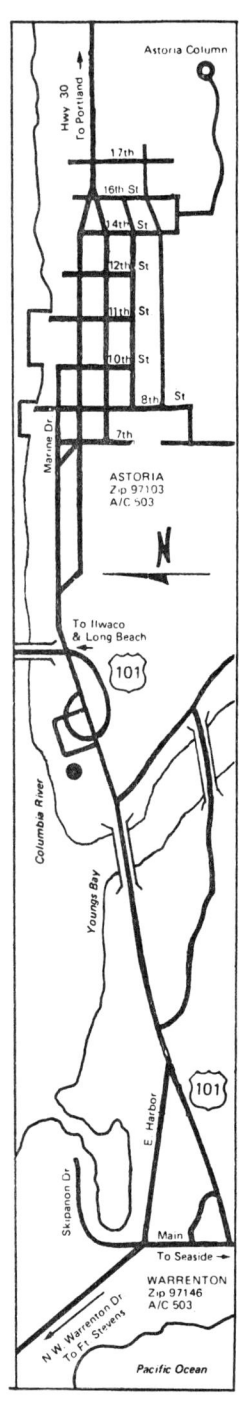

ATTRACTIONS

THE ASTORIA COLUMN
Coxcomb Hill
Astoria, Oregon

This is a must for visitors to the Northwest. Climb the 166 steps to the top of the tower for a breathtaking view of the Columbia River estuary, the surrounding countryside and dramatic coastline. The 125 foot tower was erected in 1926 by the Great Northern Railroad and is ideally poised at the top of treelined Coxcomb Hill which includes a fine park for family "lazying" amid great scenery. Pack a picnic lunch, romp in the salt air, and take in some unique history of the Astoria Column. You'll love the intricate, spiral decorations winding their way up the outside walls of the column. Artistic graffiti murals depict famous historical events that occurred within site of the tower. At night, the illumed column looks like a moon angel, visible to sailors as far out at 15 miles in the blue Pacific.

ASTORIA FLIGHT CENTER
(located at the Astoria Airport
just past the WW II blimp hangars)
Astoria, Oregon
503-861-1222 for directions and reservations

Imagine soaring high above Mt. St. Helens, then sweeping across to catch the sun dipping below our spectacular Oregon coastline. If you've always dreamed of capturing the panoramic natural beauty of Oregon from the air, then this is the place to make your fantasies come true. Donald Sokol, owner, has been flying for some 43 years. In fact, Donald tells us his flying experience dates back to WW II when he flew B-17 bombers on the longest and highest flight missions in the European theatre of Operations from southern Italy all the way to Berlin. So you can feel comfortable about the level of expertise here. The fleet includes everything from a Cessna 172 to a pressurized Baron. Numerous scenic flights are available plus an air taxi service that will whisk you up to Portland, Seattle, or any point you prefer. Fuel for aircraft is available from Dennis Williams plus flight instruction under the capable hands of Irv Allen. Prices are very reasonable and the views from up high are gorgeous. Be sure to bring the camera for some long-lasting memories.

KLAMATH HOUSE
Corner of 8th & Exchange
(diagonally across from Clatsop County Historical Museum)
Astoria, Oregon

Hours: 10am-dusk, almost every day

The Klamath House is included in a walking tour of Old Astoria, and for good reason — a long rustic, cedar shingled building, Klamath House dates back to pioneer Job Ross who constructed the house in 1852. Today it is one of the largest private pottery studios in Oregon. You'll love browsing through the unique displays of original high-fired stoneware pottery. Finish your visit outside on the deck where tea and coffee are served during summer months.

COLUMBIA RIVER BRIDGE
Astoria, Oregon

Don't miss the longest continuous truss bridge in the world. Originally opened in the summer of 1966, the Astoria Bridge boasts a truss span of 1232 feet in length and a whopping 4.12 miles of overall stretch connecting Oregon with Washington. It is even listed in the *Guinness Book of World Records*, so don't miss a drive across this one.

FORT ASTORIA
15th & Exchange Street
Astoria, Oregon

Visit the replica of the original blockhouse built in 1811 by seaman from the ship *Tonquin* sent from New York by the Pacific Fur Company to set up trade on the Columbia River. This fort became the first permanent American settlement on the Pacific Coast. You will capture a sense of real pioneer history as you smell the wood embers, musket fire and imagine the chill of hard, scanty winters lived by fur trapping adventurers of the early 1800s.

FORT CLATSOP NATIONAL MEMORIAL
Astoria, Oregon

Hours: 8-5 fall, winter & spring
8-6 mid-June thru Labor Day

Fort Clatsop was built in 1805 by the Lewis and Clark Expedition to serve as their winter quarters. Today the reconstructed fort is registered as a National Memorial and is open to visitors who will delight in reliving the pioneer days of our past. In summer, National Park Rangers dress in buckskin and offer living history demonstrations and programs. There is a visitor's center housing museum displays and exciting audio-visual programs take you back to the time of explorers blazing new trails on the journey west.

FLAVEL MANSION
8th & Duane Street
Astoria, Oregon
Hours: 10-5 daily

The year was 1883. Wealthy merchant and sailing fleet captain George Flavel decides to build the elegant home of his fancies in Astoria. Flavel commissioned a San Francisco architect to design his dream estate and then collected craftsmanship talents of a band of ship's carpenters to hand-chisel the details. The results — a splendid Victorian mansion with the elegance and workmanship of yesteryear, lovingly preserved for today's visitor. The local historical society has taken great pains to refurbish the mansion with the antique furniture and other artifacts of the period. You'll love Captain Flavel's unique fireplaces (there are six altogether), each of them framed in different mantels, exotic wood and different tile work. Don't forget to stop by the museum during your visit. Capture the distinctive flavor of the Victorian times as you stroll past period costumes, collector music boxes, dainty stoneware bone china, paintings and antique pianos. Enjoy the pioneer tools and period kitchen utensils also on display. This is definitely a best choice for you and the family during your visit to Astoria.

BAKERY

LINDSTROM'S DANISH MAID BAKERY
1132 Commercial St. (downtown)
Astoria, Oregon
503-325-3657

Hours: 5am-5:30pm Mon-Sat

When the scent of Lindstrom's fresh, ovenbaked breads mingles with crisp salt air, the result is irresistible. The bakery is steeped in Scandinavian heritage; well-tested, secret family recipes are blended with fresh ingredients and lots of tender, loving care to produce a delectable assortment of tempting baked goods. The Danish pastries and gooey cinnamon rolls have been longstanding favorites over the last 11 years. John and Jan Lindstrom create special occasion cakes, apple fritters, maple glazed buns, and a full selection of fresh bread loaves daily. You are going to have a tough time choosing from Saddle Mountain bread, whole wheat, caraway, light rye, sour dough, butter crust white and more. Absolutely no preservatives are used anywhere — just plenty of fresh eggs, butter, milk and a genuine love for baking and serving people. By the way, there is no need to rush your stay here. Sit down and relax at one of the tables and enjoy some amazing homemade soup, perhaps turkey or egg salad on fresh bread, and a warm cup of tea or coffee to round things off nicely. Prices here are very reasonable indeed.

(See special invitation in Appendix.)

CHILDREN'S APPAREL/GIFTS

YOUNG WORLD
1144 Commercial St. (downtown)
Astoria, Oregon
503-325-7722

Hours: 9:30-5:30 Mon-Sat

Some 20 years ago, owner Doris Nygaard began dreaming of a magical kingdom devoted solely to the world of children. The result is Young World, now the largest children's shop in the Northwest. It is assuring to know that all of the staff here are long-timers, loaded with experience. The newest employee started eight years ago. They bring a grandmother's touch to looking after the tender needs of our little people, and what an assortment you'll have to choose from among all the name brand articles. There is a wide selection of children's apparel ranging from infant to girls' size 14 and infants to boys' size 20. Roam around the durable, cuddly toys, clothing, accessories, and furniture which includes everything from rocking chairs, walkers, cribs, car seats to unique musical items that will delight little hands. Young World is just the place to bring out the kid hiding in all of us. By the way, prices are reasonable and the company makes a point of standing behind their products to ensure customer satisfaction. The shop has a gift wrapping service, too.

(See special invitation in Appendix.)

CRAFTS/GIFTS

NORDIC BUTIK
211 12th Street (downtown,
behind Owl Drugstore)
Astoria, Oregon
503-325-4883

Hours: 10-4 Mon-Fri, 10-2 Sat
Nov & Dec, open seven days a week

Come into this treasure of a shop and be transported into a Scandinavian hamlet of Old World gifts. Owner Ella Simonsen has been sharing warm smiles and making beautiful, delicate lace by hand here for ten years. You'll be able to watch the painstaking care as Ella works to make her beautiful bobbin lace. Then roam around the nooks and crannies of imported Nordic wares and international handcrafts. While the shop's specialties are Hardanger embroidery and bobbin lace, be sure to check out the frosted Diittala glass from Finland, intricate vases, handmade buckles, carved welcome signs and Scandanavian wall hangings. Ella carries a full line of unusual buttons, Nordic candle holders, Danish bobbins and charming Christmas decorations. Check out the Swedish sauna supplies and the Nordic book offerings. Gifts are mailed around the world; classes, supplies and instructions books in lacemaking are offered by Ella.

(See special invitation in Appendix.)

EVENTS

CLATSOP COUNTY FAIR
Astoria, Oregon

Clatsop County Fairgrounds is the place to be during the first week in August for a fantastic family hoedown. Enter the goat milking contest or the greased pig chase, and taste the beef sizzling on the barbecue pits. There are animals galore for the kids, plus livestock auctions, equestrian shows, tractor pulls and a ton of different foods, crafts, musical entertainment and educational booths. So get those cowboy hats ready for a whopping fun time, Oregon style!

REGATTA

This has to be the longest running community tradition held anywhere in the Northwest. After all, it dates back to 1894.

For about five days each summer in mid-August, the Astoria harbor area becomes one huge festival of dances, beer gardens, grand parades for children (and not so little ones), splendid foods, crafts and music. You'll be able to tour some of Astoria's historical seaside houses, check out the quarters of visiting military boats, and enjoy a unique boat parade complete with fireworks dazzling the night sky above the waterfront. The whole family will love the long list of festivities from salmon barbecues to hydroplane races and a one-eyed pirate dance. There is something for everyone at the Regatta.

SCANDANAVIAN MIDSUMMER FESTIVAL

Be transported to the Old Country for a day of Scandanavian frivolity right here in Astoria, U.S.A. Mark the third weekend in June on your calendar, for the whole family is in store for a real celebration. Delectable Danish pastries, flag raising ceremonies, parade, tug-of-war, traditional dancing 'til midnight, Swedish style, colorful costumes, music singalongs, and some of the best time-honored family style Scandanavian home cooking and folk crafts you are likely to find anywhere outside the fjords.

MUSEUMS

COLUMBIA RIVER MARITIME MUSEUM
Between 17th & 18th Streets
on Marine Drive
Astoria, Oregon

Hours: 9:30-5, every day, May 1-Oct 1
9:30-5 Tues-Sun, Oct 1-May 1

Get a salty dose of maritime heritage as the museum transports you and the family back to the exciting seafaring days of one hundred years ago where proud sternwheelers clipped the local waters and the billowing sails of elegant ships filled the coastal horizon as they glided in toward snug Oregon harbors. It is all here waiting for you during your visit to the Maritime Museum. There are remnants and relics from dozens of shipwrecks, collections of nagivation instruments, marine charts, paintings, handsome old ship figure wheels and fascinating exhibits on whaling, sealing and the Northwest maritime legacy. Check out the old revolving lens of North Head Light. The museum's collection of ship models ranging in size from a tiny three inch to a five-masted vessel measuring ten feet is one of the finest on the whole West Coast. And don't forget to venture on board Lightship 604, the *Columbia,* who after 30 years of regal service up and down the Columbia River, sits waiting for your inspection. She is moored just below the museum building as the largest artifact housed here. You'll love walking the squeaky plank deck with its proud sea dame. Good news! The moderately price museum admission tickets include climbing onto this unusual lightship. Don't miss your chance to navigate the seas through uncharted waters — the Maritime Museum in Astoria is just the place to let childhood fantasies come afloat.

PARKS

FORT STEVENS STATE PARK
Astoria, Oregon
For info, call toll free
1-800-452-5687

Imagine nature paths that lead to crystal lake water, old historic places that the kids will love exploring, jetties where you'll wash in ocean spray as the surf thrashes over boulder outcroppings, baby crabs scampering among seaweed as you sunbathe. Fort Stevens is not only one of the largest state parks in Oregon, but also one of the most historical. The Fort itself was originally built in 1864 to guard the entrance to the Columbia River. During WW II a Japanese submarine attack on this installation turned the fort into an historic landmark as the only U.S. military site to be attacked by an enemy since the War of 1812. Today the state park offers everything from superb day use picnic facilities to a huge campsite area accommodating 600 — everything from pup tents to RVs. There is a great film on Fort Stevens at the Visitor's Center plus miles of well-maintained trails for bike expeditions and peaceful nature strolls. Explore the beached wreck of the *Peter Iredale* sailing vessel. Watch the waves lick sand from your own secluded rook perch; do some bird observing in the woods; find out for yourself why this place holds a favorite reputation with local surf fishermen. The whole family will love the refreshing breezes and natural Oregon beauty ready to welcome you back to the outdoors and history here at Fort Stevens State Park.

RESTAURANT/DELI/GIFTS

PIER II MALL
Foot of 10th & 11th Streets
Astoria, Oregon
503-325-0279

There are four unique experiences in one mall location. Your trip inside Pier II will brim with the flavor of old wood and lots of hand-hewn character. Strategically placed on the Columbia River, the mall is carefully run by local owners Bill and Madonna Pitman and their three children. The fine dinner house itself has become something of a local landmark, steeped in some 30 years of Astoria's seacoast history. The restaurant and lounge area are open at 11am daily. We suggest a trip through the unusual 17 item salad bar or dip into one of the savory crab or turkey crepes smothered in cheese or mushroom topping. For dinner, we are partial to the quality you get from the prime rib and the King Neptune Casserole, a delicious blend of crab, shrimp, scallops and cod and the chef's specially prepared white sauce. The clam chowder is very good and dinners come with choice of soup or salad bar, potato or rice, rolls and coffee or tea.

Also, tucked in the mall is **Ye Olde Feed Store Deli**, a great deli featuring a wide selection of fresh meats, cheeses, salads, homemade soups and Oregon wines. Try the Washingtonian on sourdough or the Stormin' William on deli rye. There are croissants, bagels, fresh pies and cheesecake. Party catering is available and the Pitmans offer ready-to-go takeout orders when you phone ahead. Beyond all the delectable edibles, the Pier II Mall boasts a handsome kitchenware shop featuring nifty gourmet gift items and cooking pleasures, plus a shell shop which specializes in treasures from the sea. You'll have fun roaming around the displays of mugs, brass, glassware and unusual shell collectibles. The Pier II Mall, just the place for great river dining, or deliciously fast deli sandwiches, or gifts of high quality.

RESTAURANT/GIFTS

CAPTAIN FOX'S MARKETPLACE RESTAURANT AND GENERAL STORE
146 11th St. (look for the blue awning)
Astoria, Oregon
503-325-3011

Summer hours: 11-9 seven days a week
Winter hours: 11-3 Mon-Fri, 11-9 Sat

Feast your eyes on a unique view as the Columbia River flows its way to the deep blue ocean waters. Sit back, sip you wine or a cool Pina Colada, then begin another feast — this one laden with Louie Spevacek's homestyle knack of turning fresh catches-of-the-day seafood into great lunches and dinners. The Marketplace is a family-run business; the menu includes everything from fish to chicken served up with imaginative combinations of fresh vegetables, brown rice, soup and salad, all in hearty portions. For dinner, we thoroughly enjoyed the Sana De Pollo Rellinos — stuffed chicken breast served with chile rellinos. You might finish with an after-dinner cocktail as you relax in the restaurant's entertainment and soak up views of the breath-taking scenery. When you are visiting, check out the General Store where you will find lots of hand-crafted gift items, curio antiques, collectibles, mugs and a vintage slot machine collection. Banquet rooms available anytime.

(See special invitation in Appendix.)

SEAFOOD/GIFTS

JOSEPHSON'S SMOKEHOUSE AND DOCK
106 Marine Drive
Astoria, Oregon
503-325-2190
Toll free: 1-800-828-3474 in Oregon
1-800-772-3474 nationwide
Mon-Sat 8-6, Pacific Time Zone

Hours: 8-6 Mon-Fri, 9-5:30 Sat, 10-5 Sun

The Pacific Northwest's reputation here began way back in 1920 when the Josephson family first started applying traditional Swedish methods to smoking Columbia River salmon. Today, Michael and Linda Josephson have gained a nationwide reputation for the exceptional quality of their mail order specialty foods and numerous fine eateries by wholesale from Josephson's Smokehouse. The nova-style lox and traditional smoked salmon are made from the highest quality Chinook, and their tasty sides of smoked Sockeye salmon are all hand-processed in similar fashion. Michael explains that the quality curing process requires only a light dusting of salt; then the salmon is cold smoked slowly with alderwood. The natural ingredients of the salt and smoke make the use of any artificial preservatives, colors or flavoring absolutely unnecessary. The kipper products have the reputation of being unsurpassed. Only the best seafood varieties are used in them. Josephson's offers the highest standard, cold smoked Chinook, Alaska King, and Norwegian fjord salmon. Premium quality hot smoked salmon, sturgeon, black cod, Albacore tuna, trout, scallops and oysters are selected for careful processing. The smoked salmon jerky makes excellent snack and camping food. Cured products include Josephson's uniquely flavored pickled seafood. They offer salmon and sturgeon caviar and specialty items like Mediterranean-cured pepper salmon. Imagine some delectable gourmet pepper salmon, Oregon pine cured with aromatic herbs and spices the Scandanavian way with just a hint of the Oregon pine forest. You'll love your personal visit to the Smokehouse in Astoria. Copies of their handsome gift order brochures are available. There is also a current wholesale price list for all their specialty foods plus nationwide toll free numbers for customer order convenience.

(See special invitation in Appendix.)

WINERY

SHALLON WINERY
1598 Duane Street
(across from Maritime Museum on 16th St.)
Astoria, Oregon
503-325-5978

Hours: 12-6pm, seven days a week

Imagine a tasting room overlooking the mighty Columbia River where you can gingerly sip specialty wines and gaze at the ocean cruisers which seem to make the whole world look small as they float by. For Paul van der Veldt, what started as a hobby has become a consuming way of life. Little did he know when he began his passion back in 1978 that it would blossom into a full-time professional winery operation. Poised on the shores of the Columbia River, you'll be enthralled with this intimate little winery where the great taste of western woods mingles with local wild berries to produce a selection of rather unique wines. A native Astorian, Paul translates a great sense of local pride into his choice of wine ingredients. He makes more than a half dozen fruit and berry wines from the local cranberry, blackberry, peach and red huckleberries he prefers to use. In fact, the whole wine-making process is imbued with Paul's very own loving, unique story. The belief is that good vibrations encourage good wine. To this end, Paul plays trumpet music while mashing the fruit, Vivaldi's *Four Seasons* as it starts to forment, and chamber music for the duration of the long, mild fermenting process. The result — aromatic wines that recreate the rich, woodsy quality of the Clatsop forest. Try the cranberry and whey wine made here; it is exceptional and is the first of its kind. The wine tasting room is open most days from 12 to 6pm.

Note: The "Lemon Meringue Pie" wine is now out.

WOMEN'S APPAREL

BETTY'S CLOSET
1108 Commercial St. (downtown)
Astoria, Oregon
503-325-1169

BETTY'S FASHIONS
Young's Bay Plaza
just off Hwy 101
Warrenton, Oregon
503-861-1322

BETTY'S FASHIONS
Rainier Shopping Center
225 West B Street
Rainier, Oregon
503-556-2391

Hours: 10-6 Mon-Sat

When you are looking for distinctive clothing for women, you'll be hard pressed to find a more personal, quality line of apparel. Betty Bryant has lots of expertise when it comes to fashion. Her Rainier, Oregon, shop initially opened some 30 years ago. You might say that offering quality women's clothing has become a way of life for her and her whole family with daughter Patty running the downtown Astoria store, and Patty's husband, Lee Brinson, personally managing the Warrenton location. Although all three stores are slightly different, each shares the emphasis on friendly, knowledgeable staff, huge selection of women's apparel, and very attractive layouts. Together, the three of them buy many top clothing lines for the shops, everything from Catalina and Bay Club swimwear to Joyce and Wallstreet West sportswear. Slip into one of their silky evening dresses or try Jenelle lingérie and feel transported into a dream.

ASTORIA TOUR

These are suggestions for an enjoyable time in Astoria. They'll help you discover why this place is so wonderful. This tour is only an idea of what to do; you may want to make up your own tour after looking through all the best choices in the area.

TIME	PLACE	DESCRIPTION	HOW TO FIND IN BOOK
Breakfast	Danish Maid Bakery	Best breakfast treats	Astoria/Bakery
A.M.	Astoria Column	Best view	Astoria/Attractions
A.M.	The Columbia River Maritime Museum	Best museum	Astoria/Museums
Lunch	Captain Fox's Marketplace Restaurant	Best lunch	Astoria/Restaurant
P.M.	Nordic Butik	Best Scandanavian gifts/crafts	Astoria/Gifts
P.M.	Shallon Winery	Best wine/gifts	Astoria/Winery
P.M.	Josephson's Smokehouse	Best seafood/ historical	Astoria/Seafood
Dinner	Ye Old Feed Store (Pier II Mall)	Great dinner	Astoria/Restaurant/ Deli/Gifts
P.M.	Columbia River Bridge	Great view	Astoria/Bridge

GEARHART

ACCOMMODATIONS

GEARHART BY THE SEA
Ocean View Condos
10th & Marion Streets
Gearhart, Oregon
503-738-8331 or 1-800-452-9800

Restaurant, lounge, kitchens, pool, jacuzzi, fireplaces, golf.

SEASIDE

ABOUT SEASIDE

Locals aren't joking when they claim that the picturesque coastal community is the place "where good things are always happening." The range of activities and year 'round special events seems endless, but let's start with the beginning — some very old beginnings since Seaside's history dates back to pioneer days. The area was discovered back in 1805 when the Lewis and Clark expedition set foot here after many months of searching for an all-water route to the West. The Turn-a-round that exists today in Seaside is at the site where these early explorers ended their journey, and it is fittingly named *Trail's End*. In fact, it was the point of turning around for the Lewis and Clark Expedition.

Over the years, thousands of people have discovered the charm of Seaside and thrilled to the abundance of natural beauty and developed attractions here. Whether you are a brown bagging backpacker, a vacationing family or hectic businessperson, Seaside stands ready to meet your needs. Accommodations range from homestyle cabins and campsites to the finest, full-service resorts and luxury condominiums, plus everything in between. Restaurants also cover the gambit from fast food eateries to national award winners. The town has built a handsome city convention center capable of facilitating conventions up to 2000 and dining services for over 1000 people.

Beyond the hospitality and wide range of guest services, Seaside offers you even more — the beauty of the coastal outdoors and plenty of it. Enjoy beachcombing along stretches of virgin sand, try some razor clam digging, explore acres of state park or hike trails that give a glimpse of panoramic ocean vistas, lighthouses and magnificent sunsets over the Pacific. The options are endless — horseback riding, moped rentals, golf, fishing, surfing, miles of paved bicycle trails, shipwrecks to discover, roller skating or gently strolling down the two mile promenade that is right on the beach. Be sure to take a leisurely roam down the pedestrian lanes of Seaside's "million dollar walk" along which contemporary shops, intriguing emporiums and an endless selection of fun eateries wait, ready to tempt you with "out of this world" aromas. The special events offer you plenty to take advantage of throughout the year and, as locals know, although the sun dips magenta across the ocean when evening sets in, don't be too sure the sun ever really sets, for Seaside's nightlife and entertainment burn bright well into the wee hours for those with energy left from the day's adventures.

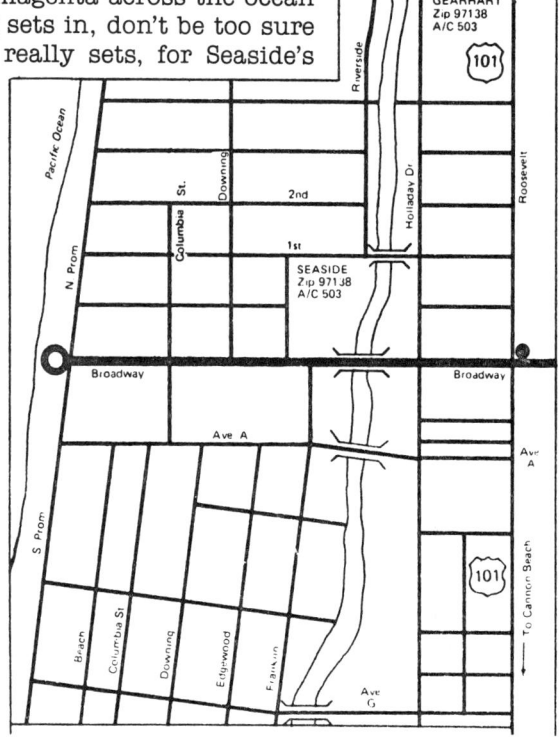

CHAMBER OF COMMERCE

The Seaside Chamber of Commerce is the place to go for all sorts of visitors' information and helpful service. Conveniently located at the intersecion of Hwy 101 and Broadway, the Chamber offers tips and brochures on accommodations, dining, area activities, side trips, special events and more. There is ample parking for cars, RVs and pickups. For visitors' convenience, they offer public restrooms and an RV dump station. For information about Seaside, call 503-738-6391 or in Oregon, call 1-800-452-6740.

ACCOMMODATIONS

HI-TIDE MOTEL
30 Avenue "G"
Seaside, Oregon 97318
503-738-8414 for reservations
    (Suggestion: call 60 days in advance
    for July, August or weekends)

Second location:
EBB TIDE MOTEL
300 North Prom
Seaside, Oregon 97318
503-738-8371 for reservations

With total ocean view on three floors, you'll find one of the best values in motel stays on the Oregon Coast. Features include indoor pool, rooms with fireplaces, comfortable beds, full bathrooms, jacuzzis (saunas at Ebb Tide), and a fantastic staff. Of the 64 units, 52 have kitchens which include pots, pans, dishes, coffee pots, reefers, two burner stoves and remote control TV, wall units. A great place to stay with the beach just outside your door, and close to shops and restaurants only blocks away. Hi-Tide is managed by Don and Norma Lichty; Rose Raniero and Barbara Lucker are managers of Ebb Tide; they are very friendly people and do all they can to make your stay enjoyable. For a best choice for relaxation and clean comfort — the Hi-Tide or Ebb Tide Motel in Seaside, Oregon.

ROYALE MOTEL
531 Avenue A (one block south of
Broadway, at the river)
Seaside, Oregon 97138
503-738-9541

Open year 'round

A motel with personality, close to everything, and a bargain for the traveling family or businessman. The view is not of the ocean, but there is a river with ducks and geese just outside your window. The rooms are always clean, all equipped with color cable TV with movie channel, phones, coffee pots and free coffee, lots of fresh towels, and good beds. The water pressure is great and I've never known of the hot water to run out. The owners, Mary and Henry Pinter, live on the premises to ensure high standards and are always available to help you find whatever you are looking for, whether it be a secluded beach, a great restaurant, or a particular gift shop. The rates will be pleasingly low, up to 75% lower than some other places in Seaside, with commercial rates promoted as the lowest in the area. A best choice for saving you money, giving you comfort and an enjoyable time — the Royale Motel. (Call in advance for reservations.) P.S., ask for one of the rooms with river view. You'll love it!

(See special invitation in Appendix.)

ADDITIONAL ACCOMMODATIONS

AMBASSADOR BY THE SEA
40 Avenue U
Seaside, Oregon
503-738-6382

Kitchens, food, view.

LANAI MOTEL
3140 Sunset Blvd.
Seaside, Oregon
503-738-6343

Phones, pool, kitchens, free movie channel.

SEASHORE MOTEL
(Best Western) On the Prom
60 N. Prom
Seaside, Oregon
503-738-6368

Pool, sauna, whirlpool.

SHILO INN
30 N. Prom — on the Turn-a-round
Seaside, Oregon
1-800-222-2244 or 503-738-9571

Lounge, restaurant, kitchens, pool, movie channel.

SUNDOWNER MOTOR INN
125 Ocean Way
Seaside Oregon
503-738-8301

Pool, jacuzzi, sauna, showtime, kitchens, phones.

ANTIQUES AND COLLECTIBLES

ANITA'S CORNER
In the Wind N' Sea Building
(Heart of Broadway)
416 Broadway
Seaside, Oregon 97138
503-738-7659

Winter hours: Open Thurs-Mon
Summer hours: Open seven days
    10:30-5 Mon-Sat, 1-5 Sun

Anita Merrill is owner of this great shop located on Broadway in Seaside, Oregon. With help from her husband, Del, Anita's Corner has become well known for very fair prices and one of the best places for toys and antique jewelry anywhere. Anita doesn't have to give discounts to anyone; her prices are already as low as she can go. Anita is a very unique person — friendly, honest and knowledgeable. Everything you purchase is guaranteed and here are just a few examples of what she carries: vintage charms, lockets, rhinestone brooches, necklaces, bracelets, rings, and much more. If your jewelry chest is full, Anita has other items to tempt you — antique garments, old books, records, salt and pepper sets, rare occupied Japan pieces, and collectible dolls. They have a nice selection, the nicest shopkeeper you'll ever want to meet, and a very convenient, easy-to-find location. Anita's Corner — a definite best choice.

(See special invitation in Appendix.)

ART GALLERY

THE WEARY FOX ART GALLERY
111 Broadway, Suite 11
Sand Dollar Square
Seaside, Oregon
503-738-3363

Summer hours: 10-6 seven days,
   Open 'til 9 on Fri & Sat
Winter hours: 10-6, closed Tues except
   closed Tues-Thurs in January & February

Second Location:
F. W. FOX ART GALLERY
2190 W. Burnside
Portland, Oregon
503-227-2775

Open Wed-Sat, noon-6, or by appointment

An outstanding gallery representing northwest and internationally known artists with fine art and quality gifts. Asian art, including Japanese wood blocks, Chinese paintings, antique furniture, fine pottery, porcelain, jewelry, sculpture, wood carving. This gallery is special because of the artistic people who own and manage it, Fred and Cathrine Maloon and Barbara Bassette. They seem to have the knowledge of art that goes beyond the normal gallery operator, with every item displayed to perfection, every artist's pieces picked for the best look of the '80s. This gallery was talked about from one end of the coast to the other. You must take time to see this display of art. Even with a limited budget or when buying for the office you will come away satisfied — a best choice for Oregon and for the lovers of beautiful things — The Weary Fox Art Gallery in Seaside and Portland.

ART STUDIO

LYNN'S ART STUDIO
317 S. Columbia
Seaside, Oregon 97318
503-738-8833 or 738-8938

Open Tues-Sat 10-5, or call for appointment

The Oregon Coast has a magnetic draw for people who have creative abilities. The beauty and the seclusion add up to a perfect place for an artist or writer to find themselves doing their best work. In Seaside, I was fortunate to meet with a very special artist, the congenial Lynn Campbell of Lynn's Art Studio. The studio is two blocks from the beach, but conveniently located in downtown Seaside on the corner of South Columbia and Avenue A. The studio is open to the public and Lynn is more than happy to have anyone stop by and watch her create a scene on canvas. Lynn's work has been shown at many fine shows and she does many commissioned paintings each year. Her specialties are landscapes, seascapes, florals and birds. She also does exceptional human or pet portraiture. She told me that she prefers to meet her subjects, but if that is not possible, she will work from a photograph. Lynn Campbell teaches custom painting and offers frames and framing. She also offers limited edition prints, notes and a personality you won't want to miss. A best choice in creativity — Lynn's Art Studio in Seaside.

See special invitation in Appendix.)

ATTRACTIONS

COVE AREA
Seaside, Oregon

At the base of Tillamook Head you'll capture a sweeping view of the beach. The "Unknown Sailor's Grave" rests here. A simple stone slab marks the gravesite of four unknown Portuguese sailors who were washed ashore in 1865. The cove area is also a favorite spot for you to enjoy some relaxed fishing or for the more daring to try some wave surfing.

LEWIS AND CLARK SALT CAIRN
Seaside, Oregon

The year was 1806 and the fierce bite of winter was setting in fast. Times were rather "inhospitable" for members of the Lewis and Clark Expedition. They were faced with scant rations, blustery winds and unsafe territory. This reconstructed salt cairn indicates the location where these pioneer men set about boiling sea water to obtain the salt they needed to weather the harsh winter climes of that yesteryear.

MILLION DOLLAR WALK

Your adventure begins at the Seaside Chamber of Commerce and extends the length of Broadway Street, right down to the Promenade and next to the billowing waves of the Pacific

Ocean. Broadway hosts a delightful assortment of eateries, gift emporiums, novel shops, everything from collector music boxes to colorful kites and wind socks. European sidewalk cafes oozing aromas of expresso coffee, scrumptious Danish pastries, specialty seafood, euphoria, truffles, and intricate scrimshaw await you. It's all here, framing your pedestrian stroll along the Seaside Million Dollar Walk.

SEASIDE AQUARIUM

Dive into the depths of aqua sea, watch an octopus change color right before your eyes, greet playful seals flapping "welcome", check out the leopard and sand sharks — lots of ocean antics here for the whole family. Moderate admission charge.

SEASIDE MUSEUM
Corner of 5th & 6th Avenues
at Necanicum
Seaside, Oregon

Open weekends and holidays 1-4

Take an historic look at Oregon's oldest resort community through the intriguing collection of photographs, memorabilia and Indian artifacts housed here. There is also an exhibit depicting the region's logging history.

SEASIDE PROM

The Turn-a-round at the end of Broadway Street marks the official end of the Lewis and Clark Trail. The 8000 foot Promenade located here was built in 1920. Enjoy a stroll, skate or bicycle ride along the amazing stretch and curl up for the evening on one of the comfy benches to watch the romantic sunset across shimmering ocean.

TILLAMOOK HEAD TRAIL

Enjoy a wonderful day's hike along this head trail which measures about six miles each way. Allow a leisurely 2-3 hours for each direction so you can have ample time to soak in the coast's beauty. A great place to spread your picnic is right around Look Out Point with Tillamook Lighthouse within your sight. The views along this trail are lovely. The hike will invigorate the whole family along with fresh sea breezes, open spaces and beautiful coastline.

BAKERY

THE CINNAMON ROLL SHOP
300 Broadway (inside front entrance,
Town Center Mall)
Seaside, Oregon
503-738-3433

Do you love cinnamon rolls? This shop could actually be called "the freshest, the gooiest, the best cinnamon roll shop in this galaxy." You see, every morning Barbara Hayward, owner, with her husband, Jim, show up to make the best cinnamon rolls from scratch anyone has ever tasted. The recipe is a guarded family secret that has been handed down for generations in Jim's family. Customers actually line up outside the window watching the rolls being prepared and coming fresh out of the oven. The cinnamon rolls come frosted or "gooey", raisins or no raisins, and that's it except for coffee or juice — that's all the Haywards sell here. You have to try this best choice, a true flavor of Oregon — The Cinnamon Roll Shop in Seaside.

BREAD AND BREAKFAST INN

THE BOARDING HOUSE BED AND BREAKFAST INN
208 N. Holladay Drive
Seaside, Oregon 97138
503-738-9055

A new experience for the modern traveler was a traditional mode of accommodation just a few years ago. Bed and breakfast inns are what people of an earlier generation affectionately called boarding houses, a place where you could get a home-cooked meal, a good night's sleep and meet other travelers. Today a renaissance of the boarding house concept has arrived in Seaside, Oregon, called The Boarding House Bed and Breakfast Inn, with the motto "This old house serves comfort" (and that could well be an understatement). The house and its hosts, Dick and Carole Rees, would have made most boarding house travelers of the past think that they were in a palace. The house has six separate rooms — enough to accommodate up to 20 people (perfect for many business conferences), a large parlor with crackling fire, gourmet breakfasts, clean fresh rooms, private baths, and new beds. There is also "The Cottage" behind the main house, fully equipped with a deck overlooking the river and loaded with country charm. It is a place for a different kind of adventure, a place for rest, fun and the meeting of new friends, an old and traditional way of spending the night away from home, but updated to the '80s thanks to Dick and Carol Rees's Boarding House Bed and Breakfast Inn.

THE GILBERT HOUSE BED AND BREAKFAST INN
341 Beach Drive (One block east of the Prom; Corner of Beach Drive and Avenue A)
Seaside, Oregon 97138
503-738-9770

Stay at The Gilbert House Bed and Breakfast Inn, and a real experience can unfold. A kind of dreamy place built in the 1800s by Alex Gilbert, a wealthy lumberman. The house is full of history and peaceful rest with room enough for small business conferences or a weekend retreat for storm watchers. The house is large enough to have a conference room, parlor and large dining room. Complimentary wine is served in the parlor. The beach is just one block away with hiking, bicycling, clamming and beachcombing. This is the closest bed and breakfast to the beach in Seaside. Your hosts, Pat and Rosemarie Link, believe in pampering their guests and will take care of your every need. Rosemarie makes a good, nourishing breakfast, offering coffee, tea, sweet rolls, plus entre. Hopefully you can be there on the day she makes her souffle — it's great! So for a best choice in comfort, call for a reservation at The Gilbert House Bed and Breakfast Inn. You'll end up with a real experience.

CANDY

PHILLIPS CANDIES
217 Broadway,
Seaside, Oregon
503-738-5402

Since 1897, people have been experiencing the sweet taste of the Oregon coast at a very special shop — a shop filled with hand-dipped chocolates, licorice ropes, tasty caramel corn, cheese corn, popcorn, gummies, jelly beans, candy corn, and most importantly, the candy that made this tasty place famous, saltwater taffy. You see, a young teenaged girl named Margurette was working at her first summer job in 1926. As her customers' good fortune would have it, she worked at the candy store until she was wed to a fine young man named Phillips. Then Mr. and Mrs. Phillips purchased the store from the original owners and began to run what was, through hard work and a knack for good taste, to become a candy store famous for quality called Phillips candies. Their calling card became saltwater taffy with flavors like butter, molasses, peppermint, strawberry, chocolate, almond, licorice, peanut butter, lime, vanilla and a special flavor that is the number one best seller, cinnamon. The boxes of chocolates that are hand-dipped by Phillips are unique with the best mixes inside, and outside, real Oregon driftwood for unique displays on the box. Candy can be shipped all over the United States and the Phillips saltwater taffy is offered in some of Oregon's most prestigious stores. Steve Phillips, Margurette's son, now manages the candy store with the same pride and care his parents had. A best choice for the sweet taste of Oregon's coast — Phillips Candies on Broadway Street in Seaside.

(See special invitation in Appendix.)

CHOCOLATES

COLUMBIA CHOCOLATES BY MORDENS
First intersection east of Broadway turnaround
Seaside, Oregon
503-738-3612

Summer hours: 10-8, seven days a week
Winter hours: 10:30-5, seven days a week

Second location:
1213 Commercial Street
Astoria, Oregon
503-325-4744

Open 10-5:30 Mon-Sat

Chocoholics will love this store, stocked full of hand-dipped chocolates and fresh-made fudge, with nothing chocolate on the shelf being over a few days old. The owners, Donald and Anne Morden, were made to be in the candy business and like fate, were brought to the northern Oregon coast with diverse backgrounds. Donald, with a degree in food technology from Iowa State, was brought to Oregon from the Carnation Company. His wife, Anne, teaches home economics. Put these two talents together and wow! what a combination for great candy. You don't have to love chocolate to enter this store. They have jelly belly beans, fancy suckers, gummy bears, and much more. But if you are visiting the coast and you need to take home the perfect gift for a chocolate lover, try the chocolate pizza. The base is loaded with peanuts and marshmallows, all chocolate coated, then jelly bellies are added. After sprinkled with coconut and white chocolate to look like mozzarelli, it is put in a pizza box. It weighs over a pound. Perhaps you would prefer more elegant boxed candies in one of their two pound boxes. A perfect place to buy chocolate on the cool, Oregon coast and a best choice for fresh candy year 'round — Columbia Chocolates by Mordens.

(See special invitation in Appendix.)

CHRISTMAS / GIFTS

MRS. CLAUS' EMPORIUM
8 North Downing Street
Seaside, Oregon 97138
503-738-3133

Open 10-6, seven days a week

The Christmas spirit is turned on year 'round in Seaside thanks to one special business and two special people who own and manage it. The place is Mrs. Claus' Emporium and the names are Marty and Jack Phillips. This shop is full of everything you've ever dreamed of for decorating your home for the holidays with old-fashioned bubble lights, ornate door hangers, Christmas trains, German nutcrackers and so many beautiful and unusual things it is impossible to mention them all. Marty Phillips started the shop eight years ago. Being an intelligent businesswoman and the original Mrs. Claus, she has turned this into the best choice in Christmas shops anywhere in the world. The store produces a quality Christmas tabloid that you can find at many Chamber of Commerce offices all over the United States. Ask your chamber for one; it will list the Christmas store closest to you. If you are going to be in Seaside, ask anyone where Mrs. Claus lives and they will show you the way to the best choice in Christmas shopping year 'round — Mrs. Claus' Emporium.

(See special invitation in Appendix.)

COLLECTIBLES

DAVID'S FINE PORCELAIN AND CRYSTAL
515 Broadway
Seaside, Oregon 97138
503-738-7372 or
738-6097 for appointment

Open 11-5 Mon-Sat, noon-2 Sun
or by appointment anytime

Finding a beautiful shell on the beach or discovering a quaint little shop full of fascinating things are moments that become unforgettable when traveling the Oregon Coast. Located on Seaside's famous Broadway, you'll find a quaint little shop that is unforgettable. It is David's Fine Porcelain and Crystal, full of pieces you would expect to find in the finest stores in New York, London or Hong Kong. David's specializes in collectible plates and has one of the largest displays of Bing and Grondahl's and Royal Copenhagen Christmas plates you'll see anywhere in the United States. David Pratt is the owner of this wonderful shop and lists 16 years in the same location. His expertise in buying beautiful items goes without saying. A quick look will give you the idea of David's taste with over 1200 plates in stock, dating back to 1895. It is a collector's paradise. David told me that he buys in enough quantity to have two to three years of inventory on hand for each piece. His shop also specializes in Cybis porcelain with over 120 pieces displayed — Children To Cherish, Woodland, Birds and Animal Kingdom, Portraits in Porcelain, just to name a few of the series in stock. Daum crystal with its marvelous texture, Baccarat and Lalique crystal from France, Moser crystal from Czechoslovakia — it is all displayed in beautiful pieces. An item you must ask to see is a hand-made paper weight made in Oregon. The shop has many other unique crystal and porcelain pieces, more than we can list, but David takes time to find other high quality, decorative and useful items. David's Fine Porcelain and Crystal is definitely an unexpected pleasure and a best choice for lasting memories and beauty on the Oregon Coast.

DEPARTMENT STORE

TEENA'S SHOES, GIFTS AND CLOTHING, INC.
600 Broadway (just before
you go over the bridge)
Seaside, Oregon
503-738-5557

Winter hours: 9:30-5:30
Summer hours: 9:30-6:30 Sun-Thurs, 9-7 Fri-Sat

New York, Houston and San Francisco are fine cities known for their great places to shop like Saks Fifth Avenue and Macy's. Those cities are also known for crowded sidewalks and bumper-to-bumper traffic. There is a city where you can find great places to shop without the crowds or traffic. It is Seaside, Oregon, and the store is not Macy's — it is Teena's Shoes, Gifts and Clothing, which would equal any fine department store in any major city in the U.S. Teena's owner is Teena Jarred, who has been in the same location for over 23 years selling "the best of everything," as she puts it: the best in clothing with beach ware, evening wear, leisure wear, sleep wear, swim wear, with brands as well-known as Cole of California, Miss Elaine, R & K originals, Alafost Iceland sweaters, LiliAnn with a line of fine colognes and perfumes by After 5 Auvergne, shoes for dress, work and fun for men, women and children. From Step and Stride, Nike, Young Set to Weyenberg dress shoes for men, Texas brand boots, Rockport for women, deerskins, Cobbie Cuddlers, and on and on. Like all fine department stores, clothing, shoes and perfume are not all Teena's has in their massive inventory. Gifts and collectibles take up a huge part of this large store — items from Belleck, hand-made leather moccasins for the whole family, a full line of Prince Gardener for him and her, jewelry for her, copper items, antique jewelry, Fostoria, Aynsley fine bone china, music boxes, Ebeling and Russ fine china and crystal, baskets, glasses, hand-carved and painted wooden ducks, German beer steins, myrtlewood, collectible lead crystal bells, Hummel dolls and plates, and more. This store has something for everyone and prices are better than you are going to find almost anywhere. A best choice for clothes, shoes and gifts — Teena's on Broadway Street in Seaside.

EVENTS

The calendar of Seaside events runs the year 'round. Every season there are special, festive goodies to keep you entertained during your visit. Here is a list of possible choices in seasonal order:

Summer—

Independence Day Fireworks Display — The Seaside Chamber plans a whole program of 4th of July fireworks by the Town Turn-a-round on the beach. Watch the magic of starbursts careening through the sky above the Pacific Ocean.

Miss Oregon Pageant — For over 39 years, this coastal community has played host to the finals competition for Miss Oregon. The pageant takes place in July when regional winners compete for the chance to be coronated as Oregon's entry in the Miss America Pageant held in Atlantic City. The event takes place at the Convention Center and performances for preliminary judging are open to the public. The town hosts a special parade to celebrate the pageant.

Seaside Beach Run — Come August, for the past 19 years, the Seaside Turn-a-round has played host to a lot of run arounds where recreational as well as seasoned pro runners have enjoyed running on gorgeous expanses of beachfront as part of this unique event. Aside from plenty of fun runs and a challenging 10K meet, there will be all manner of new games being played throughout the day. Playful is the main name of the game and there is plenty of it, so plan to be there.

Volleyball Tournament on the beach — This event has become rather infamous as the largest event of its kind in the whole Pacific Northwest. Last year about 900 players showed up in August to participate in the sport of the day. There are categories of all levels of volleyball experience. The location is Seaside Beach off the Turn-a-round.

Dahlia Parade — Imagine a parade held each August where only children 13 and under are allowed to participate. The idea is to promote positive family involvement and honor all our wonderful little people. By the way, only "kid power" vehicles permitted, of course.

Fall Events

Cruisin' the Turn-a-round — Imagine a crisp, September day marked by some 90 cars—everything from specialty vintage models to Corvettes and hotrods all doing the annual cruise around the Seaside Turn-a-round.

Oktoberfest — In late September, Seaside's community sets aside a weekend of German festivities that can't be beat. Hear the yodels of another era. Step back into the Old Country atmosphere of German music, street dancing, knockwurst and kraut, rich pastries and, of course, the clanking of beer steins as everyone toasts the love, laughter and gaity that is life.

Great Pumpkin Festival — This special Halloween Party has become a tradition among locals. Children from throughout the Seaside community arrive at the Convention Center for a spooky assortment of ghostly games and caramel apple fun.

Winter Events—

Christmas Gift Fair — The magic of this special fair comes from the local people. It is a warm community gathering aimed at celebrating the holiday spirit of caring and sharing. Held annually at the end of November, the event features a huge selection of strictly homemade craft items just in time for the yuletide season.

Christmas at the Beach — In Seaside, a whole month of activities deck the joys of the holiday season. The yuletide merriment is ushered in with "grand illumination" in a lighting ceremony on Friday after Thanksgiving. There is old-fashioned caroling, traditional children's Santa programs, a window decorating contest and scrumptious holiday feasts.

The North Coast Barbershop Quartet Cabaret — Imagine over 700 of the Northwest's top barbershop singers gathering together in January for a tunefull evening of listening pleasure. Plan to enjoy a full evening of harmony and nostalgia at the Seaside Convention Center.

Trail's End Marathon — February marks one of the West Coast's oldest and finest runs. Marathon runners from coast to coast arrive in Seaside to pound their way over 26 miles toward the hope of victory.

Spring Events—

North Coast Home and Garden Show — Seaside Convention Center plays host each March to this event where you'll get a chance to check out the latest in home and garden ideas.

Country Western Dance — Dust off your dancing shoes and cowboy hats to get ready for a hoedown. Springtime fever in late March sets Seaside a-stompin'. There is live music, dancing lessons, square dance and western dance shows, and plenty of family fun for everyone.

GALLERY

DIMENSIONS WEST GALLERY
2020 S. Holladay (Hwy 101)
Seaside, Oregon 97138
503-738-6431

Winter hours: Fri-Sun 1-5 or by appointment
Summer hours: Fri-Tues 11-5 or by appointment

Like a walk on a lonely beach, the experience of Dimensions West will give you that creative feeling from inside. This gallery is operated by artists Richard and Barbara Hall. Through their own mastery of metal and jewelry, the Halls can help a person rediscover the need for art in one's life, and that is the main reason the gallery has opened. Metal sculpturing is chemicals, heat and hammer working to form something from within the artist. The real reason has been found by the Halls. With their creative wisdom they design jewelry and metal sculpture to fit your own personality, your lifestyle. Or, if you have an office and you want to promote a certain feeling, the Halls can custom design a sculpture for a specific space that will emit that feeling you want to project. The Halls have been at their art for many years and have taught others the skill it takes to perform the task of pleasing others. At present, a local community college has an accredited program taught by the Halls in their gallery workshop. Richard and Barbara are available for individual workshops from two days to two weeks. These classes are offered primarily for professionals and others seeking indepth knowledge and very specialized skills. Among the many beautiful items shown to me as I toured the gallery is the body sculpture the gallery produces. One piece fits around the neck, forged hollow from gold and silver, flowing with your body lines — a magically appealing sculpture that is worn with beauty and pride. If you are ever in need of a crown for a wedding or other occasion, they have crowns available which look as if they could have been worn by a medieval queen. They work with almost any metal including gold, silver, bronze, titanium, the ancient Japanese metal technique Mokume-gane, aluminum and steel. The Halls even have a unique leasing program set up so you can lease sculptured pieces and rotate them throughout a given time period. Barbara and Richard Hall's Dimensions West Gallery is a best choice for you to open your creative senses and to help you find art you can identify with. (If it is a storm-free day, ask to see the Japanese Gardens just behind the gallery.)

GIFTS

GRANDERSON'S
210 S. Columbia
(½ block south of Broadway)
Seaside, Oregon
503-738-8265
Open Mon-Sat 9:30-5:30, Sun noon-4

With only quality merchandise, unforgettable displays, a friendly, intelligent staff, and gifts for the entire home, you can hardly believe such a store can be in such a remote coastal town. But Seaside, Oregon, has it all and then some with Granderson's. This gift shop is the kind you look for all over Portland or San Francisco and never find. Prices are fair and the inventory is huge. The five specialty departments are kitchen, dining, bath, bedroom and gifts. Ken Grant and Shirley Anderson are the two creative owners of Granderson's with a total of 40 years experience in retail between the two of them. Ken is on an advisory board of a retailers' publication called *Gifts and Decorative Accessories* which advises other similar retailers throughout the nation. You know before you ever walk into Granderson's that the shopping experience is going to be fun because the window displays are the best you'll see on the coast (and maybe in the whole Northwest)! Inside, everything is displayed by departments, so if you have a friend who needs bath items or a gourmet chef on your list, you can enter into a whole section of whatever you need. In the kitchen department, you will find cooking demos by nationally famous or local authors of cookbooks. In the gift area, you will find collectible items you never dreamed you could find. If you are a teddy bear collector, you must see the Granderbears, made exclusively for Granderson's, very elegant bears with velvet tucks and bowties, dated and signed. A best choice may be an understatement! You can see for yourself — something for men, women, children, everyone — a great store in a remote coastal village which has everything because of Granderson's, and then some.

OREGON ONLY
3111 Highway 101 North Gearhart
Seaside, Oregon 97138
503-738-3396

When you are traveling in Oregon, it is great to find gifts which are authentic, Oregon-made arts, crafts, foods and inventions. That is all you'll find in Oregon Only, a unique store full of great smells, great sights, great tastes and great experiences of Oregon. The smells you get come from the in-store bakery, baking up wholesome breads and pastries strictly from natural ingredients, with some of the recipes being endorsed by Oregon's own late James Beard. The great sights come from a special artwork — sculpture, pottery, ceramics, paintings, and more that fill up the store. Great tastes are from the bakery and Oregon-made candies, jams, jellies and honeys. The great experiences will be at every turn, as you watch local artists actually performing their art — etched glass, potters and artists, to name a few. The store has Oregon-made toys, furniture and original creations, the prices are very, very fair. So if you think Oregon is a best choice, try Oregon Only for gifts and goodies — it is definitely a best choice.

(See special invitation in Appendix.)

SEASIDE AGATE SHOP
408 Broadway
Seaside, Oregon 97318
503-738-5633

Summer hours: 8am-11pm seven days a week
Winter hours: 10-6 Mon-Fri
9am-closing on weekends

I knew Seaside well as a child from my grandfather, Al Carter, who retired and lived on the promenade for years until his death recently. I remember a lot of enjoyable times playing on the beach, roller skating on the prom, and shopping in the small shops up and down Broadway Street. One of the shops I remember most is Seaside Agate Shop. As a child I thought it held everything on earth anyone would want to give or receive, and I spent a lot of time in the store dreaming about who I would give each gift to or hoping someone would give something to me. You see, "agate shop" is sort of a misnomer —the shop has very few agates but lots of toys, wind chimes, Myrtlewood, shells, jewelry, beach wear, mugs, sweatshirts, and one of the best selections of miniatures anywhere in Oregon. Allen, Cliff and Joyce Erikson are the knowledgeable and exceptionally friendly owners of the shop, with help from their two daughters, Meagan and Debbie. Everything is enjoyable to look at and fun to buy for those land-locked friends and relatives back home. They have a large selection of things people want. It is a shop that has been a best choice for years and now is even better, thanks to the Ericksons — Seaside Agate Shop on Broadway, downtown Seaside.

(See special invitation in Appendix.)

GOLF

SEASIDE GOLF COURSE
451 Avenue U
Seaside, Oregon
phone 503-738-5261 for start time

Open seven days a week,
daylight to dusk

A very friendly course that can almost be played 365 days a year. Everything is available for the pro or novice, from a hearty breakfast at the clubhouse to rental or sale of clubs, electric golf carts, shoes and, naturally, balls and tees. The course is a nine-hole challenge of water and natural elements. Owner Fred Fulmer recommends that you have a golfer's special breakfast before you go out — a three-egg omelette, hash browns and toast. If you want to golf late and meet your friends for dinner, the golf course offers the Putter Room and Lounge, a fine dining room with full bar. Try the prime rib, choice of potato, salad and vegetable. It is filling and absolutely delicious. Fred has help from his two sons, Fred, Jr. and Wayne, who help out at Seaside Golf Course and the course they own in Vernonia, Oregon. Fred has owned the Seaside Course for 16 years and with that kind of knowledge, knows how to keep the green perfect. For a best choice in fun and recreation, it is Seaside Golf Course.

NURSERY AND GIFTS

THE RAIN TREE GARDEN AND GIFT CENTER
At the junction of Hwy 101
to Seaside and Cannon Beach
Seaside, Oregon
503-738-6980

When traveling the northern Oregon coast, you can't help but realize you're in a lush garden of greenery with wild rhododendrons, coastal pines, Douglas fir and wildflowers at every turn. There is a wonderful place from which you can actually carry a part of this beauty home with you. It is called Rain Tree Garden and Gift Center and the location couldn't be better — just off Highway 101 at the junction to Cannon Beach, Seaside and Portland. The Garden Center will pleasingly surprise you. It is not just bags of fertilizer and plastic pots. It is more like a garden of Eden with fantastic gifts, collectibles, outdoor furniture, potted plants of the highest quality, perennials, and a huge assortment of trees, along with knowledgeable help. The owners of this remarkable center are Dennis and Marylee Saulsbury, who have been in the business for over ten years. Dennis is an Oregon certified nurseryman. With that kind of knowledge, it helps you to know if the coastal plants that you buy will grow in your particular climate and the care needed for the plants, fertilizers required, etc. This way, they save you money with their knowledge so you don't buy something that does your lawn or plants absolutely no good. At the nursery, you will find indoor and covered areas are always open for your browsing pleasure. No matter what the weather, this is a very warm place to be. The main building is full of fantastic gifts — Chinese lacquered trays, Oregon-made products like delicate pine needle baskets, antique pieces, classy displays, and even a nice collection of toys for the young ones. So take part of the northern coast home with you. Stop at the best choice for flora, fauna and fun things — the beautiful Rain Tree Garden and Gift Center.

RESTAURANTS

DOOGER'S SEAFOOD AND GRILL
505 Broadway
Seaside, Oregon
503-738-3773

Open daily, 11am to closing
Winter: Tues-Sun, 11am to closing
Closed the months of Nov., Dec. and Jan.

Dining out is part of the experience in enjoying Oregon's coast. Seafood is the natural fare, and one of the most famous places for eating on the North Coast is Dooger's Seafood and Grill in Seaside. Owners Mary Wiese and son, Doug (Dooger) and wife, Mary Jean Wiese, have created a perfect kind of restaurant for families on a budget, couples on a honeymoon, and local residents (or anyone else) who want high quality, low prices and a warm, hometown atmosphere. You won't go wrong here. Many dishes are sauteed, but if you prefer deep frying, a light coating is used to ensure the flavor you want. I had fried oysters for lunch, accompanied with a salad sprinkled with some fresh Oregon shrimp. I received a full plate of food including a very generous portion of oysters, and all for $3.95. Lunch is served from 11 am until 4 pm. Dinner prices are not much higher, and dinner is served from 4 pm until closing. The owners do all of the cooking, so you know you are going to have the highest quality. Only the best leaves the kitchen with Doug. I asked Doug to recommend something for dinner off the menu, and he named the Sauteed Prawns with shrimp salad, garlic toast and potato wedges. He also recommends a special recipe clam chowder that makes chowder fans rave and is always at prices you can afford. Dooger's is a triple best choice, so experience dining out that will bring you back to Oregon's beautiful coast over and over. Try dinner at Dooger's Seafood and Grill. They have high chairs and booster chairs, and most major credit cards are taken for your convenience.

THE LIGHT HOUSE RESTAURANT
220 Avenue U (first light on 101 going north
to Seaside or last light south leaving Seaside)
Seaside, Oregon
503-738-7471

Winter hours: 11:30-9, Sun 8-8, closed Wed
Summer hours: 11:30-10, Sun 8am-9pm,
    closed Wed

When I am writing about a given area, I check with a lot of local people and ask them about the best place to dine. Almost all the local people insisted that I try The Light House Restaurant. Although it is really not hard to find, it is a little more hidden away than restaurants in the downtown area of Seaside and a lot of visitors might not know how to find Avenue U. Ask anyone local where Seaside's golf course is located. Then about one block west is where you'll find this delightful restaurant. The owners are George and Tomika Stecher, and they have been in the restaurant business for over 22 years. Their daughter, Louise, helps, too, and the service is as close to perfect as you would expect in a family-style restaurant. The menu, a combination of favorites the Stechers have found when traveling worldwide. George recommended some things off the menu you should try when in Seaside. All soups are homemade from scratch, including their famous clam chowder. For lunch, he recommends their great taco sandwich — meat with seasoned sour cream, chopped olives, peppers and cheese. It comes with cole slaw and fries. For dinner, he suggests Seaside's famous razor clams cooked to perfection with soup and salad, a vegetable, potato or rice pilaf. If you should order a steak, it is all choice, midwest, corn fed beef. Another specialty is grilled calves liver and onions. Yes, take it from the local residents, this restaurant is a best choice for best food and service.

(See special invitation in Appendix.)

LUMPY'S FISHWORKS RESTAURANT
104 Broadway (½ block from turnaround)
Seaside, Oregon
503-738-7176

Winter hours: 11-8 weekdays, closed Tues,
   8-8 weekends
Summer hours: 8am-9pm, 7 days a week

Seaside, Oregon, is blessed with a lot of greats! Great beaches, great clam digging, great people, and great restaurants! Lumpy's Fishworks Restaurant is not "just" great — it is one of the greatest — family fare with a flare. If you are a coffee person (and who isn't on the cool, Oregon coast), try Lumpy's. They serve the most delicious coffee in the largest mug you've ever seen. More than coffee, though, are the great eats, with breakfast, lunch and dinner offered at their best and at prices you'll love. Lee and JoAnne Sayles are the owners and managers of the restaurant. Young and innovative, they have created a unique dining experience. You have to try the clam chowder. It's as close to the best you'll find. The fish and chips not only taste good but fill the plate. (No little chunks of fish here; very generous portions is an understatement.) For breakfast, Lee Sayles suggested the unique creation called Stuffed French Toast which is stuffed with cream cheese and walnuts. For lunch, Lee says his fish and chips will bring you back — and I agree. He always offers malt vinegar or ketchup for the chips, and homemade tartar sauce for the fish. For dinner, he suggests Seafood Combo — scallops, prawns and cod sauteed or deep fried with your choice of potato, cup of chowder and salad. If you need to sweeten up your life, how about a slice of dark chocolate cake for which Lumpy's is known by almost anyone who lives in the Seaside area. Wine and beer are available, and coffee is just 50 cents a cup (or should we say pot). A best choice and another great place for Seaside — Lumpy's Fishworks. I'll see you there. P.S., make sure you ask about Lumpy's story.

(See special invitation in Appendix.)

PAPA G'S ITALIAN RESTAURANT
300 Broadway (inside Town Center Mall)
Seaside, Oregon
503-738-3372

Summer hours: 11:30am-10pm, Sun-Thurs
   11:30am-midnight, Fri & Sat
Winter hours: 11:30am-closing, 7 days a week

The whole family will enjoy this restaurant. Located inside a very nice mall with many quaint little shops, you'll find Papa G's on the main floor just north of the real merry-go-round that fills the mall with children's laughter and old-fashioned organ music. The menu will please almost anyone and so will the prices. They are open for lunch and dinner. Italian fare is offered — pizza, lasagna, minestrone soup, salads, garlic bread and, naturally, spaghetti, with soft drinks, beer and wine served to quench your thirst. Real cheese and the best ingredients are used in preparing their meals. The added bonus is a big screen TV and, as far as I know, it is the only big screen in Seaside. So if your motel TV is on the blink or if a great sports event is coming up, go to Papa G's, the TV is bound to be on. The staff is friendly, all members of the Hayward family, Charles, Karen, and daughter, Jodene. They work hard to deliver high quality food and service to your table. Bring the whole family and enjoy a best choice for food and fun — Papa G's Italian Restaurant in Seaside.

PIG N PANCAKE
323 Broadway
Seaside, Oregon 97138
503-738-7243
(Original restaurant)

Summer hours: Sun & Mon, 6am-10pm,
   Tues-Sat, open 24 hours
Winter hours: 6 days, 6am-10pm,

In Astoria: 146 W. Bond
503-325-3144
Open 24 hours, Tues-Sat

In Portland:
12110 122nd N.E. (122nd and Glissan)
503-252-3457
Open 5:30am-3pm, seven days a week

This restaurant and its owners are a story of success. Bob Poole and his wife, Marianne, started with less than $1000 cash, a purple 1930 Model A dotted with pink pigs, and an ambition and work ethic, and through hard work and determination turned the Pig N Pancake in Seaside into an institution on the north coast. "Meet me at the Pig!" has been a byword of locals on the northern coast since 1961 when the first Pig N Pancake opened. Astorians were asked to drive quite a way for a good breakfast, so the Pooles decided to open Astoria's own restaurant in 1967. Their Portland restaurant opened in 1982. Why has it been such a success? It takes more than $1000, a purple car and hard work. It takes high quality, good food served consistently, along with help so good they last for years. If you happen in on the right day, the mayor of Seaside herself will seat you at a very clean and comfortable table. The mayor is Joyce Williams and she has worked at the Seaside location for years. Owners Bob and Marianne Poole are the kind of people who make America what it is today, and their children are helping shape the future. Linda, Wayne and Rebecca all have college educations and are working hard at the restaurant. Restaurants in Seaside and Astoria are open for breakfast, lunch and dinner. (Try the prime rib at dinner; you'll find it exceptional!) The Portland location is open for breakfast and lunch. Whenever you are in Seaside, Astoria, or northeast Portland for a meal, you can't go wrong at the Pig, a best choice for high-quality food at very fair prices.

SPORTING GOODS AND GIFTS

ERNIE'S SPORTS, GIFTS AND FINE JEWELRY
1803 South Holladay (Hwy 101)
Seaside, Oregon
503-738-7901

Winter hours: 9-6 Mon-Thurs, 9-7 Fri-Sun
Summer hours: 8-8, seven days a week

Welcome to Bigfoot Country, where Bigfoot and friends live in a real live building. Ernie's Sports, Gifts and Fine Jewelry has something for everyone with the largest selection of sporting goods in the Seaside area. Fishing, hunting, backpacking, golf, tennis, baseball, basketball — they have it all — beach wear for men and women, rain gear, crab rings, clam diggers, bait, ammunition and more. Then there are the gifts of all kinds including collectibles and fine jewelry. You won't find a better store in which to shop for quality, selection and the unusual, a store Mom, Dad and the kids will love. Remember, Bigfoot is actually is inside the store in a special section called Bigfoot Museum. For a very nominal fee, you can have a "Bigfoot Experience". So when headed for the northern coast, stop at this famous sporting goods store for all your needs — Ernie's Sports, Gifts and Fine Jewelry. See you there.

SEASIDE TOUR

For an unforgettable time in Seaside, try our tour which starts at dawn and ends at sunset. It's mere suggestion, but you'll enjoy all the exciting places we have on this tour. Also, we have tried to keep their locations as close together as possible so you can visit one best choice right after another.

TIME	PLACE	DESCRIPTION	HOW TO FIND IN BOOK
Dawn	The Promenade	Best exercise/view	Seaside/Attractions
Breakfast	Pig N Pancake	Best breakfast	Seaside/Restaurant
A.M.	The Cinnamon Roll Shop	Best cinnamon rolls	Seaside/Bakery
A.M.	Mrs. Claus Emporium	Best Christmas gifts	Seaside/Gifts
A.M.	Seaside Beach	Best beach	Seaside/Beach
Lunch toss up	Doogen's Seafood	Best lunch	Seaside/Restaurant
Lunch	Lumpy's Seafood	Best lunch	Seaside/Restaurant
P.M.	Granderson's	Best gifts for home	Seaside/Gifts
P.M.	Seaside Agate Shop	Best gifts/coastal memorabilia	Seaside/Gifts
P.M.	Anita's Corner	Antiques/jewelry	Seaside/Antiques
P.M.	David's Fine Porcelain	Best gifts/collectibles	Seaside/Collectibles
Snack	Phillips Candies	Best candy	Seaside/Candy
Snack	Chocolate by Mordens	Best chocolate	Seaside/Candy
Dinner	The Light House Restaurant	Best dinner	Seaside/Restaurant
Sunset	Stroll on Promenade	Best romantic atmosphere	Seaside/Attractions

CANNON BEACH

ABOUT CANNON BEACH

Nestled on the beach just south of Seaside sits an intimate, all-year resort town loved by visitors and natives for its quaint charm and laid back atmosphere. The town name was coined for several cannons which washed ashore just south of the city in 1846 as part of the shipwreck of the Sloop of War *Shark*. The setting is idyllic — silvery mornings, spun gold late afternoons, beautiful sunsets and a full cultural program of summertime music and art happenings. As a growing art and craft colony, Cannon Beach boasts a downtown professional live theater, the Coaster Theater, which stages some of the finest drama to be had anywhere up and down the Oregon Coast.

Another addition to the unique charm of this little hamlet is "The Haystack" program hosted each summer by Portland State University. The town's picturesque seven mile stretch of beach is flanked by the imposing 235 foot Haystack Rock, one of the world's largest monoliths. The rock is a protected wildlife refuge and a great place in which to investigate tidepool marine life. The beach is great, too; perfect for beachcombing, surf fishing, clamming, kite flying, horseback riding and cozy evenings for fires.

Make a point of checking out Whale Park on the north end of downtown. Run your fingers along the smooth finish of an eight foot whale sculpture erected to commemorate the spot where members of the Lewis and Clark Expedition found a beached whale over a century ago.

For a great day's picnic outing and trail hike, head over to Ecola State Park, a gorgeous, 1300 acre park that surrounds Tillamook Head. There are two accessible beaches, picnic areas, and plenty of hiking trails. Be sure to catch the panoramic view of Tillamook Head Lighthouse perched out on the offshore rocks.

The main street of Cannon Beach features lots of unique curio shops, distinctive art galleries along Hemlock Street, shops featuring everything from pottery to painting, sculpture and handsome stitchery creations. Eateries range from sidewalk cafes to gourmet dining establishments. The town boasts an impressive array of lodging options whether your plans call for staying one night, a weekend or a summer. There are hotels, motels, cottages, and simple, moderately priced cottages right up to luxury condominium suites with all the amenities. Annual Cannon Beach activities include the infamous Sand Castle Contest held early each summer and the old-fashioned Dickens Yuletide Festivities hosted here each Christmas. Experience the unpretentious lure of an intimate, relaxed art colony set amid the scenic splendor of Oregon's rugged coastline.

CHAMBER OF COMMERCE
P.O. Box 64
Cannon Beach, Oregon 97110
503-436-2623

The Chamber will be happy to provide you with information regarding various lodging facilities, restaurants, sight-seeing attractions, parks and camping facilities, plus special cultural events planned throughout the summer. Check with them regarding the Coaster Theater's live productions scheduled for the summer season and the various music and art performances planned.

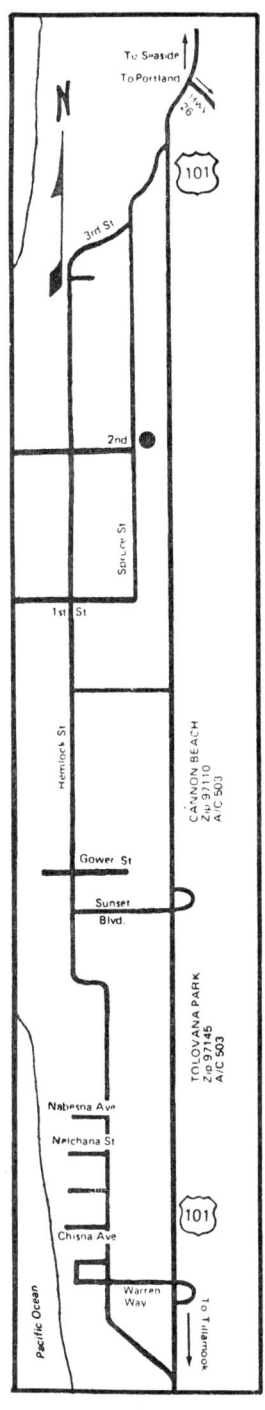

ACCOMMODATIONS

TOLOVANA INN
at Tolovana Beach
Cannon Beach, Oregon
503-436-2211 or
In Oregon, WATTS 800-452-9402
outside Oregon, 800-547-9059

The comfort of your own home and within a short walk to hiking, beachcombing, fabulous sunsets, swimming, sauna, sunbathing, playground and the blue-green Pacific Ocean — does this sound like Hawaii? Maybe you need more hints. Just a short drive from where you live with no bumper-to-bumper traffic, live theater, wine shops, unique shops, galleries and parks located in the middle of the most beautiful rain forest you've ever seen. Maybe this is Tahiti? No, this is Cannon Beach and the place to stay is the Tolovana Inn, a condominium resort with 170 units which include fireplaces, fully equipped kitchens, indoor pool, sauna, outdoor playground, green lawns, an ocean view from just about every room, and one of the most beautiful settings on Oregon's northern coast. Conference rooms and hospitality rooms are available also — a great retreat for family, winter storm-watching, remote getaway, or just plain old, summer beach roaming. You won't find a better choice — clean, comfortable and managed expertly by Jack and Teddi Heck and opertated by Vacation Village of America, Inc. Call Teddi Heck and ask about the fun things to do around Cannon Beach. She loves to tell you why this is the best place on earth to spend the night or a whole month — Tolovana Beach. (Take that exit off Highway 101.) Call two weeks ahead in winter and two months ahead in summer for reservations.

(See special invitation in Appendix.)

ADDITIONAL ACCOMMODATIONS

LANDS END MOTEL
263 W. Second
Cannon Beach, Oregon
503-436-2264

Kitchens, TV, jacuzzis, fireplaces, phones.

NEW SURFVIEW RESORT
1400 Hemlock
Cannon Beach, Oregon
503-436-2511 or 1-800-446-6900

In-room spas, pool, fireplaces, recreation center.

SURF SAND MOTEL
(Best Western) Grower Street
Cannon Beach, Oregon
503-436-2274 or 1-800-452-4470

ANTIQUES

LILLIE'S ANTIQUES
(Turn at major motel sign,
just off Hemlock, 1 block west)
179 Chisana Street
Cannon Beach, OR 97110
503-436-1259

Mailing address: P.O. Box 345
Tolovana Park, OR 97145

Open 10-9, seven days a week, winter & summer

Antique enthusiasts will find a special place and special people at Lillie's Antiques. Lillie Major and her husband, Dale, are the congenial owners of this well-stocked shop. This is the kind of hidden away shop where you might hope to find that unusual piece you've been searching for year after year, and at a price you can afford. Sure enough, Lillie's is such a place. Just read on for the kinds of things she specializes in: children's dishes, toys, furniture, Pennsylvania Dutch items, lots of glass (Fostoria, depression and fiesta ware), mixing bowls, coffee services, and cups and saucers. You'll also find a nice selection of antique collector dolls and china all over the shop and at fantastic prices! The most unusual and exciting thing for collectors of Belleek china figurine pieces is that Lillie easily has the largest selection on the Oregon Coast. If you worry about honesty, no need at Lillie's Antiques. They will be glad to show you values of pieces and confirm age. For a best choice in places and people, drop in at Lillie's Antiques, winter or summer, for antique surprises.

(See special invitation in Appendix.)

CANDY

BRUCE'S CANDY KITCHEN
256 N. Hemlock
Cannon Beach, Oregon
503-436-2641

Winter hours: 10-5, seven days a week
Summer hours: 10-8, seven days a week

With many artists, actors, and other creative people in Cannon Beach, the local eateries have to be more than just usual to attract attention and a following. It must be a place where quality and freshness are served for many creative people have traveled the world and tried the very best. Bruce's Candy Kitchen serves nothing but candy and any world traveler would know that this candy is definitely a best choice. Along with being a tradition in Cannon Beach for over 22 years, the store has been owned and operated by the Bruce Haskell family, perfectionists at their trade, making the best salt water taffy in Oregon according to *Oregon Magazine*. I agree — it's fantastic because it is fresh and no one can make salt water taffy like you find on the Oregon coast. Hand-dipped chocolates are made fresh every day, not like boxed chocolates. Almost all the candy at Bruce's is no more than one to four days old. There are jelly beans, gummy bears, licorice, rich mix, popcorn, caramel corn, caramel apples and candied apples — all fresh. Peanut brittle is a very popular item along with a chocolate, crunchy combo called Seafoam. Chocolates can be shipped anywhere and they are sent in one to two pound boxes with a choice of dark, light or assorted. Gift items to buy are also offered. Mugs, t-shirts, quality things; but if you need a special gift, ask Heidi (next door) and a great gift shop called **The Gift Shop** which is also a part of Bruce's. It has the same reputation for quality as the candy store. For a best choice of the creative people who live in Cannon Beach (and anywhere else), try Bruce's Candy Kitchen — it will turn you into an artist of fine eats.

(See special invitation in Appendix.)

EVENTS

THE ANNUAL SAND CASTLE CONTEST

This event has made Cannon Beach famous. Held in late June, early July every summer, this special festivity began as a bit of local fun and has blossomed into a major festival. Over 500 beach artists blend their imagination to the task of creating intricate sand castles as spectators cheer them on. Imagine sand taking on the shape of people's wildest fantasies. You'll marvel as true works of masterful sand art take shape on the beach. Teams work on incredible, well-conceived sculptures. The categories are then judged while visitors watch. Finally, the tide edges in ever closer and the mighty ocean reclaims her own treasures, leaving you with memories that will live vividly for a lifetime of sand castle imaginings. Don't miss this one. Plan to arrive early and stay late at the beach so you can take in all of it. Check with the Chamber for exact contest dates this summer.

GALLERY/GIFTS

S. CLAY DESIGN GALLERY AND GIFTS
164 Hemlock (Sand Piper Square, downtown)
Cannon Beach, Oregon
503-436-2210

Open 11-5, seven days a week

Walk into S. Clay Design Gallery and Gifts in Cannon Beach and experience expressions from all over the world — beautiful, delicate decorative things, all to make our personal environment more fulfilling. Lasting a lifetime — no plastic things, no phony things — they are all real things thanks to Bill and Sally Steidel, the creative owners of this fantastic shop. The Steidels are both artists. Bill's art, oil on canvas, could very well be as near to genius as you'll see anywhere. The big trouble is that his paintings sell out as fast as the canvas dries. The gallery carries limited prints and other works by Bill. Even if you flunked "Art Appreciation I" you must make this a stop on your coastal journey — a best choice that can't be written about. There are no words to describe the total feeling you'll receive at S. Clay Design Gallery and Gifts. Make sure you ask about Bill's studio which is open to the public, offering limited prints, framed or not. Don't leave the coast until you see what Bill and Sally Steidel can do for you and for the rest of your life.

GIFTS

THE BUTTERY
Sand Piper Square
Cannon Beach, Oregon
503-436-2723

Open: 10-5, seven days a week

Something for everyone who cares about good food and a beautiful kitchen can be found at The Buttery in Cannon Beach — a store full of useful and decorative wares for the gourmet to the decorator. The Deuber family, owners, and manager Elizabeth Goss, have years of experience and their beautifully displayed store proves that experience pays off. Customers will find whole sections of what they're looking for, and with friendly assistance in addition to a well-chosen selection, you won't go away still looking. For fun, quality, merchandise, try The Buttery — a gift store that is outstanding and, naturally, a best choice on Oregon's coast.

THE WILD DAISY
(delightfully different gifts)
200 Hemlock (corner of 2nd & Hemlock)
Cannon Beach, Oregon
503-436-1888

Summer hours: 10-9, seven days a week
Winter hours: 10-6, seven days a week

Cannon Beach has many unique shops and restaurants dotted along its narrow streets, and just about in the middle of all of them is a gift shop you must visit — The Wild Daisy. It is full of fun things to take back home for decorating or great gifts for the unfortunate ones who could not make the trip with you. Plus, you'll find the friendliest owners and managers of any store in Cannon Beach, Doug and Sandra Larson, with Heidi, their daughter and manager, all creative people who craft many of the special things in the store. For example, there are finger puppets that are characters from famous fairy tales, made by Hedi and Sandra, and wooden toys made by Doug and painted by his wife, Sandra. But there is much more in The Wild Daisy: one-of-a-kind imported gifts, prints, cards, collectibles, fun things for kids and adults. There is even a pattern for a vacuum cleaner cover doll. If you love to browse through stores that are delightfully different, you've come to the right best choice for gifts — The Wild Daisy in Cannon Beach.

GIFTS / TOYS / CARDS / APPAREL

DEUBER'S FOR VARIETY
Sandpiper Square
Cannon Beach, Oregon
503-436-2271

Hours: 9:30-6, seven days a week

Deuber's is not your typical variety store, but rather a series of intriguing departments rolled into one delightful shop.

Variety: A beautiful shell department that will please both the child and the collector, with prices that begin at 15 cents. A marvelous beach and toy department to add to your fun in the sun with postcards, games, puzzles and activity books galore for the not so sunny days at the beach.

Card Company: Absolutely the finest collection of greeting cards in Oregon... over 600 square feet of unique card displays that earn this department a four star rating!

Clothing: For fashion and fun at the beach, Deuber's presents this department especially for women. Unique styles and colorful basics for those who might have forgotten their suitcases at home. They are quality-minded and proud to announce that they are open seven days a week.

Art Shirt: One of the most innovative sections of the store is the shirt department. The Duebers hire local artists to design original drawings on quality t-shirts and sweatshirts — scenes from Cannon Beach, all hand silk screened on the most up-to-date color choices you'll find anywhere.

Dueber's is definitely worth looking into. Peter, Paul and Meg Dueber have had years of experience and their beautifully and originally displayed store proves that experience pays off. Customers will find friendly assitance in addition to a huge selection.

RESTAURANTS

THE DRIFTWOOD INN
(Across from Sand Piper Square)
179 N. Hemlock (downtown)
Cannon Beach, Oregon
503-436-2439

Hours: 4-10 Wed, Thurs & Fri; 12-10 Sat & Sun

A tradition in Cannon Beach for fine dining is The Driftwood Inn, serving delightful meals for over 25 years. The Inn is owned by John Ward, an expert in what makes a restaurant successful because over the years, more people have talked about the great food at Cannon Beach because of The Driftwood Inn. The menu includes light, seafood dishes to thick, juicy steaks cooked to perfection. When Dave was asked to recommend something from the lunch menu, it was the Crab Sandwich — an English muffin loaded with fresh cracked crab and then melted Tillamook. It also comes with fries and cole slaw. I've heard from others that their Turkey Dip is exceptional for lunch. I did not need any suggestions for dinner. I tried their prawns — they were top grade, large, cooked by the pro with a light batter. There was a choice of soup or salad, baked potato or rice, and a mini-loaf of French, sourdough bread or hot garlic bread. I tried the salad with the Inn's house dressing — perfect. When the baked potato came, they also put a large bowl of sour cream on the table so I could use all I wanted — just the way I like it. I chose the garlic bread and it was done the way I like it. With a full bar, beverage was no problem. I picked a white wine to go with the seafood plate. The whole meal was picture perfect and the service was even better. For a traditional best choice, try the Inn — just remember Driftwood in Cannon Beach.

GRANDMA LEE'S CHOWDER HOUSE
1235 S. Hemlock (south end,
across from liquor store)
Cannon Beach, Oregon
503-436-1762

Winter hours: 8-8, closed Wednesdays
Summer hours: 7am-9:30pm, seven days a week

If you like your own grandma's cooking, you'll love Grandma Lee's Chowder House in Cannon Beach. Just like all grandmas, they make food the old-fashioned way from quality scratch ingredients and hard work. The store was named after a real grandma who is the mother of Sally Rea, co-owner with her husband, Bill. There is even a table set aside for Grandma Lee at the restaurant. The Reas both cook and both have their own specialties. Bill cooks some of the best chowder you've ever put a spoon into and Sally's pies will melt in your mouth. The food offered is old-fashioned homemade chowders, pies and jams. Open for breakfast, lunch and dinner, you have a wide selection of plain and delicious American/Oregon foods. For breakfast, try a traditional breakfast of eggs the way you like them, a pile of hash browns, bacon, ham or links, toast and homemade jam. I guarantee you won't leave hungry. For lunch, try the 5½ inch, juicy, deluxe hamburger — again, just like Grandma's best. Along with that, a cup or bowl of chowder. You must like clams though, because it is overflowing with them. For dinner, try fish and chips with cole slaw or tossed salad and bread — delectable, and a lot of it. The prices at Grandma Lee's are a few years outdated, being very modest. The food is great and the Reas are very friendly. Don't pass up a meal at everyone's favorite grandma in Cannon Beach and a best choice on the Oregon coast — Grandma Lee's Chowder House.

(See special invitation in Appendix.)

THE WHALER RESTAURANT
200 Hemlock (downtown)
Cannon Beach, Oregon
503-436-2821

Summer hours: Open seven days a week,
   Breakfast, lunch and dinner
Winter hours: closed Wednesdays & Thursdays
   Open other days, breakfast, lunch and dinner

If you love bouillabaisse, try the dish that won top honors in a place where they know good food — San Francisco. Doug and Sandra Larson, owners of The Whaler Restaurant, entered their recipe in a crab cooking contest in a prestigious event in San Francisco and took first place. The Whaler is open for breakfast, lunch and dinner, with the dinner meal being their specialty — full bar open until 2:30 am with entertainment every night and open mike on Sunday nights. The seafood is sauteed and only the freshest is served. Lighter fare includes Shrimp or Crab Louies and the most delicious homemade cinnamon rolls you've ever tasted. There is a children's menu and they accept most major credit cards. Bouillabaise paradise — The Whaler Restaurant, Cannon Beach.

(See special invitation in Appendix.)

SEAFOOD

CANNON BEACH SEAFOOD
123 S. Hemlock (corner of
Hemlock and First)
Cannon Beach, Oregon
503-436-2272

Winter hours: 11-6, closed Mon
Summer hours: 10:30-7 seven days a week

Oregon's coastal waters are abundant in what makes the best seafood restaurants around the world famous — Dungeness crab, shrimp, salmon and more. Just a few people on this large earth are lucky enough to live close enough to enjoy seafood caught on the same day. When traveling the coast, a must stop is at a seafood market and, on the north Oregon coast, the best choice for fresh Oregon seafood is Cannon Beach Seafood located conveniently in downtown Cannon Beach. Lyman Hawken and his wife, Ruth, own this fine shop full of fresh crab, shrimp, oysters and salmon, all from Oregon waters. Lyman and Ruth's son, Richard, fishes for the store and when weather permits, is out catching the fresh seafood for the family-run shop. Richard also offers charter fishing for the sportsmen wanting to catch their own. (Just contact the store for more details.) Summer is a busy time in Cannon Beach, and Lyman and Ruth offer takeout foods such as seafood cocktails and fish and chips. The store also has cook books, sauces, wine, juices, soft drinks, ice, beer, crackers, cheese and all you'll need for a gourmet picnic on an Oregon beach. If you are a sportsman, Lyman smokes salmon and always gives you your own fish back. Since the smoking is done on the premises, it is done with high quality and the supervision of pros. Make sure you treat yourself to what makes restaurants famous all over the world — Oregon's own seafood at the best choice — Cannon Beach Seafood. (Try the peppered smoked salmon or the pickled herring. They're great!)

STAINED GLASS

HANNEN STAINED GLASS
987 S. Hemlock
Cannon Beach, Oregon
503-436-2761

A gallery of beautiful pieces of art is open, free to the public, at Cannon Beach. It is Hannen Stained Glass Gallery where you will find artists Jim and Deborah Hannen hard at work creating beautiful stained glass windows and lampshades. Jim and Deborah have over 20 years combined experience in the craft and have become known for their exceptional designs and superior quality craftsmanship. The Hannens have exhibited and sold their work nationwide. They have completed several thousand commissions in Oregon and elsewhere, and are known for making that extra effort to ensure customer satisfaction. Jim and Deborah are friendly and welcome people to visit their studio. You are sure to be fascinated by the dazzling display of finished work always on hand in the gallery area of the studio. Hannen Stained Glass — a best choice on the Oregon Coast. Stop by and see their colorful art.

THEATER

COASTER THEATER
108 N. Hemlock
P.O. Box 643
Cannon Beach, Oregon 97110
503-436-1242

A year 'round live theater located in a rural coastal village with a population of not much over 1,000 — Fimpossible? Not in Cannon Beach, Oregon, a city known for creativity and community support. The theater is warm and hospitable, constructed from cedar wood which makes the acoustics fantastic, and has comfortable, movie theater-type seating on raised floor. It is better than a lot of theaters in San Francisco and the talent and energy may even be better thanks to Stephen Diehl, producer and manager of the theater. The Coaster's traditional events include the annual Dickens Festival which is celebrated with a community Christmas play each December. For coming winter or summer performances, call for a schedule. One will be mailed at no charge. For a best choice in live entertainment on the entire Oregon Coast, go the The Coaster Theater — don't miss it.

Clatsop County 55

TOY SHOP

GEPPETTO'S TOY SHOPPE
247 N. Hemlock (across from
Bruce's Candy Kitchen)
Cannon Beach, Oregon
503-436-2467

Winter hours: 11-5 seven days a week
Summer hours: 11-6 seven days a week

Sand castles and children are part of Oregon's sandy beaches. A village on the coast famous for sand sculpture is Cannon Beach with its annual Sand Castle Contest that brings people of all ages from miles around to create artwork in the sand. Children with wide eyes are everywhere, helping and watching the artists at work. A shop at Cannon Beach especially meant for little ones is Geppetto's Toy Shoppe. The shop is co-owned and managed by a lady who could pass as the real Mrs. Claus of Santa Claus fame. Her name is Cheryl Johnson, and she has owned the store for over three years with help from her father-in-law (who reminds me of the real Geppetto), her husband and four children. Parents described Geppetto's Toy Shoppe like this: fun, puzzles, cars, games, dolls, blocks, and most of all, hands-on. The shop is not just for people under two feet. Cheryl carries toys for all ages. Appealing items carried in the shop are German clocks made in the Black Forest, cuckoo clocks and other fun things for adults. Most importantly, Geppetto's has all those fun beach toys that no one should go to the beach without. Oregon's coast is for children, sand castles, and best choices like Geppetto's Toy Shoppe in Cannon Beach.

(See special invitation in Appendix.)

WINE SHOP

LAUREL'S WINE SHOP
263 N. Hemlock (across from
Bruce's Candy Kitchen)
Cannon Beach, Oregon
503-436-1666

A good wine shop reflects its owner. The person buying the wine for the shop needs to have knowledge of the science of wine making and have a good palate for tasting wine. If you find a wine shop like that, you're almost ensured the wine you buy will be perfect for your needs. With Laurel Hood, owner and manager of Laurel's Wine Shop, you will have that kind of knowledge. Laurel has tasted thousands of wines, studied winemaking, and has been working to expand her knowledge of wine for almost 12 years. Her shop is well stocked with most wines for which you will be looking. There is wine tasting every day with an emphasis on Northwest wines and during the summer, local vinters are on hand for special event tasting (call for schedule). Prices are fair, the shop is displayed well, the clerks are extra friendly and knowledgeable and the best imported and domestic beers are offered. Case discounts are available. Take a little bit of Oregon home with you in the form of a fine wine from a best choice wine shop, Laurel's Wine Shop in Cannon Beach.

CANNON BEACH TOUR

Cannon Beach is a special place and you won't want to miss any of it. This tour is just a suggestion on how to enjoy your day in and around Cannon Beach. If you follow it to the letter, we know you can't help but have a great day in this scenic area.

TIME	PLACE	DESCRIPTION	HOW TO FIND IN BOOK
Dawn	Stroll on Tolavana Beach	Best beach	Cannon Beach/Beach
Breakfast	The Whaler Restaurant	Best breakfast	Cannon Beach/Restaurant
A.M.	Wild Daisy	Best gifts	Cannon Beach/Gifts
A.M.	Deuber's for Variety	Best gifts	Cannon Beach/Gifts/Toys
A.M.	The Buttery	Best kitchen gifts	Cannon Beach/Gifts
A.M.	S. Clay Design	Best art/gifts	Can. Beach/Gallery/Gifts
Lunch	Grandma Lee's Chowder House	Best lunch	Cannon Beach/Restaurant
P.M.	Hannen Stained Glass	Best stained glass	Can. Beach/Stained Glass
P.M.	Geppetto's Toy Shoppe	Best toys	Can. Beach/Toy Shop
P.M.	Laurel's Wine Shop	Best wines	Can. Beach/Wine Shop
P.M. Snack	Bruce's Candy Kitchen	Best candy/gifts	Cannon Beach/Candy
P.M. Snack	Cannon Beach Seafood	Best seafood	Cannon Beach/Seafood
P.M.	Lillie's Antiques	Best antiques	Cannon Beach/Antiques
Dinner	The Driftwood Inn	Best dinner	Cannon Beach/Restaurant
P.M.	The Coaster Theater	Best live entertainment	Cannon Beach/Theater

Chapter Two

TILLAMOOK COUNTY

ABOUT TILLAMOOK COUNTY

The land of trees, cheese and ocean breeze! Captain Robert Grey, the first white American to land in Oregon, did so in what is now known in Tillamook Bay in 1788. What Captain Grey saw there was the same breathtaking panorama of beaches, coastal wild flowers and green forests we can see today. The first settler in Tillamook County was Joe Chapman, who lived in a hollow tree for two months in 1851. There were several others, mostly rough mountain men who lived in this area and either made their way via the turkey trails of the Neah-Kah-Nie Mountain or, like Joe Chapman, came by the sea on ships. The pioneers of this area got along with their Indian neighbors probably because of the wise diplomacy of Chief Kilchis and his fairness and kindness toward the courageous pioneers. While other tribes were waging war on other Oregon pioneers, Chief Kilchis kept the peace in Tillamook County.

There are many things to see in Tillamook County, like colorful Cape Kiwanda and Cape Lookout, as well as the Cape Meares Lighthouse and the Umpqua Seven Trees in One featured in *Ripley's Believe It or Not*. You can visit the Dougherty Fleet of Pacific City or the largest wooden structures in the world, blimp hangers of the former U.S. Naval Air Base located just south of Tillamook on Highway 101. These amazing structures are 1080 feet long, 300 feet wide and 190 feet high.

For the outdoor enthusiast, this beautiful country offers some of the best hiking and beachcombing to be found anywhere. Trails run along streams, amid cool breezes, peaceful forests and green meadows. Throughout the county the beaches offer miles of hard sand and oceanside trails where you can find small treasures like glass floats, driftwood, Indian relics and shells. There are numerous parks in Tillamook County and are operated by the state, county and Forest Service as well as the Bureau of Land Management and private companies. In March, Tillamook becomes a fisherman's homeland. Along the ocean shores and from jetties are some of the best fishing spots on the coast. Rock cod, ling cod, sea bass and kelpfish are easily caught. You can even charter boats in Garibaldi and Pacific City for you who like deep sea trolling off the coast. Trappers will enjoy their favorite sport at Netarts, Tillamook, Nestucca and Nahalem Bay. Boats and crab rings can also be rented in these localities.

For a different kind of hunter, elk, deer and bear are the big game to be found in the county. Ducks and geese can be found in the lakes and bays. Pigeon hunting is also excellent. For regulations concerning hunting, consult the Oregon Game Department.

Don't forget to visit cheese country. Throughout Tillamook County amongst the beautiful hills and fields you will find hard-working dairy farmers producing milk to be processed into some of the finest cheese made on the West Coast. Captain Robert Groy and Joe Chapman knew Oregon was special, but could they have envisioned the beauty and bounty of the land? Oregon, and especially Tillamook County, is indeed the land of trees, cheese and ocean breeze.

ATTRACTIONS

CAPE LOOKOUT STATE PARK

Located on Three Capes Drive, Cape Lookout State Park has every geologic and natural feature found on the Oregon coast. You can enjoy green forests and easy-to-walk trails through shadowy glens which open onto spectacular views of the coastline and the cape. The trail also has nearly 20 stations showing typical coastal rain forest vegetation as well as, if you are observant, local birds and animals in the area. If you would rather spend your time at the beach, you can look for driftwood, jasper, agates and Japanese fishing floats as well as enjoy fishing from the surf.

Cape Lookout itself is a rocky headland that extends 1¾ miles into the ocean. It was formed by molten lava from a vent in the earth's crust which hardened into layers making the salt cliffs that have resisted the wind and sea for over 20,000,000 years. The vegetation of the cape and surrounding area is much like the tropical rain forest. You can find Sitka spruce, western hemlock and red cedar along with salal, box blueberry, salmon berry and Pacific wax myrtle.

If you want to do a little camping, two sites are available. There are campsites with water, picnic tables and fire rings, and those with full hook-ups for electricity, water and sewer in addition to tables and fire rings. Restrooms and utility buildings with hot showers are conveniently located throughout the camp.

Spectacular views, thundering surf, cliffs and quiet beaches await you and your family when you visit Cape Lookout State Park.

CAPE MEARES STATE PARK

Ten miles west of Tillamook on the north end of the beautiful 20 miles through Three Capes Scenic Loop is Cape Meares State Park. You won't want to miss the beautiful, large Sitka spruce, thundering surf and Cape Meares Lighthouse. You will especially want to see the marvel of nature called the Octopus Tree. This tree is more than ten feet in diameter at its base. Unlike most trees, this one has no center trunk. Instead, limbs from 3 to 5 feet thick branch out close to the ground, much like the large tentacles of an octopus. The Cape Meares Lighthouse is a 40 foot tower that was built in 1890 with a light visible 21 miles out to sea. The first light was provided by a flame from a heavy bronze, five wick kerosene lantern. After 20 years, it was replaced by an incandescent oil vapor lamp. A system of gears and weights kept the lens turning throughout the night.

Sightseeing on Three Capes Scenic Drive begins in Tillamook and skirts the bay before climbing to Cape Meares. Ten miles to the south through Oceanside and Netarts is Cape Lookout State Park with miles of beaches for beachcombers and trails for hikers. Further south are fun sand dunes and Sand Lake. Then you come to Cape Kiwanda, the third cape on the scenic drive, and home of the Doy fishing fleet. This is a fine place to bring your camera to photograph spectacular wave action. The scenic drive finishes through Pacific City where it joins Highway 101 25 miles south of Tillamook. Beautiful scenery, trees and ocean breezes invite you to Cape Meares State Park.

TILLAMOOK COUNTY PIONEER MUSEUM

Take a trip into Tillamook County's rich past at this fascinating pioneer museum. You can see old gun collections, pump organs, Indian baskets, rock collections, photos of county settlers, old wagons, a replica of a pioneer home, and a replica of a great-grandmother's kitchen. The library also houses a research library for those of you who want to do some historical research, trace genealogies, or pursue older book volumes. This building is on the site of Tillamook County's first courthouse which was built in 1887 and burned down in 1903. The building was built in 1905 and was used in 1932 when a new courthouse was built. With the help of the Tillamook County Pioneer Association, this museum was started with 400 artifacts. It is now administered by the county. Visit a piece of Old West history Oregon style and appreciate the richness of our pioneer past. Admission is inexpensive.

TILLAMOOK STATE FOREST

The Tillamook State Forest wasn't always called a forest. For several years this area was known as the Tillamook Burn. Because of a series of catastrophic fires which destroyed the forest starting in August of 1933 and continuing to reappear in a fire cycle in 1939, 1945 and 1951, a total of 350,000 acres were blackened and more than 13,000,000 board feet of timber were lost as well as an immeasurable amount of fish and wildlife which have since repopulated the forest after many years. In 1948, Oregon voters passed a constitutional amendment which authorized $12,000,000 in bonds to restore the forest in the most expensive reforestation project ever undertaken by any state. Large scale seeding took place and now that initial $12,000,000 investment is worth $350,000,000 in revenue for the state. Evidence of the old burn is still visible. For the most part, however, the young timber covers the area. The Tillamook Burn was officially renamed the Tillamook State Forest on July 18, 1973. Enjoy nature but please, as Smokey so often says, "Be careful with fire."

MANZANITA

ACCOMMODATIONS

SUNSET SURF MOTEL
456 Ocean Way
Manzanita, Oregon

Kitchens, pool, fireplaces, new units, secluded, beach.

BEACHES

Beaches, beaches and more beautiful beaches for family fun are here at the charming little village south of Cannon Beach on Highway 101. You will be able to hear stories of the fabled Spanish galleon that is reputed to have wrecked just offshore in the deep and gives up lumps of beeswax which are occasionally found washed ashore. So do a little combing, listen to the stories and listen for the ghosts of those who may have lost their lives below the surf.

NEHALEM

ABOUT NEHALEM

The little village of Nehalem offers a little something for everyone. Located between Manzanita and Garibaldi on the Oregon Coast and nestled on the bank of the Nehalem River, this sleepy town offers visitors interesting shops and galleries as well as the Nehalem Arts Festival in July and Nehalem Duck Days in mid-February. The Nehalem River and Bay offer anglers silver and Chinook salmon, native cutthroat trout and steelhead fishing. It is also popular for crabbing and clamming enthusiasts. So don't just drive through. Stop awhile at the little village of Nehalem.

PARKS

NEHALEM BAY STATE PARK

Enjoy camping, hiking, beachcombing, bicycling and horseback riding on trails (provided you bring your own bike or horse), or just plain relax at Nehalem Bay State Park located

62 Tillamook County

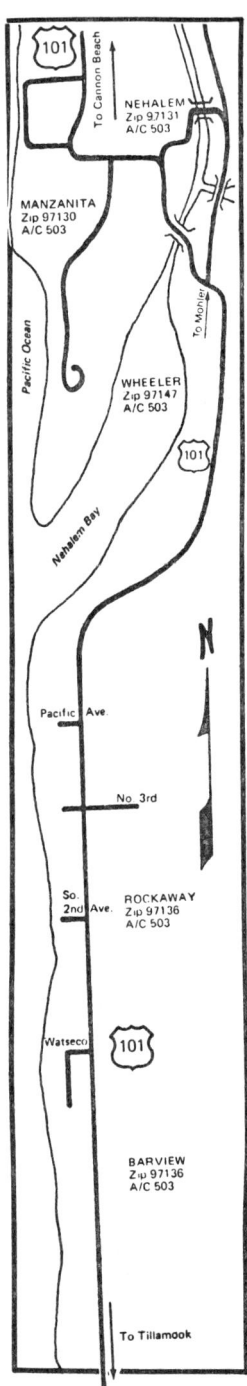

2½ miles off Highway 101 at the Bayshore Junction north of Tillamook. The overnight campground has 242 electrical hookup campsites as well as picnic tables, fireplaces and water at each site. There are also utility buildings which provide restroom facilities and hot showers. The Nehalem State Beach extends the full length of the four mile Nehalem Bay spit. At the end of the spit is a nice and quiet little picnic area that is accessible only by boat or by foot. Another picnic area is near the campground and overlooks Nehalem Bay and offers a view of boats against the backdrop of coastal mountains. The camp for horseback riders has 18 tie stalls for horses, picnic tables, fire rings and sanitary facilities for the riders. Horses are allowed only on designated beaches and trails. Nehalem Bay State Park is one of the few that is accessible by air. Not far away is Nehalem Airport, less than ¼ mile from the park entrance. So camp out on the Oregon Coast and relax to the sound of surf and ocean breezes at this fun state park.

ROCKAWAY BEACH

ABOUT ROCKAWAY BEACH

For the fisherman, hiker, beachcomber, clammer, crabber and sightseer, Rockaway Beach and its beautiful five mile stretch of sand and surf is indeed a treasure for any lover of nature and relaxing fun. Located just two hours west of Portland, Rockaway Beach is secluded yet very accessible to the majority of people in Oregon. With over 250 bedroom units, almost all of them overlooking the ocean, you'll also find gift shops, old time bumper cars, restaurants and friendly people who are happy to make your stay a most enjoyable one. As we were saying, you are not going to want to miss your stroll along the ocean's edge to collect a variety of souvenirs. If you enjoy eating crab or clamming and you don't feel like digging for them, try some of the several seafood restaurants which will satisfy your taste for this scrappy little critters. But if you do want to do a litle digging, many sport outfitters in Rockaway will be able to support you with a variety of equipment to do the job from crab rings and boats to clam shovels and clam guns. They'll be more than happy to tell you the best spots in which to hunt. If you are an angler at heart, there are countless fishing holes and lakes within minutes of

Rockaway to satisfy your every fishing need. Whether ocean or fresh water, your frying pan is going to be full of fish. So enjoy a relaxing time sightseeing in and around Rockaway Beach, one of Oregon's best kept secrets in the center of Tillamook County's vacationland.

ACCOMMODATION LIST

LAKE LYTLE MOTEL
101 N.W. 11th
Rockaway Beach, Oregon
503-355-2312

Kitchen, pool, HBO.

SILVER SANDS MOTEL
215 Pacific Street
Rockaway Beach, Oregon
503-355-2206

Kitchen, pool, HBO.

ANTIQUES

TRASH AND TREASURES
Highway 101
Rockaway Beach, Oregon
503-355-2790

You can find just about anything you want for men, women and the little folks at Trash and Treasures. This is definitely a fun place to shop where you can always find something within your budget with lots of smiles. Owner Phyllis Underwood and her assistant, Ruth Eckhart, make sure you can find something to have fun with or something you've needed around the house for quite some time. You can find glassware, collectibles, and other things; generally, things people are looking for such as children's toys, baby cribs, strollers, book shelves, and pots and pans. Almost all the items in the store have been bought from local people. Trash and Treasures is full of fun things, bargains, antiques and collectibles. It is a great place to spend a little time and a best choice for spending just a little money because everything is priced very reasonably.

BED AND BREAKFAST

THE CAPTAIN'S LADY BED AND BREAKFAST
Located off Hwy 101 in the heart of
Rockaway Beach, Oregon
503-355-2966 for reservations

Open year 'round

Stay as close to home as you can get without being home. In lovely bedrooms, sleep under real, handsewn quilts in warm, comfortable beds and among antique furnishings in a home built in 1909. This wonderful place is The Captain's Lady Bed and Breakfast in Rockaway Beach. For two years, Dan and Laurie Utterson have made sure everyone's needs are well taken care of at "The Lady". An unusual and delicious egg dish is served for breakfast with homemade, sour dough cinnamon rolls or sour dough blueberry muffins. There is no better food anywhere. Homelike comfort, great hospitality, and delicious food make The Captain's Lady a "must" stay. If you need a haircut, Laurie is also the owner of Driftwood House of Hair Design, just steps away from the Bed and Breakfast. Not only is she a great chef, but also a great hairdresser.

(See special invitation in Appendix.)

GIFTS

SHELLAY GIFT SHOP
South end of Rockaway Beach
On Highway 101
Rockaway Beach, Oregon
503-355-8248

Summer hours: 10-6 seven days a week
Winter hours: 10-5, Tues-Sat

It's the music from the wind chimes made from seashells that first lures you into the wonder and beauty of this charming gift shop devoted to, of course, shells. Marie Gruver, owner of this fascinating shop for almost three years, has just about anything your heart could desire made out of shells. Hanging on the ceiling are some of the most beautiful shell chandeliers to be seen anywhere. They hang three to four feet and are made from the most beautiful, delicate shells imaginable. No other shop in Oregon has this inventory of shell products, and many are shipped especially from the Orient for Marie's shop. But again, there is much, much more. There is a fine collection of myrtlewood products, plant chandeliers, shell lamps, jewelry, gold and silver jewelry, porcelain ceramics, and lots of other craft items. There are also miniature wind chimes making beautiful music and shell night lights as well as local, Oregon-made products like wine and jellies.

(See special invitation in Appendix.)

KITES

THE KITE SHOP
116 Highway 101 South
P.O. Box 517
Rockaway Beach, Oregon 97136
000-000-8088

You don't have to ask yourself too many times what a long sandy beach with no power lines and the wind blowing from a constant direction is good for — kite flying! Kites are a serious business in many parts of the world and have been for several thousand years. In this country, kites have always been considered toys for children, but in areas like the sea coast where conditions are ideal, that is changing. Kite shops like The Kite Shop at Rockaway Beach sell sophisticated kites of all price ranges, from children's basic kites to sophisticated adult kites. Roger and Ardella Lovitt, owners of one of the many kite specialty stores on the coast, sell a full range of kites, books on kites, and also give patient advice on controlling and flying the high performance models. On one of my trips to the coast, I bought an interesting airplane-like kite with rotating wings. It looked so pretty I was afraid to fly it. I hung it on a wall in my den instead, but that's okay, kites are as decorative on walls as they are in the clear blue sky. The Kite Shop also has wind socks and beautiful windspinners. So for a best choice for fun on the beach, stop at The Kite Shop in Rockaway Beach.

RESTAURANTS

KELLY'S BAR AND GRILL
Highway 101, downtown
Rockaway Beach, Oregon
503-355-2790

Hours: 7am-10pm Sun-Thurs
Open 'til 11 Fri & Sat, full bar open 'til 2:30

For family dining, great food and live entertainment in Rockaway Beach, Kelly's Bar and Grill is the place to be. For eighteen years in the restaurant business, serving people with a smile has been Number One in John Underwoods' family-oriented business. The specialties of the house are many: steak, seafood and practically everything else. For breakfast, John recommends the Grill's hearty two or three-egg omelette, called Cactus Kelly; or ham and cheese with jalapeno, salsa, cheese, onions and spices as well as extra large homemade muffins and honey. For lunch, fish and chips with locally bought fish, fresh halibut, dipped in a light beer batter with tartar sauce and lemon wedges. Ah! And for dinner, Bay City oysters with soup or salad, rice or fries, and clam chowder. For dessert, any of the homemade pies with a big scoop of Tillamook ice cream are recommended, or shakes and sundaes. On summer nights, the lounge and dance floor are packed with fun-loving people. So stop by and enjoy Kelly's Bar and Grill, a best choice for good food and entertainment in Rockaway Beach, Oregon.

WOMEN'S APPAREL

THE CLOTHES HANGER
On Highway 101, north end of town
Rockaway Beach, Oregon
503-355-2451

If you like clothes you can play in, this is the place. Susan May has been personally buying clothes in which to enjoy the Oregon Coast for over 18 years. With a wide selection of sportswear, beachwear, swim suits, lingerie and so much more. She also has a wonderful line of a brand called Play Me — they are shirts that actually have games printed right on them and come with a bag of things for playing the game. Also in the store are some fine antique pieces to take note of, such as an old copper washer up front and wagon wheel racks for a lot of the clothing to hang on. A fun place to shop and a best choice for style — The Clothes Hanger in Rockaway Beach.

(See special invitation in Appendix.)

GARIBALDI

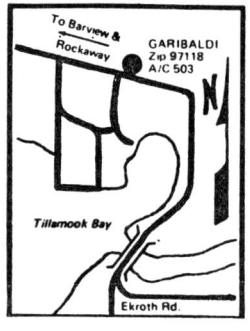

BAKERY

BAY FRONT BAKERY AND DELI
Highway 101, downtown
Garibaldi, Oregon
503-322-3787

Winter hours: 4:30am-5:30pm Tues-Sat
Summer hours: 4:30am-5:30pm Tues-Sun

You can smell the mouth-watering freshness of newly baked breads and pastries while taking an early morning stroll through Garibaldi. The aroma in the air leads you in an almost dreamlike trance to the Bay Front Bakery and Deli where Carl and Cathie Obermeier have been mixing their batches of recipes for more than 7 years. Just walk into the bakery and take a deep breath. There is no doubt that everything is freshly made every morning at sunrise — wonderful sourdough and sheepherder bread the size of bowling balls; eight-grain bread with the texture and smell of Grandmother's homebaked. There are also pastries galore with bear claws, prune Danish, poppyseed strudel, cinnamon rolls, and doughnuts of every kind. There is also a delicious cheese pocket, a Danish pastry filled with cream cheese (so good it will make your eyes water!). Pies are also a specialty, made from local fresh fruit in season, as well as custom cakes made for birthdays, anniversaries and weddings. If you want a meal, they serve delicious deli sandwiches on your choice of freshly baked bread, with soup and your favorite beverage. For some of the best smells on the Oregon coast, try the best choice bakery — Bay Front Bakery and Deli in Garibaldi.

EVENTS

Garibaldi has borrowed a little tradition from the Old World to keep the fishermen safe from the dangers of the sea. Imported from Portugal, the March Blessing of the Garibaldi Fleet opens the new fishing season with a beautiful ceremony of prayers at the sea wall asking for the safety of the fishermen and a plentiful. Then led by a Coast Guard cutter from Tillamook Bay, fleet ships move slowly from the harbor into the bar as wreaths are tossed into the sea from the boats to pay respect to those lost at sea. After the blessing of the fleet, participants celebrate the new season with food, music and entertainment offered at booths at the boat basin. Blessing comes as the new fishing season begins during the last weekend in March, so join in the celebration in beautiful Garibaldi.

GIFTS

VIRGINIA'S GIFTS
Highway 101
Garibaldi, Oregon
503-322-3779

Summer hours: 10-6 Wed-Mon
Winter hours: 11-5 Wed-Mon

If you enjoy finding a truly unique or beautiful gift for a best friend, from people who smile, you will find it here at Virginia's Gifts. Virginia and Bud Underhill have been collecting a fine and large inventory of collectibles for years. There is something for everyone, including collectible pencil sharpeners, wind chimes, tools for the male shopper, sand toys, buckets, inflatables, lots of music boxes (200 or more from which to choose), lamps (unusual fiber optic lamps), stained glass items for great gifts, mugs, seaside memorabilia, jewelry, T-shirts with coastal scenes, etched glass pieces, unicorns, and belt buckles. There is just about every kind of knickknack and collectible gift you could think of, along with the kind smiles of down-to-earth people. For one of the largest selections of unusual gifts on the north Oregon coast, try the friendliest best choice — Virginia's Gifts in downtown Garibaldi.

(See special invitation in Appendix.)

RESTAURANTS

THE OLD MILL RESTAURANT
(from south on Hwy 101, first left hand turn; from the north, turn at sign to Old Mill Marina)
Garibaldi, Oregon
503-322-0222

The old lumber mill is gone, but historic echoes remain fresh in the friendly taste of the hometown family cooking at The Old Mill Restaurant overlooking beautiful Tillamook Bay. Joe and Judy West and their friendly staff have brought smiles and good food (made from scratch) to the old mill site for four years now, with a generous breakfast, lunch and dinner menu fit for all food lovers. For breakfast, Joe and Judy recommend their mix and match omelette with three eggs and Tillamook cheese, served with hash browns, toast and jam (breakfast is served until 11:30am). For lunch, they recommend their delicious oyster burger made from local Bay City oysters, or their Shrimp or Crab Louie with a hot loaf of sourdough bread. You can eat dinner at any time you please, with beer and wine available. You might like to try the large cut of prime rib on special nights, with soup, salad or clam chowder, a relish tray with a choice of potato, and a loaf of sourdough bread. For seafood lovers, there is a jumbo plate with lightly breaded, deep-fried scallops, prawns, Bay City oysters and fresh fish. Great service is the rule here, as you can sit on the dock and enjoy a beautiful view of Tillamook Bay. For dessert, don't pass up the delicious pies such as sour cream with fresh fruit when in season (they also have cobbler). The Wests want everyone to leave well fed — that is, if you ever want to leave because the beautiful view, the good food, the clean restaurant and the great atmosphere at The Old Mill Restaurant.

TILLAMOOK

ACCOMMODATIONS

EL RAY SANDS MOTEL
815 Main
Tillamook, Oregon
503-842-7511

Restaurant, TV, phones.

MAR-CLAIE MOTEL
11 Main Avenue
Tillamook, Oregon
503-542-7571

Restaurant, kitchens, pool.

CHEESE/GIFTS

BLUE HERON FRENCH CHEESE FACTORY
One mile north of Tillamook
on Hwy 101
Tillamook, Oregon
503-842-8281

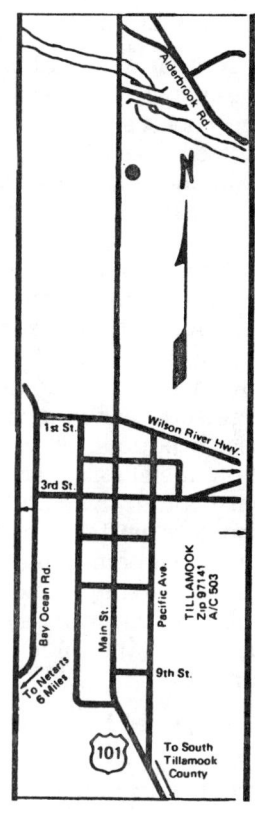

There are special places around the world which become famous for producing the best of a certain food or drink. France is famous for wine, Wisconsin for cheese, Maine for lobsters. Oregon, because of its short history of a mere 100 or so years, has not had enough time to create the fame as these other places. However, in small but evergrowing numbers, gourmets in the know have found Oregon's wines and cheeses surpassing the best of those in France or Wisconsin. The tasty cheeses of Tillamook County have a quality that is bringing increasing fame to Oregon. The cheeses we speak of are the tangy cheddars from Tillamook County Creamery and the Brie of Blue Heron Cheese Factory, two cheese factories less than a mile apart in the small coastal community of Tillamook. In recent tastings, Oregon wines have won over the more famous of France's best and sell for less than half the price. The wineries of Oregon have turned many wine connoisseurs' heads and thus, Oregon is becoming more and more famous. Give us a thousand year history to boast about (as in France) and we will be the wines and cheeses to beat!

There is a special place in Tillamook where you can sample these great cheeses and wines (it happens to be where one of the cheeses is made). It is the Blue Heron Cheese Factory located on Highway 101 just one mile north of downtown Tillamook. Mario and Denny Pastega are the owners of this fantastic place with manager, Louey Minisce, always present to help answer your questions about cheesemaking. Besides every gourmet cheese you could want, the Cheese Factory offers free wine tasting of Knudsen Erath Winery, the largest and one of the most award-winning wineries in Oregon. The factory is open to all and is located inside a huge, old-fashioned Dutch barn. Inside this authentic barn you'll find a deli with great creations, cheese samples, gifts offered from Oregon's best products, and soft drinks and wines by the glass. You must insist on ordering the Toasted Brie Sandwich that comes with potato salad and a crispy dill pickle. You'll find "flavored popcorn" with lots of flavors such as cherry, chocolate peanut, or sour cream and onion — all great treats for an afternoon snack. Scrumptious box lunches are available for picnicking and the staff is always friendly and helpful. A best choice for Oregon — the Blue Heron's Brie cheese — it's making us famous!

(See special invitation in appendix.)

CHEESE / RESTAURANT / GIFTS

TILLAMOOK COUNTY CREAMERY ASSOCIATION
(Home of the famous Tillamook Cheese)
Highway 101, just two miles north of Tillamook
P.O. Box 313
Tillamook, Oregon 97141
503-842-4481

The air, the climate, the lush green valleys and the people are all in perfect unison to create a perfect product. It comes from the land — the land of Tillamook. The product is famous and so is the creamery; it is from the land of cheese, trees and ocean breezes. You've guessed by now — Oregon's most famous commodity, Tillamook Cheese. To anyone who has consumed even an ounce will proclaim its superiority of taste and texture. As a small child, I was raised on the stuff and didn't know there were any other brands. Cheddars, medium to sharp, are the specialties, but Tillamook Creamery boasts masterful Monterey Jack and smoked cheddar, too. A group of hardy pioneers settled this small coastal valley around 1850 and began to process dairy products and the now famous cheeses. At the present time, the creamery boasts a newly remodeled facility with large gift shop, a viewing area for watching the actual cheesemaking process, and a clean, bright restaurant where you can buy a toasted Tillamook cheese sandwich, have a big glass of Tillamook milk, and a bowl of delicious Tillamook ice cream with your favorite toppings for dessert. It is a "must" stop for travelers and the restaurant is good enough to be popular with the local residents — a best choice for the perfect product —Tillamook Creamery. (Call or write for free cheese gift pack catalog.)

(See special invitation in appendix.)

GIFTS

KITCH-N-IDEAS
115 Main
Tillamook, Oregon
503-842-2209

Hours: 9:30-5:30 Mon-Fri, 9:30-5 Sat

The tantalizing aroma of fresh coffee beans, bulk tea and spices, and freshly baked croissants are all that is needed to lure any lover of great food into this charming kitchenware paradise. Zoe Naegeli provides not only the greatest aromas which can be inhaled in downtown Tillamook, but everything and anything that has to do with your kitchen with a fine selection of gourmet or old-fashioned cookware, Robot Coupe food processors, coffee makers, grinders, tablecloths, placemats, woks, electric crepe and omelette makers, cook books, and more — This shop has it all! Zoe also caters for weddings and parties from the smallest get together to the largest banquet. Low prices, smiles and a huge selection are what this store is all about. Kitch-N-Ideas — a best choice for tantalizing aromas and super gifts. Stop in for a cup of gourmet coffee.

(See special invitation in appendix.)

GIFTS/SPORTING GOODS

KIMMEL'S SPORTING GOODS AND GIFTS
1812 First Street
Tillamook, Oregon
503-842-4281

Hours: 8:30-6 Mon-Sat, 9-4 Sun

The worlds of indoors and outdoors come together in a special way at a wonderful store that has something for everyone. Yes, Tillamook has a gift finder's and sportsman's dream store, nicely rolled right into one. Iris and Ron Quick, owners of Kimmel's, have a store that is hard to compare because there is nothing quite like it anywhere else on the Oregon coast. The variety of gifts includes fine china and crystal, a full bath shop, wall decor and candles — in fact, they have one of the largest selections of top quality gifts in Oregon. Kimmel's is a doll collector's paradise with a selection of beautiful dolls.

But this isn't all! Walk through a door and you arrive in a different world — one of outdoor adventure. The Quick's sons, Rock and Kim, run the sporting goods part of the store which has everything from team sports to archery, hunting equipment to raingear, hiking equipment to weights, to information on where to catch the big fish or track the biggest elk. As a matter of fact, they have the five top salmon streams, three of the top ten steelhead streams, and some of the largest elk herds in Oregon almost outside the door. They also have a remarkable guide service to lend a helpful hand in finding those favored streams.

For both indoor and outdoor adventure, you won't want to miss this best choice — Kimmel's Sporting Goods and Gifts in downtown Tillamook.

RESTAURANTS

HADLEY HOUSE RESTAURANT
2203 Third Street
(across from the Court House)
Tillamook, Oregon
503-842-2101

The Hadley House Restaurant is located in the most beautiful old mansion in downtown Tillamook, and Harold and Betty Schild, owners, invite the whole family to come-as-you-are, bring the kids, so you can feel the warmth of this special restaurant. The charm is from another era and a special blend of "good old home cooking and fine cuisine" is the way people in Tillamook describe the Hadley House. The house has been a landmark in Tillamook for over 80 years, having been built in 1905 by pioneer C. B. Hadley, and was owned by the Hadley family until Harold and Betty bought it in 1977. The house was then converted into a restaurant complete with family pictures and period furnishings to add to the comfortable atmosphere. There is a wide choice of seafood and meat entrees with a light eaters section available and a children's menu, too. A recommendation for lunch from the chef is the grilled crab and Tillamook cheese sandwich served open face on an English muffin. Included with that is a tossed green salad, potato salad or fries. For dinner, she suggests the grilled Pacific Razor Clams, lightly breaded and grilled at a high temperature. Included in the dinners are an all-you-can-eat at the large salad bar, rice pilaf or baked potato, and warm, home-baked bread. Another dinner treat is Teriyaki Chicken Breast served with rice pilaf, salad bar and warm bread. Now for the suggested desserts: cakes of all kinds — carrot, apple, cheese and mousse — all prepared by dessert expert Carol Young. Everyone is crazy about the pies at the Hadley House, also. The Hadley House is a special place and definitely a best choice for a special blend of old-fashioned home cooking and fine cuisine.

(See special invitation in appendix.)

VICTORY HOUSE
First and Pacific
Tillamook, Oregon
503-842-4111

Hours: 11:30-10 Mon-Sat, 11:30-9 Sun
All major credit cards are accepted.

As the Victory House's name indicates, you can't lose here with the freshest and best ingredients Oregon's sea and countryside can offer your palates and at moderate prices. This nicely decorated, comfortable restaurant has been serving mouth-watering seafood and steak entrees since the 1940s. Specialties of the Victory House include homemade soups, oyster stew and clam chowder, and they are made with the very best of ingredients. For lunch, the friendly owners, Larry and Janet Silva, recommend their special recipe fish and chips or thinly sliced, deli-style ham, beef or turkey sandwiches with the soup of the day. For those with lighter appetites, try the Victory House's fish sauteed in garlic butter with seasoning and a side of cole slaw. For dinner, the Silvas recommend their delicious seafood from Tillamook Bay, especially the Deep Sea Delight with shrimp, cod, scallops and oysters; or enjoy the choicest of filet mignon steak with all the trimmings. A full bar is always available and they have special prices from 5pm-6:30pm Monday through Friday on your favorite beverages. Let us not forget dessert. Choose from homemade pies, bread pudding or rum cake. Just remember — it's all in a name — your meal is always a winner at the Victory House, a best choice for great food!

NETARTS

ACCOMMODATIONS

TERIMORE MOTEL
5105 Crab Avenue
Netarts, Oregon
503-842-4623

Fireplaces, HBO.

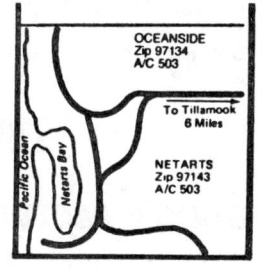

OCEANSIDE

ACCOMMODATIONS

HOUSE ON THE HILL MOTEL
(look up)
Oceanside, Oregon
503-842-6030 for reservations
toll free 1-800-235-6030

Imagine yourself flying high above the earth like a sea bird, looking down on some of the most beautiful views that can be seen while the ocean wind softly caresses your face. You can get that feeling on the House on the Hill Motel. Overlooking the ocean, this motel remarkably rests on a dramatic projection of land reaching like a finger out into the ocean, 200 to 250 feet above the rocky Oregon coast. You actually feel as if you are walking on an earthen tightrope with breathtaking, shear drops on each side where, far below, you can see two beautiful beaches, one of the largest bird rookeries on the West Coast, and lumbering sea lions among the dark, coastal rocks. Bob and Marile Thurmond are the wonderful hosts of this fine motel. They hail from Texas and have 15 years of experience in making people feel comfortable. The motel rooms all have spectacular views and are fully equipped with kitchens and comfortable beds. All you need are food and binoculars to enjoy the spectacular scenery. The motel is close to fishing, sunbathing and restaurants, and is above some of the best beaches on the Oregon coast. The whole picturesque city of Oceanside is just steps away and could very well be one of the most beautiful villages on the Oregon coast. For a best choice in comfort and breathtaking views, don't miss a stay at the House on the Hill Motel in Oceanside — you'll never forget it.

(See special invitation in appendix.)

PACIFIC CITY

ABOUT PACIFIC CITY

Pacific City, home of the Dory Fleet, surf fishing, boating, hiking, camping and golfing. For dune buggy lovers, a trip to Sand Lake is a must. In the summertime when the fishing is in full swing, enjoy a little swimming, surfing, hang gliding, horseback riding, whale watching or beachcombing for treasures of the sea. This year 'round family playground offers views from Cape Meares, Cape Lookout and Cape Kiwanda, along with their beautiful trails and wildlife. You can also enjoy fresh seafood from a fine restaurant or seafood market. Get away from it all — Pacific City is the place to do some good old relaxing by the sea.

ACCOMMODATIONS

O'SHANNON MOTEL
35280 Brouten Road
Pacific City, Oregon
503-965-6464

Kitchens, airport.

NESKOWIN

ACCOMMODATIONS

PACIFIC SANDS RESORT
48250 Breaker Blvd.
Neskowin, Oregon
503-392-3701

Decks, pool, golf, horseback riding.

PROPOSAL ROCK INN
Off Highway 101
Neskowin, Oregon
503-392-3115

Pool, sauna, TV, recreation room, restaurant, lounge.

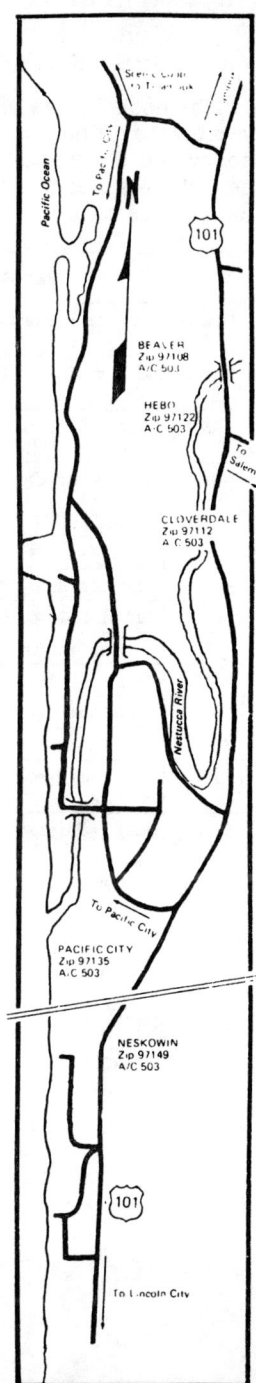

TILLAMOOK COUNTY TOUR

Tillamook County is rural, friendly and beautiful. From walks on a beach to dinner at a fine restaurant, you won't miss much if you follow our suggestions on this tour. Make sure you check the book for all the towns in Tillamook County and their best choices so you won't miss a thing.

TIME	PLACE	DESCRIPTION	HOW TO FIND IN BOOK
Dawn	Walk on Rockaway Beach	Best beach	Rockaway Beach/Beach
Breakfast	Kelly's Bar & Grill	Best family style breakfast	Rockaway Beach/Restaurant
A.M.	Trash and Treasures	Antiques	Rockaway Beach Antiques
A.M.	Shellay Gift Store	Fantastic Gifts	Rockaway Beach/Gifts
A.M.	The Clothes Hanger	Best women's apparel	Rockaway Beach/Women's Apparel
A.M.	The Kite Shop	Best kites	Rockaway Beach/Kites
Lunch	Old Mill Restaurant	Best lunch	Garibaldi/Restaurant
P.M.	Virginia's Gifts	Best gifts/toys	Garibaldi/Gifts
P.M.	Tillamook Creamery	Best cheese/gifts	Tillamook/Cheese/Gifts
P.M.	Blue Heron Cheese	Best cheese/gifts	Tillamook/Gifts
P.M.	Kitch-n-ideas	Best kitchen/gifts	Tillamook/Gifts
P.M.	Kimmel's Sporting Goods & Gifts	Best sporting goods/gifts	Tillamook/Sporting Goods/Gifts
Dinner toss up	Hadley House Restaurant	Best dinner	Tillamook/Restaurant
Dinner toss up	Victory House Restaurant	Best dinner	Tillamook/Restaurant

Chapter Three

LINCOLN COUNTY

ABOUT LINCOLN COUNTY

Stretching over 60 miles along the majestic Pacific Ocean from tranquil Cape Perpetua north to scenic Cascade Head, Lincoln County abounds in outdoor adventures and attractions. It is not surprising that the county has been coined "Oregon's Sea Country". For generations, farms, forests and fishermen have chosen the simple, natural lifestyle which abounds here amid clear, babbling brooks and rivers, towering forests, the endless unspoiled coastline and deep blue water bays. Imagine massive mountains, forested lush green by the moisture-rich marine air and separated by narrow, steep-sided river valleys. Perch yourself atop commanding rock cliffs, sit among a profusion of wild flowers strewn over grassy hill tops, stroll along broad, sandy beaches as your senses beckon to the whisper of restless ocean and surging surf. You'll love the diverse fishing opportunities awaiting you — everything from ocean fishing charters to bay fishing for flounder, perch, bass, crab or fly fishing in the upper rivers and great salmon and steelhead fishing in the main waters.

Various museums and aquariums like the OSU Marine Science Center on the south shore of Yaquina Bay offer you the opportunity to learn more about the geology, history, sea lions, seals and other sea life native to the Oregon Coast. More than 60 public and private parks are scattered throughout Lincoln County to afford visitors the opportunity for camping, hiking, picnics and scenic beach adventures. Accommodations are excellent with a host of modern lodging options waiting to welcome you.

There are plenty of modestly priced inns and restaurants to serve you everything from the freshest Oregon seafood entrees to terrific gourmet ice cream cones and every type of food imaginable in between. Lincoln County — the tranquil beauty of "Sea Country" along with the warm, Oregon hospitality of locals who know how to lay on the best for the enjoyment of visitors who stop here. For additional information, contact Lincoln County Chamber of Commerce, P.O. Box 68, Newport, Oregon 97365.

ATTRACTIONS

BURROWS HOUSE MUSEUM

Located just north of the Log Cabin, this house was originally built in 1895 by John and Susan Burrows at a cost of $1400. It was utilized as a boarding house until 1914. The house was then sold to a funeral parlor business until 1976 when the Bank of Newport purchased the property. Rather than destroy the antique house, the bank presented it to Lincoln County Historical Society and it was moved to its present location. Today the museum here features exhibits highlighting the household furnishings, clothing and history of Lincoln County.

LINCOLN COUNTY HISTORICAL MUSEUM COMPLEX
579 S.W. 9th Street
Newport, Oregon
503-265-7509

Open from 10am-5pm June-Sept and 11am-4pm Oct-May; closed Mondays.

LOG CABIN MUSEUM

Located just behind the Armory, this cabin was built in the early 1960s through donated materials and volunteer labor. It houses the unique collection of artifacts from the Siletz Indian Reservation as well as logging, maritime and farming exhibits.

EVENTS

SPRING EVENTS

March — Yachats Arts and Crafts Festival; Blessing of the Fleet; Newport Porthole Players Theatre Performances; Lincoln County Home Show.

April — Farmer's Market, April-Oct, every Sat at Fairgrounds.

May — Loyalty Days and Sea Faire Festival in Newport; the Sailing Regatta, Newport; Depoe Bay Fleet of Flowers; Porthole Players Theatre Performances; annual Spring Kite Festival, Lincoln City.

SUMMER EVENTS

July — Independence Day Parade, fireworks over Siletz Bay in Lincoln City; Arts and Crafts Fair, Lincoln City, third Sunday in the park, Regatta Gardens, Devils Lake; Independence Day Parade and fireworks over Siletz Bay, Lincoln City; Yaquina Bay Yacht Club Fun Boat Race, fireworks; Lincoln County Fair at the fairgrounds; City of Newport Tennis Tournament; Bullhead Days, Toledo; The Porthole Players Theatre Performances, third Sunday in the park, Regatta Gardens, Devils Lake; Lincoln City Sand Castle Building Contest.

August — Toledo Family Festival; City of Newport Tennis Tournament; Beach Blast, Newport, racquetball; Toledo Summer Festival; Summer Children's Festival, Lincoln City.

AUTUMN EVENTS

September — Yaquina River Boating Marathon and Celebration; Depoe Bay Salmon Bake; Annual Fall Kite Festival, Newport; Annual Lincoln City Kite Festival; Yachats Annual Smelt Fry; Salmon Derby, Waldport.

October — Yachats Annual Fall Kite Festival; Annual Clam Chowder Bake-off, Lincoln City; Annual Driftwood Derby, horses race on beach, Lincoln City.

November — Fishermen Wives' Annual Benefit Ball; Daniel Toledo Christmas Craft Fair, Santa Claus comes to town, Newport.

WINTER EVENTS

December & January — Lincoln City Christmas Festival and Parade; Yachats, Christmas Is Yachats—one month of yuletide celebration.

February — Depoe Bay Coastal Run, 10,000 meter warmup run; Newport Seafood and Wine Festival; Porthole Players Theatre Performances.

LINCOLN CITY

ABOUT LINCOLN CITY

Would you believe that at one time Lincoln City was five distinct communities? It's true all right. In 1964, three incorporated cities, Oceanlake, D Lake and Taft, merged with the communities of Cutler City and Nescott to form the friendly resort of Lincoln City. Here you have several excellent beach accesses, fishing, and water sports in Devil's Lake, fishing and crabbing in Siletz Bay and Taft Dock, a fine selection of art galleries and craft shops, and an award winning statue of Abraham Lincoln in Kirtsis Park, as well as a fine selection of resorts, motels, restaurants and other facilities. Don't forget to see the "D" River, the world's shortest at the mouth of Devil's Lake Park. If you love golf, you'll find four excellent golf courses within minutes. For kite lovers, there are kite flying contests; if you like fast excitement, there are speed boat races. You can also find fresh seafood at roadside stands or eat out at one of the several excellent restaurants. This is truly a taste of three fine cities plus two — Lincoln City.

CHAMBER OF COMMERCE
3070 N.W. Highway 101
(P.O. Box 787X)
Lincoln City, Oregon 97367
503-994-3070, or phone toll free in Oregon
1-800-452-2151

Promoting business, community and competitive enterprises are only a few of the services the Lincoln City Chamber of Commerce offers the community and visitors, ensuring everyone a wonderful stay in Lincoln City. For more information concerning Lincoln City accommodations or demographic information, please contact the Lincoln City Chamber of Commerce, people who are always ready to help with a smile.

Lincoln County 85

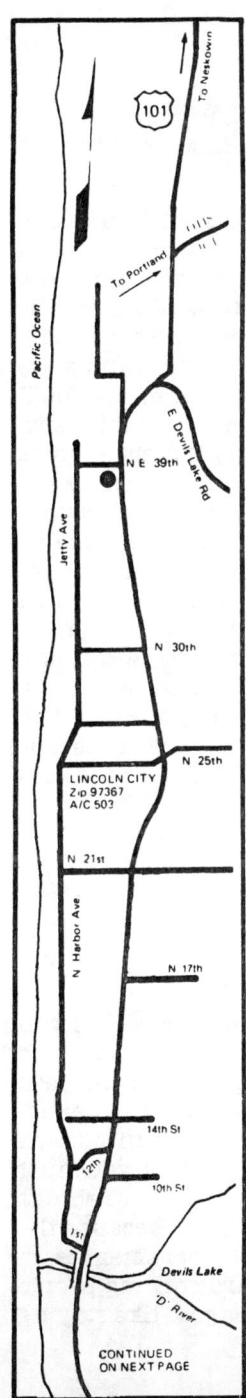
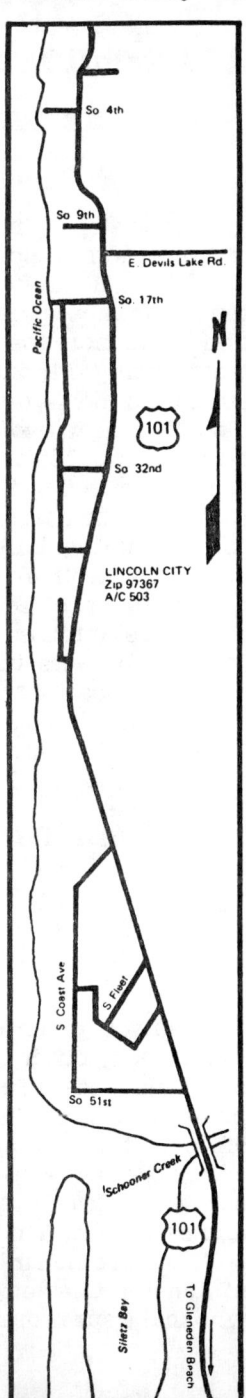

ACCOMMODATIONS

THE INN AT SPANISH HEAD
Located on Hwy 101, midway to Lincoln City
Lincoln City, Oregon

You can step right onto the beach from the front floor at one of Oregon's most spectacular cliffside ocean resorts, The Inn at Spanish Head. If you like a higher view, this fine inn rises ten stories above the changing moods and tides of the Pacific and offers more than relaxation. You will find, on the beachfront setting, 146 individually decorated condominium-style suites and rooms, each with stunning views of the coast. You'll also find one to two-bedroom suites, fully equipped kitchens, telephones and color TVs to make you feel almost more at home than at home. But if you are anything like me, you will want to head to the beach for a little beachcombing, sunset watching, swimming, building sand castles, or a little romance on a twilight stroll. You can also do some swimming in an outdoor heated pool, relax in a sauna or have fun in a recreation room. Just minutes away are fascinating art and craft galleries, glass blowers, intriguing shops, live summer theater, and beautiful, coastal trails for hiking. Also available are tennis, deep sea fishing and golf. So feel the breeze in your face and the wonderful solitude of sand and surf — the perfect escape from it all at The Inn at Spanish Head in Lincoln City.

SEA GYPSY MOTEL
145 N.W. Inlet
Lincoln City, Oregon 97367
503-994-5266
Oregon WATTS 1-800-452-6929
Outside Oregon WATTS 800-341-2142

When you go for a trip to the beach, where else would you want to stay but in a modern luxury condo, 20 feet from one of the most beautiful sandy beaches in Oregon, with enclosed pool, saunas, kitchen facilities, color cable TVs, and refrigerators. It is extremely quiet, being tucked away in its own cove, and is at a rate you can afford. The place where you must stay is the Sea Gypsy in Lincoln City. It has all these things and even more. The rooms are kept immaculate because the staff is run efficiently by the husband-wife management team of Ken and Charlotte Cuff, friendly and hardworking people who make sure your stay at the Sea Gypsy is just like staying at your own home, only they do all the work. The Sea Gypsy is located just off Highway 101, right before the north side of the world's shortest river's bridge, the "D" River. Because of the popularity, please call 15 days in advance during the peak summer season for reservations. I stayed at the Sea Gypsy on a cold, December day, but the Cuffs made it a warm visit. The pool is open year 'round. For a great place to stay — a best choice with everything to offer — try the Sea Gypsy Motel in Lincoln City.

(See special invitation in Appendix.)

ADDITIONAL ACCOMMODATIONS

COZY COVE MOTEL
515 N.W. Inlet Ave.
Lincoln City, Oregon
503-994-2950

Beach acces, showtime, in-room jacuzzis.

"D" SANDS MOTEL
171 S.W. Highway 101
Lincoln City, Oregon
503-994-5244

Kitchens, showtime, beach access.

NORDIC MOTEL
2133 N.W. Inlet Ave.
Lincoln City, Oregon
503-994-8145

Kitchens, pool, saunas, fireplace, beach access.

ANTIQUES/GIFTS

SEAFAIRE ANTIQUES AND GIFTS
304 S. Highway 101
Lincoln City, Oregon 97367
503-994-3765

We've all had friends over eighty years of age, and what you can say without hesitation about each one of them is that they become more valuable every day. Things these "oldsters" can teach us — how to bake a delicious loaf of bread, make handmade lace, or churn milk into fresh butter — yes, the older they become, the more they have to share with the modern society that has moved so fast and left some of the best things behind. Just like these special people, some items from the past become more valuable every day, things we now call antiques. Real things, none of which is called electronic or computerized or space age, and all made from real material — wood, china, natural things from the earth. A shop on the Oregon coast that is doing one of the best jobs preserving these valued items of the past is Seafaire Antiques. The shop is owned and operated by Glenn and Sue Tingley, a friendly couple who, after raising a family, decided to settle in Lincoln City and open this fantastic antique emporium. The shop is full of antique furniture, glassware, Indian artifacts, ivory pieces, collectibles, old victrolas — everything old and gaining value each day. Glenn and Sue are very congenial and are more than happy to help you in any way. They both are experienced antique buffs with over nine years in the business. Almost everything they sell is from the local area, things you cannot find anywhere else. I love antiques, and this shop has to be a best choice for me, and like our friends over 80 years of age, this shop will get better day after day with people like Glenn and Sue Tingley as the owners.

ART GALLERY

MOSSY CREEK POTTERY
Just off Highway 101, look for state highway signs at south end of Siletz Bay at Immonen Road, first road north of Salishan.
Lincoln City, Oregon
503-996-2415

Open year 'round, seven days a week, 9-5

Located on a beautiful wooded lane, well worth the drive by itself, a treat is in store for anyone who visits this unique pottery studio and gallery, where the beauty of the surroundings is reflected in the work of the several fine Oregon potters represented here. Owners and resident potters Tom and Joanne Davis create much of the pottery on display at Mossy Creek in the charming studio next to the gallery, and visitors are always welcome to watch through the window while they work. As you walk into the gallery, you will be struck by the stunning glazes Tom has developed, including brilliant copper reds, cobalt blues, celadon greens, caramel golds, and many others you'll have to see to appreciate. You'll be pleased with the excellent craftsmanship and reasonable prices. Joanne was quick to tell me that their work is prices so people will be comfortable using it in their daily lives and won't be tempted to put it away somewhere to protect it. All the pottery is, of course, food safe and can be used in the oven, microwave and dishwasher. The variety seems endless, with unique butter safes, sauce warmers, casseroles, cannisters, dinnerware, bird feeders, planters, exquisite vases, huge punch bowls and much more. If you happen to be on the coast Thanksgiving weekend, don't miss Mossy Creek's annual three-day Open House and Sale! All the local folks, as well as people from all over the state, flock to the gallery for this special gala event which includes lavish refreshments, festive decorations, and sale prices on everything. Do take the ⅓ mile drive up beautiful Immonen Road from Highway 101 to find the best choice of earth and artist — Mossy Creek Pottery, Lincoln City.

ART GALLERY/GIFTS

OCEAN LAKE STUDIO GALLERY
(across from the "D" River wayside
in Boatyard Village)
Lincoln City, Oregon
503-994-5335

Artists Marv and Julie Taylor have created an art gallery "par excellence" featuring some of the finest original work by Northwest artists, plus an impressive selection of one-of-a-kind collectibles. Paintings and oils, water colors, pastels and pencil drawings grace the gallery walls. Check out the full Goebel line of German miniatures, Hummel figurines and collector plates. Marvel at the elegant pewter sculptures and the miniatures cast in bronze, gorgeous sea life and wood sculptures created by John Perry. The gallery boasts fine, handblown art glass, handpainted figurines from Scotland, a beautiful selection of stained glass, fine European porcelain gifts, bone china and crystal. You'll love the handblown glass hummingbirds created by one of our local Oregon artists. There are also scrimshaw engravings, intricate crystal jewelry and one-of-a-kind gold figurines. Imagine, over 3,000 square feet of space here housing the largest collection you'll find anywhere of original creations of local, coastal Northwest artists. Marv even offers a custom framing and matting service for customers.

There is a unique added attraction you won't want to miss. Go through the "Hall of Living Light", a masterpiece collection featuring the work of John Plumer Ludlum. His series of exquisite paintings is valued at more than seven million dollars. You will be amazed as you watch the canvasses change before your very eyes. Art by day, changing color tones by dusk and again by night, the paintings are part of a unique process which transforms the visual moods of their paintings according to the amount of sunlight or evening light touching the canvass. This is an experience you are not likely to easily forget. Ocean Lake Studio Gallery — a best choice for fine original artwork right here on the mid-Oregon Coast.

(See special invitation in Appendix.)

ATTRACTIONS

DEVIL'S LAKE

Enjoy the sea and fresh water almost hand-in-hand at Devil's Lake near Lincoln City. Small creeks and underwater springs feed this beautiful lake in its relatively shallow, thus warm, water, luring swimmers and water skiers throughout the summer to this 640 acre lake. You can also do a little fishing for large mountain bass, trout, yellow perch, bullhead and catfish. The lake empties into the Pacific Ocean via the "D" River, the smallest river in the world. So enjoy a little fresh water action near Lincoln City at Devil's Lake.

EVENTS

CLAM CHOWDER COOK-OFF

In October, enjoy a taste of the Oregon Coast at the Lincoln City Clam Chowder Cook- off featuring locally made clam chowders from restaurants, organizations, and individuals as well as several booths featuring smoked meats, breads, Oregon wines, and on and on. One you won't want to miss is out at Lincoln Square Shopping Mall — come and enjoy a little good cooking and fun, Oregon style.

DRIFTWOOD DERBY

If you have horses, this event is for you. There is a wide range of events including walking, obstacle jumping, sprints and relays. There is also a special triathalon event which includes a canoe race across Devil's Lake, a 2½ mile bicycle race, and a 2 mile horseback race. You might like to enter an endurance race sponsored by the Lincoln City Chamber of Commerce and the North Lincoln County Equestrian Society. Oh yes! To start things off right, the Derby Breakfast will be served at the Lincoln City Plaza — eggs, pancakes, sausage, coffee, juice and lots of fun company, so join in.

OREGON WINE FESTIVAL

Join us in tasting the best of Oregon wines and food at the Oregon Wine Festival held on Mother's Day weekend in May at Surftide Beach Resort. Sixteen Oregon wineries display their best for tasting while area civic organizations and businesses provide tasty treats like shrimp cocktail, smoked meats, fresh fruit, shortcake, and fried rice. The Festival is held indoors at the Surftide's tennis courts, a comfortable setting for enjoying fine wine and excellent food. Special features are accordion players and other musicians who stroll around the festival grounds, and display booths showing jewels and sea shells. The Festival is co-sponsored by Surftide Resort and the Oceanlake Elks Lodge No. 1886 at Lincoln City. So come enjoy some fine wine and food at this fun festival in Lincoln City.

GIFTS

ALDER HOUSE II
(½ mile east of Hwy 101
on Immonen Road)
P.O. Box 2191
Lincoln City, Oregon 97367

A fascinating experience is what you'll find at the Alder House II. You can watch while the 2,000 year old tradition of shaping beautiful objects of glass is performed. Owner Buzz Williams has been perfecting his craft for over 18 years. He creates one-of-a-kind vases, bowls, goblets, glasses, oil lamps, paperweights, and many other gift items, as well as doing customized work. There is a tempting price range of $20 to $200 which makes it nearly impossible to walk away empty-handed. Alder House II is open to the public March 15 through the end of November. The hours are 10am to 5pm, seven days a week. The Alder House II is an exciting best choice of the Oregon Coast.

THE CHRISTMAS COTTAGE
(In the Nelscott Strip)
3305 S.W. Highway 101
Lincoln City, Oregon 97367
503-996-2230

Open: 10-5, seven days
except Jan-Feb, weekends only

'Twas the night before Christmas, and all through the condo, everything was beautiful, yes even the packages with their bright colored bows. Condos, log cabins, or plain, old, rambling ranch can all look beautiful the night before Christmas thanks to one special lady in Lincoln City, Barbara Jenkins, owner of The Christmas Cottage. Barbara was one of the first entrepreneurs to open the year 'round Christmas shop and, like others, has found it to be an astounding success. If you are like me and love the Christmas holiday season or love to shop and have a little Christmas in June or even January, The Christmas Cottage is completely bursting with the things to make Christmas more special. The shop has a variety of things from hand-blown Christmas ornaments to German nutcrackers and smokers, hand-painted glass ornaments to special wrap, Christmas cards to East German candle pyramids. It is a shop full of good will all because of the holiday spirit brought on by Barbara and her sparkling personality. Everything you buy will please and is fully guaranteed, with hard-to-find items just one of Barbara's specialties. The shop will ship anywhere and there are mailing tubes and other boxes in stock to make sure your gift arrives in perfect condition. You can call Barbara and order things like bubble lights, collectible ornaments, and Nativity scenes of all sizes. For a best choice for that wonderful spirit Christmas brings year 'round, visit Barbara Jenkins' Christmas Cottage in Lincoln City. (While you are there, you will meet a new friend named Priscilla. Just ask.)

(See special invitation in Appendix.)

PARLOR BEARS
1423 N.W. Highway 101
(north of "D" River on Hwy 101,
across from Copeland Lumber)
Lincoln City, Oregon 97367
503-994-2082

Hours: 10-5 seven days a week

You are about to enter "teddy bear heaven" when you set foot in this unique bear shop featuring one of the best selections in imported and limited edition teddy bears anywhere. A host of the Northwest's most lovable handcrafted bears are jumping up and down ready to greet you. Teddies from 40 different manufacturers throughout the world plus 25 western bear artists present a combination of huggable, furry fellow that seems endless. There are electronic bears that talk and some that purr, rollerskating bears, drumming bears and dancing bears as well as bear puppets and just huggy bears. Collectors are delighted with the variety of Lucy and Me porcelain bears. Bear posters, books, stationery, t-shirts and sweatshirts are just part of the bearaphernalia available.

Marge and Tom Adolphson began this creative shop three years ago. Their amazing collection of cuddly creatures runs the gambit. The shop is delightfully laid out and offers customers a mail order shipping service plus special collector's discounts and newsletter with bear update information. Parlor Bears is unbearably good fun. MasterCard and Visa accepted.

(See special invitation in Appendix.)

SEAGULL FACTORY
(Next to kite shop on Highway 101)
1020 S.E. Third Street
Lincoln City, Oregon 97367
503-994-2660

Open: 10am-5pm, Mon thru Sat

The Oregon coast is one of the most breathtaking places on earth with jagged, rocky shores, long, secluded sandy beaches, and abundant wildlife. The most famous of all the wildlife on Oregon's coast are the ever present, friendly seagulls. Many of these beautiful birds will fly right up to you and, with pleading calls and looks, beg you out of your entire picnic lunch. Most people are willing to give up a little food just to see these art acrobats of the sea breeze come so close. These seagulls give us a feeling we can't get from any other bird or animal — a special feeling of freedom. Just think — to be able to fly over beaches all day and eat nothing but fresh, Oregon seafood! Thanks to the Seagull Factory in Lincoln City, you can take that idea home with you. The factory, or should we say, art studio, is owned and operated by Paul and Denise Mosier. You'll find Paul hard at work in the shop crafting seagulls — seagulls standing on rocks, seagulls flying, seagulls everywhere! Paul explained that it takes more than pouring and casting to obtain the perfect seagull. It takes years of trying to come up with the right casting materials that hold up to weather and all the chemicals found in the air. All seagulls at the factory are cast from a special cement with qualities that will make your gull last a long time. All are hand-painted and are slightly different. Even the climate at Lincoln City is perfect to make gulls, as if we wouldn't have guessed. You see, to set the concrete mixture right, the temperature should not go over 75 degrees Fahrenheit, and it nearly never does in the Lincoln City area. The shop is more than seagulls. They also have pelicans, small seabirds, and the most authentic dogs and cats you've ever seen. This best choice has quality that lasts, creative designs, and best of all, you take that part of the Oregon coast home with you that reminds you of a perfect dream — true freedom.

(See special invitation in Appendix.)

GOLF

DEVIL'S LAKE GOLF AND RACQUET CLUB
3445 Clubhouse Drive
Lincoln City, Oregon 97367
503-994-8442

Lincoln City is known for its sparkling clean beaches, the cool climate, and warm people. Lincoln City seems to have just about everything in one place to enjoy a for weekend or a lifetime. This city even has more thanks to Carl and Betty Mason who recently purchased Lincoln City's sleepy little Devil's Lake Golf Course and transformed it into a mecca for fun, health and fitness. The course jumped from nine holes to 12 almost overnight, and a full 18 holes will be completed as fast. The small clubhouse was abandoned for a modern, football field size building that offers a fine restaurant with banquet facilities (can accommodate up to 350 guests), six racquetball courts of the latest design, an exercise room that would make the largest big city club envious, two well-lighted indoor tennis courts, a delightful snack bar, and a fully equipped pro shop for all your sporting needs including pros to help you shave strokes off your game. With saunas, jacuzzis, classes offered for aerobics and tennis, and even a resident massage therapist, the Masons have turned Devil's Lake Golf Course into the most modern and beautiful sports facility on the Oregon coast. They are sharing their beauty with others by building single family dwellings and townhouses along the timbered borders of the well-kept golf course. Call for more details. Sparkling clean beaches, fresh air, cool climate, warm and healthy people — Carl and Betty Mason's new Devil's Lake Golf and Racquet Club — a best choice for health on the Oregon Coast.

LEATHER

NELSCOTT LEATHER WORKS
(On the Nelscott Strip)
3259 S. Highway 101
Lincoln City, Oregon 97367
503-996-3316

"Turning the leathers of today into personal leather goods to last you a thousand tomorrows," a quote directly from Nelscott Leatherworks' owners Joan and Wayne Gordon. The Gordons are a bit modest with this quote. What they need to add is that the leather they "turn" is of only the best quality. The way they "turn it" into leather goods is through years of skill, hard work and artistic talent. At their shop in Lincoln City, they turn out some of the most beautiful leather work you'll find anywhere in the world. If you love the soft leathers from Italy, but believe in *Made in the U.S.A.*, then you'll find this shop to your liking. Even though they make traditional leather belts, wallets and carry a large line of buckles, they also have a large inventory of original design work and fashion leather pieces like clutch bags, handbags, and luggage — all in the softest 100% cowhide with over 15 yummy colors to choose from. One of the specialties of the shop is copying any soft leather bag, no matter how old. As an example, if you have loved a purse for years and it is falling apart but you just don't want to give it up, bring it in and let Joan's talent go to work for you. She will draw up a pattern from the old purse and make you a new one exactly like the original — all in leather, even inside pockets and dividers. You might think this shop will be high priced. Quite the contrary! Their prices are more than fair and that could well be an understatement.

Nelscott Leatherworks carries more than just leather crafted by the Gordons. They also have a fine line of pottery from a few select Central Oregon Coast potters: Michael Soeby, well-known for his perfection in stoneware and for his funny-headed oil lamps; his wife, Linda, known for her one-of-a-kind hangings and small clay animal whistles; and her sister, Barbara Adams, gaining renown for her stoneware impressed with cedar leaves. If you love things of quality made by some of the most adept craftsmen in the industry, try this best choice — Nelscott Leatherworks — making things you love so much you'll want to have last a thousand tomorrows.

MUSEUM

LACEY'S DOLL MUSEUM
3400 N.E. Highway 101
Lincoln City, Oregon 97367
503-994-2392

Lincoln City has many interesting, beautiful places to visit. One of the most interesting is Lacey's Doll Museum which has been open to the public for 33 years. Some dolls are beautiful, some stately, and all unique in one way or another. There are 3,000 to 4,000 dolls in one of the largest private collections of dolls in the western United States. The museum, run by Hazel Lacey and her son, Dean, have been a "must" stop for anyone interested in dolls and antiques. Some dolls date back over 100 years, while some are as modern as the Cabbage Patch Doll of today. The largest doll is Linda Susan, a 48" tall, black haired china doll over 100 years old, wearing a dress of the 1860s. The whole museum takes on a mystical, antique 1930s look with a touch of a magic toy box. As you wander through, you'll find a life-size replica of Queen Elizabeth, Dolly Parton dolls, Shirley Temple dolls, and many more — thousands of dolls. I'm sure that when the last museum patron leaves and the lights go out for the evening, the dolls all start dancing, drinking tea and talking about the tourists that wandered through that particular day. So, for an unusual, interesting experience, try Lacey's Doll Museum — a best choice for anyone who loves beautiful things from the past. (Admission rates are 1950s prices.)

(See special invitation in Appendix.)

RESTAURANTS

GALLUCCI'S PIZZERIA
2845 N.W. Highway 101
Lincoln City, Oregon 97367
503-994-3411

Open: Mon-Thurs 11-10
noon-midnight Fri-Sat, noon-10 Sun

If you want a fun, clean and moderately priced place to take the whole group, you won't find a better choice than Gallucci's Pizzeria in Lincoln City. The building is large, the decor is turn-of-the-century, and the pizza is excellent. People who live in the Lincoln City area prefer this pizza parlor over all others. The pizza is top-notch with only fresh and real ingredients used. Beer, wine and your favorite soft drinks are offered. Sharon Gallucci, owner, has been in the business for 12 years and she cares about every bite of food you eat. Her staff is excellent and you don't feel out of place in shorts and thongs. Sharon's suggestion for lunch was the Big Irving sandwich made on toasted French bread with olives, ground beef, cheese, onions and tomato (it is a local favorite). For dinner, try the seafood pizza with shrimp, clams, oysters, mushrooms, onions, olives, green peppers, cheese and French tomato slices — a gourmet delight! If you are into antiques, you must see the over 100 year old bar. It was the bar out of the old Shaniko Hotel in central Oregon. The tables are from the twenties and from the eighties. There are movies nightly, news from 5 to 6pm, and music videos Friday and Saturday nights on the "Big Screen" — free! Major sporting events are also shown. For a best choice for fun, moderate prices, plus high quality food, come to Gallucci's Pizzeria in Lincoln City.

(See special invitation in Appendix.)

LIL' SAMBO RESTAURANT
3262 N.E. Highway 101
Lincoln City, Oregon
503-994-3626

Open: 6am-8pm daily

A fairy tale written by Helen Bannerman set in East India was the reason the world's third pancake style restaurant opened in Lincoln City in 1957. The restaurant was named after the East Indian boy who made pancakes famous by eating 169 of them. Since the restaurant opened, millions of pancakes have been served to the people who lived in Lincoln City because it is the favorite place to eat breakfast or lunch by the local people and tradesmen in the area. Plus, year after year the same tourists have returned to enjoy breakfast, lunch and dinner. It is called Lil' Sambo and has nothing to do with the past Sambo's chain of restaurants which opened in the early sixties. Lil' Sambo was opened by a remarkable entrepreneur, Ron Krieger, who is seen running the restaurant on a day-by-day basis to this day. Ron explained that from the first day they opened, nothing but the finest quality has been served and most everything is made from scratch. For breakfast, try banana, blueberry, Swedish, French or German pancakes. Or if you want a filling, high protein breakfast, try a giant omelette made with four fresh eggs and melted Tillamook cheese. For lunch, deli-style sandwiches stacked high with thin-sliced meat and cheeses, are served with your choice of bread, soup or salad, baked beans or French fries. For dinner, select from any of these favorites — barbecued ribs or any seafood dish with full salad bar, soup, choice of potato, fresh bread and a choice of coffee or tea.

There is a real "family feeling" at this restaurant. All of Ron's children worked in the restaurant as they were growing up, and one daughter has stayed on as a cook. The manager has been with Ron for 20 years and her children have also worked here. One of her sons remains as night cook/supervisor. Most of the waitresses started out as busgirls in their teens, grew up and became waitresses. They hire a lot of local teenagers and are proud that they have been able to help finance a number of college educations by providing work. There is a large gift shop area full of fun coast memorabilia and other items for children and adults. Always clean with low prices and top quality foods served expertly — you can't find a better choice for a family style restaurant in Lincoln City. High chairs, booster chairs are available and all major credit cards accepted. (Ask about the strawberry waffles. They are top-notch and so-o-o good!)

(See special invitation in Appendix.)

WINE TASTING/GIFTS

THE SHIPWRECK CELLARS
3521 S.W. Highway 101
(On the Nelscott Strip)
Lincoln City, Oregon
503-996-3221

Hours: 11-5 Mon-Sat, noon-5 Sun

If you love fine wines, The Shipwreck Cellars in Lincoln City offers 50 different wines from dry to sweet, all from the excellent vineyards of Oregon. Harry and Mary Lockwood have been in the wine business, serving the best, since 1981. If you want to sample some of the best in Oregon wines, Harry and Mary will make sure you get enough of a sample to really taste the difference. There are so many vintages you'll not want to miss, but one to try is Oregon's own five star rated Oak Knoll 1982 vintage select made from pinot noir grapes and aged in French oak, or the several fine Riesling wines. If you're interested in something different, try some fruit wine; you just might change your mind about it. If you want to take some wine home with you, you can buy it by the bottle or there are good discounts when you buy by the case or mixed case. There are also gift items, such as t- shirts, gift wine boxes, and hand-crafted wine cabinets. You'll enjoy the wines from almost all of Oregon's finest vineyards, as well as the friendly, down-to-earth help offered by Harry and Mary at Shipwreck Cellars, definitely a perfect place to be shipwrecked.

(See special invitation in Appendix.)

LINCOLN CITY TOUR

Stroll along the banks of the smallest river in the world, the "D", in the early morning hours. Visit one of the largest doll museums anywhere. Watch a glass blower create objects of beauty and dine at one of the finest resorts on the Oregon Coast. This tour has some of the *musts* along the Oregon Coast. Follow it and you'll have a day long remembered.

TIME	PLACE	DESCRIPTION	HOW TO FIND IN BOOK
Dawn	D River Beach	Best beach	Lincoln City/Beach
Breakfast	Lil' Sambo	Best breakfast	Lincoln City/Restaurant
A.M.	Lacey's Doll Museum	Best doll museum	Lincoln City/Museum
A.M.	Parlor Bears	Best bears/gifts	Lincoln City/Gifts
A.M.	Ocean Lake Studio Gallery	Best gallery/gifts	Lin. City/Art Gallery
A.M.	Seagull Factory	Best gulls in town	Lincoln City/Gifts
A.M.	Sea Faire Antiques	Best antiques	Lincoln City/Antiques
A.M.	The Christmas Cottage	Best Christmas gifts	Lincoln City/Gifts
A.M.	Nelscott Leather Works	Best leather work	Lincoln City/Leather
Lunch	Chez Jeannette	Best lunch	Gleneden Beach/Restaurant
P.M.	Alder House	Best glass blowing	Gleneden Beach/Glass
P.M.	Mossy Creek Pottery	Best pottery	Glen. Beach/Pottery
Coffee Break	Coast Roast Coffee Company	Best coffee	Gleneden Beach/Gourmet Coffee
P.M.	Hot Pots	Best kitchen gifts	Gleneden Beach/Gifts
P.M.	The Wooden Duck	Best toys	Gleneden Beach/Toys
Dinner	Salishan Resort	Best dinner	Gleneden Beach/Resort

GLENEDEN BEACH

ACCOMMODATIONS

SALISHAN LODGE
(located on Hwy 101,
three miles south of Lincoln City)
Gleneden Beach, Oregon
503-764-3600 for reservations
503-764-3635 for dining reservations

When the most pleasant surroundings are what you deserve, treat yourself to the most pleasing resort on the Oregon coast. Salishan Lodge is not only pleasant, it has what it takes to make a five star rating with Mobil Travel Guide. Five star ratings are hard to get, but with a championship 18 hole oceanside golf course, indoor tennis, elegant accommodations with fireplaces, the largest wine cellar found in any resort on the West Coast, and superb cuisine prepared by a chef who knows how what to do with the many fresh edibles that Oregon is famous for. Salishan Lodge is located between Lincoln City and Depoe Bay on Highway 101, situated on a tree-lined hill overlooking Siletz Bay and the Pacific Ocean. Convenient shopping or beachcombing are within walking distance. The resort offers dining at its best with three full dining rooms to serve you. Soft entertainment and a full bar complement the lodge, service is as good as you'll find at the best in San Francisco and the food is excellent. Try the Oregon rack of lamb or a fresh shellfish dish. The head chef, Robert Pounding, is known for creating dishes from Oregon's best of what the local seas and local farms in the Willamette Valley have to offer. To complement your meal, every bottle of wine available and made in Oregon is found in the resort's extensive wine cellar. Most restaurants offer 5 to 15 wine offerings; Salishan offers 1500 plus. The wine list is most distinctive with the best from France, Germany, Italy, California and especially, the Northwest. Ask if you can visit the wine cellar — it's impressive. The golf course is always in perfect playable condition and there isn't a day that goes by, rain or shine, but that you'll see someone out shooting a white ball around the scenic course. This is the only oceanside course in Oregon. Between Russ Cleveland, general manager of Salishan, and his staff, good care is given to thousands of first time visitors to Oregon. We would like to thank Russ and his staff for the many people who consider Oregon their best choice because their first experience with Oregon was so satisfying. Salishan Lodge — you deserve this best choice! Call for reservations and give yourself a pleasing time.

ADDITIONAL ACCOMMODATIONS

BEACHCOMBERS HAVEN
P.O. Box 275
Gleneden Beach, Oregon
503-764-2252

Two and three bedroom units, kitchens, fireplaces.

CAVALIER CONDOMINIUMS
Highway 101
Gleneden Beach, Oregon
503-764-2353

Pool, kitchens.

GOURMET COFFEE

COAST ROAST COFFEE COMPANY
In the Market Place at Salishan
(3½ miles south of Lincoln City
on Highway 101, across from Salishan Lodge)
Gleneden Beach, Oregon
503-764-3330

Step inside and you'll feel transported into the flavor of an Italian coffee house complete with custom wood cabinetry, green plants, imported teas, shelves brimming with a selection of internationally blended coffee beans, and the penetrating aroma of some of the best brewed coffee we've tasted anywhere. Owner Ellie Kringer, who also operates her Hot Pots cookware shop next door, loves offering visitors a taste of gourmet coffee. Try one of her toddies or specialty espresso drinks like the Italian Supus served in attractive glass coffee cups. The house blend is also a sure bet, a rich blend of Mexican espresso and Kenyan coffee beans. There is a daily board that features two specialty coffees plus a large selection of fresh coffee beans in regular or Swiss water process decaf, all available for purchase by the pound. Ellie also stocks a full line of coffee brewing systems, including Bosch and Braun, Melitta and Chemex coffee makers. The imported mugs from England fit nicely with the attractive, relaxed feel of the place as you sit back and enjoy an afternoon cup of coffee. The toughest part will be in choosing which one.

(See special invitation in Appendix.)

KITCHEN GIFTS

HOT POTS COOKWARE
Located in the Market Place at Salishan
(3½ miles south of Lincoln City on Hwy 101)
Gleneden Beach, Oregon
503-764-2000

Owner Ellie Kringer has been working hard for the past seven years to come up with a great line of culinary cookware that offers the best for your favorite gourmet. Ellie originally graduated from UCLA with a degree in home economics and ever since then, she has been whipping up great recipes and sharing her love for cooking. She offers specialty cooking classes at the store and they are all fully accredited. Every Saturday at 2:00 you can catch some tantalizing aromas as an adventure takes place with free demonstrations right here in the shop. You'll delight at the gourmet line of imported pots, pans and kitchen gadgetry that line the colorful shelves. Superb cookware featuring heavy gauge aluminum for even cooking, cookware by Fissler boasting the highest grade stainless steel with a lifetime warranty, rolled steel woks, imported French copperware, country style aprons, glassware, professional black bakeware, fine Cuisinart kitchen appliances, plus lots more. Hot Pots — just the place to help make you feel like playing gourmet chef in your own kitchen.

(See special invitation in Appendix.)

RESTAURANTS

CHEZ JEANNETTE
Turn west across from Salishan
on old Highway 101, ½ mile
Gleneden Beach, Oregon
503-764-3434 for reservations

Winter hours: Tues-Fri 11:30am-2pm for lunch,
 Open at 5:30 Sat only for dinner
Summer hours: Mon-Fri 11:30-2 for lunch,
 Open at 5:30 for dinner, seven days a week

For the ultimate in fine dining, get dressed up and enjoy the intimate luxury and great food at Chez Jeannette in Gleneden Beach. For well over a year, Joan and Larry Westerberg have been serving up the best in fresh Oregon seafood, steaks, poultry, lamb and great desserts for those who want a very special experience in dining. If you stop in for lunch, you'll be able to enjoy a wide range of good food. The chef suggests trying a delicious Oregon bay shrimp crepe, served with a special Chez Jeannette French bread, soup de jour or salad, and butter parsley potatos. I tried the Petit Filet Mignon served in the French style — it was absolutely delicious. If you feel more like having a sandwich, you can try their hot, thin sliced roast beef sprinkled with Oregon blue cheese on French bread, or ham and swiss with mayonnaise on French bread. Then there's a wonderful selection of salads; one is the hot seafood salad with bay shrimp cooked in olive oil, with different seafoods in season; another is the Greek salad with herbs, grated Parmesan cheese and mixed greens. For dinner, the chef suggests excellent appetizers like escargot, Oregon bay shrimp cocktail, fresh homemade soups or salad maison. For your dining entrees, try the fresh seafood dinner in which selections and preparation change nightly and is priced accordingly. Filet mignon with red wine and mushroom sauce, medallion of beef, fresh Oregon quail and rack of lamb served with bearnaise sauce and fresh mint. All entrees are served with Chez Jeannette French bread, soup de jour or salad maison and a banquet of seasonal vegetables. Don't forget dessert. You'll find cheesecake, fruit tarts, chocolate desserts and homemade ice cream. All this good food needs wine and they have one of the finest Oregon and French wine lists from which to choose. So come hungry and ready to enjoy a fine, intimate dining experience at Chez Jeannette — definitely a best choice on the Oregon coast.

TOYS

THE WOODEN DUCK
Located at the Market Place at Salishan
(just off Hwy 101)
Gleneden Beach, Oregon
503-764-2489

Second location:
957 Wall Street
Bend, Oregon
503-388-1118

Go inside the Market Place, the skylit mall at Salishan, and take a peek at a most unique toy shop. Local owner Jane Greenbaum began business five years ago and tells us that people from all over the state seem to seek out her shop when they are looking for an original toy. This doesn't surprise us since Jane has 20 years of experience in education, including five as principal of an elementary school. She has translated her great love for little people into a shop brimming with different whimsical gifts. There is an emphasis on imaginative, educational toys and constructive, high quality imported materials, plus a strong infant toy section, huggable bears, Brio wooden toys, and lovely dolls. The shop features games, puzzles, art materials, constructions sets, puppets, and lots more smile provoking cherishables for kids of all ages (and grown-up kids, too). A strong suit of the shop is the friendly, accommodating service by staff who care to help people find just the right gift or toy item. Along with the good service, The Wooden Duck offers gift wrapping and a special order service. The Wooden Duck — a best choice for creative toys and a place where the whole family will enjoy shopping on the Oregon Coast.

106 Lincoln County

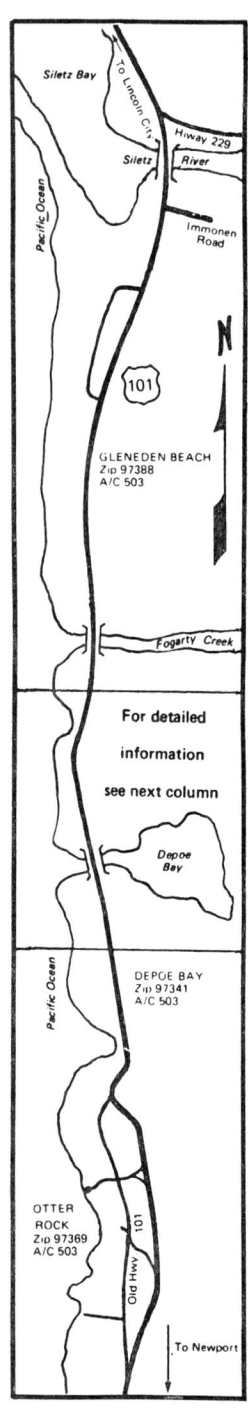

DEPOE BAY

ABOUT DEPOE BAY

Overlooking the Pacific Ocean, the rock-rimmed bay and near the rugged cliffs is the small fishing village and the officially recognized *World's Smallest Harbor* (six square acres) of Depoe Bay. The village is surrounded by coastal beauty from spectacular spouting horns, sea geysers that powerfully spout water through crevices and holes in the rocky cliffs, to the tranquility of marine gardens, town galleries and gift shops. Depoe Bay owes its name to Chief Charlie Depoe of the Siletz tribe to whom the federal government granted 200 acres encompassing the harbor and townsite about a century ago. Just as the pioneers were welcomed by the peaceful natives, mild temperatures year 'round welcome the traveler. Spring and summer are filled with cool ocean breezes and dazzling displays of colorful flowers and, as it was a century ago, autumn is the season of sunny days, golden sunsets and cool nights. The winter is also beautiful to behold. Snow is rare and temperatures rarely go below freezing. Winter storms with their awe-inspiring power offer one of nature's most spectacular performances of sea slashing its fury against the rocky coast.

Depoe Bay is in a unique location with fine fishing areas just a short distance out to sea. Here fishermen troll salmon, Albacore tuna and bottom fish that abound near the shore. For sportsmen, salmon season lasts from May 1 to Oct. 15, tuna fishing is best from mid-July through September, and bass, cod and red snapper are caught throughout the year. For whale watchers, marvel at the spectacle of gray whales playing and spouting just offshore during the semi- annual migration each winter and spring. In town you can enjoy the charming art galleries, gift shops, fine restaurants and accommodations as well as stores and shops.

ACCOMMODATIONS

HOLIDAY SURF LODGE AND HOLIDAY RV PARK
Highway 101
Depoe Bay, Oregon
503-765-2133

Enjoy the serenity, the relaxing sound of surf against rugged coastal rocks, or watch whales playing just offshore. Where can you find such a private hideaway with a great view of the ocean? The answer is simple enough...you can enjoy all of these from either the warmth of a nice motel room or the coziness of your own RV at the Holiday Surf Lodge and RV Park. Not only a beautiful view of the coastline, but close access to deep sea fishing, restaurants, shopping in downtown Depoe Bay, beautiful beaches and even golf courses and tennis courts. At the lodge, there are kitchens, TV, pool and conference room. The RV park features full hookups, cable, LP gas, laundry facilities, and a convenient market. With the charm of a quaint fishing village, the beautiful ocean view and the relaxing sound of the surf, your Holiday stay will leave you with enchanting memories.

ADDITIONAL ACCOMMODATIONS

CHANNEL HOUSE BED AND BREAKFAST
Depoe Bay, Oregon
503-765-2140

ATTRACTIONS

THE DEPOE BAY AQUARIUM

If just one of the Three Stooges makes you laugh with delight, imagine having a whole herd of them perform for you in person. You and your family will be delighted as the fun-loving herd of harbor seals perform numerous tricks for all and talk up a storm at the Depoe Bay Aquarium. But that's not all. There are fascinating collections of octopus and other marine life to be seen for your enjoyment. This is a place at which you can learn about life of the sea and have fun doing it. Located in downtown Depoe Bay.

THUNDERING SEAS

If you close your eyes once you enter the workshop, you immediately think that this is what elves must be doing right around Christmas. But instead of toys, imagine opening your eyes and looking right into some swashbuckler's treasure chest overflowing with silver, gold and precious gems. If you are a lover of fine jewelry and would like to see how it is made, visit the workshop of Thundering Seas, Oregon State University's School for the Crafts housed in a mansion perched on a rocky ledge 60 feet above the ocean. Talented students learn the fine art of gold and silversmithing surrounded by the beauty of Oregon's coast. Above the tapping of hammers, the whirring of drills and the soft, gentle movement of finger work, school director Delphine L. Kreielsheimer welcomes visitors to the busy workshop where you can observe firsthand the incredible skills needed to produce fine jewelry. If you have a gift idea for that someone special, custom crafted pieces may be arranged with the student smiths. The making of jewelry, flatware, ornaments and table sculpture are just a few of the skills students learn in their stay at Thundering Seas, and you, too, can enjoy seeing some of Oregon's finest craftsmen at work.

CHARTER FISHING

DOCKSIDE CHARTER
Located on the bay
Depoe Bay, Oregon
503-765-2545 (call for reservations anytime until 9pm)

Feel the wind against your face and the tremendous power of the sea as you fish the depths for salmon or tuna on the Oregon coast. Watch your fishing pole bend with a strike and listen to the whiz of your reel as your fish makes a run in the cold coastal waters. You can feel it all with Dockside Charters. You'll find that they are absolutely honest — if the fish are not biting, they'll tell you. With over 72 years of experience between three skippers, Lars Robison, Jim Tate or Fred Robison will take you out for the best in Oregon coast sport fishing and sea air. You can go on either a five hour salmon and bottom fishing charter, or all day tuna trip in clean and comfortable, six and ten passenger boats, with all tackle furnished and free coffee. Snack foods, ice, fish bags and no mess are the rule, and only two minutes to the place where they will process your catch. There is also easy access to the boats, no stairs to climb and the boats are not overcrowded. Everyone has a deck chair. Dockside is one of the lower priced charters on the Oregon coast with the best boats. Their offices are conveniently located right on the bay (it is the only charter service located on the small bay at Depoe Bay), and the boats are easily accessible for handicapped or elderly people. At their offices, you can also meet a lot of retired fishermen. This seems to be a good place to meet and talk over the catch from yesterday, or find out where the fish are biting.

EVENTS

ANNUAL FLEET OF FLOWERS CEREMONY

Each Memorial Day, Depoe Bay literally becomes a beautiful sea of flowers dedicated to the memory of those who have lost their lives at sea. After services on shore, the flowers are carried out to sea aboard the fishing fleet from Depoe Bay. They then receive the Chaplain's blessing and are cast upon the water, forming a colorful blanket on the sea — a silent and beautiful tribute to those who sleep beneath the waters.

INDIAN-STYLE SALMON BAKE

Just as the Siletz tribe had done over 100 years ago, Depoe Bay citizens put out all the fixings at Fogarty Creek State Park on the third Saturday of every September. Fresh ocean-caught salmon are then cooked Indian-style before an open fire, served with all the trimmings buffet style alongside the ghosts of the tribe and the sea. Everyone is welcome.

QUALITY SEAFOOD

NEPTUNE'S RESERVE
Located on Hwy 101 just south
of Depoe Bay bridge
Depoe Bay, Oregon
503-765-2286 or 765-2212

The cold, clear, bountiful North Pacific Ocean provides some of the finest seafood in the world, and Neptune's Reserve can ship it to you anywhere, or you can stop at their conveniently located seafood market on Highway 101 in Depoe Bay. The freshest seafood possible is available at Neptune's Reserve where Jim and Debbie Woodard and Fritz Ford select only the finest product from the catch of Depoe Bay's fishing fleet. This seafood can be purchased fresh, season and weather permitting. The same superior quality fresh seafood is vacuum packed and flash frozen, guaranteed as delicious as the day it was packaged, making it available year around. Also available at Neptune's Reserve are choice fillets, smoked using vine maple cut from Oregon's coastal forests, producing a flavor distinctively "Oregon". In addition, you'll find premium quality hand packed canned fish in 7¾ oz. cans. Albacore Tuna, Coho and Chinook Salmon (salt free upon request), are available fresh packed. Vine maple smoked fish is available in the above products in addition to Sturgeon and Pink Salmon. Gift packs are wonderfully packaged with salt water taffy and sea shells. They can be customized to your taste. For more information, call or write to Neptune's Reserve (P.O. Box 273, Depoe Bay, OR 97341).

(See special invitation in Appendix.)

RESTAURANT/ACCOMMODATIONS

THE WHALE COVE INN RESTAURANT AND MOTEL
1½ miles south of Depoe Bay on Hwy 101
Depoe Bay, Oregon
503-765-2255

Summer hours: 7am-9pm, bar open until closing
Winter hours: 9-9, bar open until closing

Watch the whales play in the beautiful cove and enjoy one of the most enchanting vantage points for viewing the Oregon coast you can find. Super, friendly people, a great atmosphere, and good food make Whale Cove Inn a must for any visitor to the Oregon coast. Joe and Steve Irvin and Linda McBeth, a brothers and sister team, own the Inn and have fun doing it. Their smiles and laughter bring a wonderful charm to the already spectacular scenery and, along with "Auntie Marilyn" and "Uncle Darrell" and 16 years of business experience, assure you of a wonderful stay. The recommendation from the gang for breakfast is the big Mexican omelette with sausage, peppers, salsa, sour cream, onions, mushrooms, and good ol'

Tillamook cheese. For lunch the concensus seems to be the chowder — customers rave about it. Then there is the delicious "Whale of a Crab Melt" with delicious crab served open face on French bread, topped with melted cheese and accompanied with fries. For dinner, try bouillabaisse, an assortment of seafoods poached in a special recipe. Also, there is a children's menu for the little appetites, and a full bar for those older in age where there is also entertainment. The motel is rustically fashioned with comfortable rooms and beautiful views of the cove. Call one week in advance for reservations.

(See special invitation in Appendix.)

RESTAURANT/LOUNGE

THE SEA HAG RESTAURANT
In the middle of downtown Depoe Bay, Hwy 101
Depoe Bay, Oregon
503-765-7901

Winter hours: Sun-Thurs 6am-10pm,
   Fri & Sat open until 11pm
Summer hours: Sun-Thurs 3:30am-lounge closing
   at 2:30am; food available to 2:30am Fri & Sat

The byword in this wonderful restaurant is that "the seafood is so fresh the ocean hasn't missed it yet!" And that's not all you're treated to — you'll immediately know you're in the friendliest place on the Oregon coast when Gracie Strom, alias "The Sea Hag" will entertain you with her life-loving exuberance by playing songs with her famous spoons and bottles. For 24 years, Gracie (who is also known as the friendliest person in Oregon) has tapped out song after song using two long spoons on half- filled bottles behind the bar, much to everyone's delight. When Gracie plays *Roll Out the Barrel*, using her combined talents of playing spoons, whistling, playing bells and banging on her washboard, everyone in the restaurant comes to see what is happening. Gracie's food is as good as her friendliness, featuring homemade from scratch soups and a large fresh, crisp salad bar with chilled plates which sits inside of a Coast Guard rowboat.

The interior of the restaurant reminds you of a sea captain's bedroom with real sails dividing the restaurant, solid wood tables and comfortable booth seating. The full bar is separate and is decorated with brass ship wheels and old sailing ship memorabilia. Even the dinner plates are shaped like fish and service is excellent. Gracie makes sure there is live music and lots of laughter and fun every night, even in the winter months.

Some breakfast suggestions from Gracie are delicious homemade biscuits and gravy or a crab and shrimp omelette with fresh, country-fried potatoes, toast and jelly. For lunch, try Gracie's avocado salad with kiwi fruit, bananas, watermelon, cantalope and grapes served with a cup of her famous clam chowder; or try the Sea Hag crab and Tillamook cheese sandwich served with exotic fruit. For dinner, have the bouillabaisse seafood stew with crab, shrimp, scallops, butter clams, fillet of sole and cod. All of Gracie's entrees have very low prices and are served with your choice of rice pilaf, baked potato or vegetable, a loaf of delicious, crusty bread, and a visit to the salad bar. There are great drinks from the bar, too, featuring sea drinks, wine by the glass, and Oregon wines by the bottle. On Friday evenings from 5 to 10, Gracie invites you to her Seafood Buffet, all you can eat. On Sunday, there is a wonderful Champagne Brunch from 9am-2pm. For the pint-sized appetites, there is a portion of the menu for you as well as high chairs and booster chairs for the little visitors of the friendly Sea Hag.

NEWPORT

ABOUT NEWPORT

The graceful Yaquina Bay Bridge has been welcoming visitors to this colorful coastal community for over 50 years. The bustling waterfront of Newport is alive with salty air charm. Stroll amid the town's unique shops and distinctive art galleries, catch the drifting aromas of fresh seafood entrees, pastries and rich expresso coffees. There are plenty of great eateries here to satisfy everyone from the most discerning epicurean diners to lovers of the good old American charbroiled hamburger.

Accommodations in Newport are also impressive. You can camp, enjoy a crackling fire in your own log cabin, or opt for a luxurious resort room or condominium suite complete with all the finest guest amenities.

114 Lincoln County

Besides the colorful vitality of Newport, there is lots of great outdoors ready to beckon you. Beachcomb along Agate Beach, check out the deep blue bay and picturesque harbor area where fishing boats sit gently bobbing in the sun and sleek vessels wave gracefully across the coastal horizon. Head over to old Yaquina Bay Lighthouse and enjoy a picnic basket lunch amid wild flower covered slopes. Have a look at the unusual rock formations, "Jump-off Joe", which lies just north of Nye Creek. Why not play some golf, treat yourself to a scenic air flight, or spend the afternoon clamming? The Newport area is known among fishermen for its plentiful flounder, perch and bass, so you may just want to head over to south Yaquina Bay jetty for a chance of reeling in some big ones. Newport Bay area offers boat cruises and rentals, great rock hunting for agates, jasper and petrified wood, bicycle trails and a perfect base for exploring the myriad of attractions and areas of natural beauty that lie within easy access. Experience

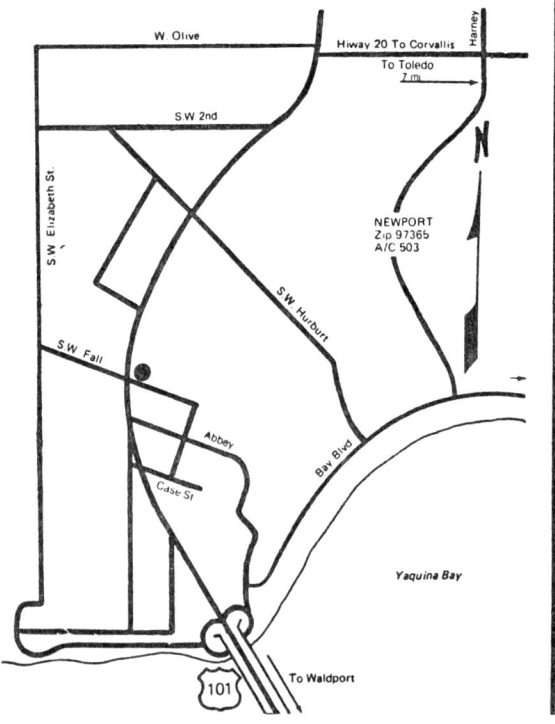

Newport, a place where the abundance of coastal color and guest amenities are matched by the warmth and friendliness of the local people who are ready to welcome you Oregon style. For additional information, contact Greater Newport Chamber of Commerce, 555 S.W. Coast Highway, Newport, OR 97365, phone 503-265-8801.

ACCOMMODATIONS

LITTLE CREEK COVE
Just off U.S. Highway 101
North of Newport, across from golf course
Newport, Oregon
503-265-8587 for reservations, or
Write Little Creek Cove
3641 N.E. Ocean View Drive
Newport, Oregon 97365

Nestled in its own secluded cove, Little Creek Cove Resort offers the vacationer all the best of accommodations and ambience of the Oregon coast. Located right on famous Agate Beach where you find spectacular ocean and mountain vistas, three miles of wide sandy beaches for beachcombing, walking and exploring, as well as golf courses and gift shops nearby. You will love Little Creek's distinctive condominium atmosphere and comfort. Unusual in design, each unit has its own great ocean view, one or two bedrooms or studio, full kitchen facilities, bath, TV and fireplaces. There are even sliding glass doors which open onto your own private deck. Deep sea fishing is not far away at picturesque Yaquina Bay and neither is Newport's Old Town, a browser's and photographer's favorite. So enjoy a little peace and relaxation in beautiful surroundings all within a short distance of fine restaurants, shops and much more at Little Creek Cove Resort where you can enjoy your own ocean world.

MOOLACK SHORES MOTEL
Located three miles north of Newport
Newport, Oregon
503-265-2326 for reservations

Moolack Shores Motel is a great place in which to put a little bit of make-believe back into your life. You can indulge your Walter Mitty fantasies for a particular time or place by choosing a room with the decor to fit whatever yearning you have.

Those who crave the thrill of competition and dream of Indy, the Kentucky Derby or being first down a mountain will like the Racer's Room with its representations of the glorious moments in competitive sports. On the other hand, you might like a Western Room which has a Winchester rifle on the wall along with branding irons, spurs and cowboy art. Altogether, there are 12 different themes from which to choose. They even offer a separate beach house and guest house on a wooded ocean front lot. The owners, John and Barbara Rieschel, are planning to add an Aviator's Room in the near future. Moolack Shores is definitely not the usual run of the mill motel. It is small, secluded and friendly. All rooms have beamed ceilings, fireplaces and decks, along with a view that is second to none. This coupled with two of the friendliest hosts on the Oregon Coast makes this motel a must. Due to demand, reservations are suggested.

ADDITIONAL ACCOMMODATIONS

EMBARCADERO RESORT HOTEL
1000 S.E. Bay Blvd.
Newport, Oregon
503-265-8521

Suites, kitchens, restaurant/lounge, convention facilities, pool, sauna.

HILTON AT AGATE BEACH
3019 N. Coast Highway
Newport, Oregon
503-265-5341

Restaurant/Lounge, pool, jacuzzi.

THE WAVES MOTEL
820 N.W. Coast
Newport, Oregon
503-265-4661

New, ocean view, TV, phones.

WHALER MOTEL
155 S.W. Elizabeth
Newport, Oregon
503-265-9261

TV, phones, kitchens, fireplaces, view.

THE WINDJAMMER MOTEL
Best Western
744 S.W. Elizabeth
Newport, Oregon
503-265-8863

Ocean front, TV, phones.

ART GALLERY

OCEANIC ARTS
444 S.W. Bay Blvd. on the bay front
Newport, Oregon
503-265-5963

The ideal location for an art gallery would have to be Newport's bay front — breathtaking scenery with every turn and scenes right out of the best paintings like the Yaquina Bay Bridge looming out of the early morning mist, small fishing boats chugging on the bay and grey-white gulls filling the air. Situated in the middle of the busiest part of Yaquina Bay is Oceanic Arts Gallery full of art to help you remember your trip to Newport and Yaquina Bay. The gallery offers clay, porcelain, sculptures, wood turnings, water colors, oils, pastels and glass, fine art from some of the best Oregon and Northwest artists. Stan Pickens, the knowledgeable and friendly owner, has been showing art at the gallery for over ten years. His expertise in display has gained him recognition from artists all over the United States. He offers museum quality framing and artistic matting, services which draw professionals and lovers of art from all over Oregon to his gallery. His glass section is the largest on the Oregon coast, all beautiful, handblown originals in art pieces and functionals. A nice array of prints, some framed, some not, a wonderful gallery in a wonderful location — Oceanic Arts — a best choice for the Northwest and the Oregon coast.

THE WOOD GALLERY
818 S.W. Bay Blvd., on the bay front
Newport, Oregon
503-265-6843

Get a special, comfortable feeling you probably won't find at other art galleries. Here you can actually sit, touch and use the art work. You'll find oil paintings, fine pottery, wonderful woodwork, furniture, metal and wood sculptures, textiles, water colors and pastels to enjoy by over 300 artists from throughout the Northwest and the United States. You'll also find fine gold, silver and other rare gem jewelry. Don't miss the stained glass pieces, large stoneware furniture you can actually sit in, carved driftwood and the Alpine Vineyards wine tasting room where you can taste fine wines made from four noble grapes — pinot noir, white riesling, cabernet sauvignon, and chardonnay. You'll find everything of the highest quality from wood sculpture to wine, all with the philosophy to make everyone who walks into the gallery feel comfortable just to browse. Since 1979, owner Kelly Barker, who owns a second gallery in Seattle called Legends, has been creating a reputation for showing some of the best works of the Northwest, all fairly priced, which makes The Wood Gallery a best choice for the lover of art in all of us — truly a unique experience in art.

YAQUINA ART CENTER AND NEWPORT VISUAL ART CENTER
Turnaround at Nye Beach
Newport, Oregon
503-265-5133

Visit all kinds of art at the Yaquina Art Center and Newport Visual Art Center. Not only will you find the beautiful works of art by various local and statewide artists, but the new Newport Visual Art Center building is a work of art all in itself. The Yaquina Art Center not only houses great local oil and water color paintings, crafts, quilts, beach craft sculptures, and more, it also has the best view of the Pacific Ocean outside its windows. Open since 1947 and operated by local Newport artists, it is a fine display of how much talent resides in just one area of the Oregon coast. Director Lillian Christensen makes sure there is something for everyone and admission is free. The two art galleries located side by side at beautiful Nye Beach — a treat and a best choice for those who don't want to miss fine art.

ATTRACTIONS

EMBARCADERO DOCK
At the Embarcadero on the bay front
Newport, Oregon
503-265-5435

Summer hours: 5am-8pm seven days a week
Winter hours: 8am-5pm seven days a week

One of the most enjoyable and memorable excursions on the Oregon coast was the day I discovered the Embarcadero Dock. My family was with me and we had been to the beach, eaten a great breakfast, and like many other people were wondering what to do next. The Embarcadero Dock answered our question. The dock is a full-fledged convenience store stocked full of things you need for a day of fun: snack foods, warm weather gear, rainwear, and so much more. The "more" is what they rent: fishing poles, crab rings and boats with motors. You've guessed it — my older sons and I couldn't have hoped for a more exciting adventure of fishing and crabbing on beautiful Yaquina Bay. My wife was also thrilled to find that they rent Honda scooters so you can putt freely about stopping at the nice shops and galleries all over Newport. We can thank Clyde and Rhonda Hamstreet, for they own the Embarcadero Dock. People around town told me Clyde was the original contractor who built the beautiful Embarcadero Resort in which this fun business is located. So for an unforgettable day, don't miss this best choice in Newport, the Embarcadero Dock on the bay front.

(See special invitation in Appendix.)

MARINE SCIENCE CENTER
South side of Yaquina Bay
Newport, Oregon
503-867-3011

Winter hours: 10-4
Summer hours: 10-6
Open every day except Christmas

There is no greater source of wide-eyed wonder in a child's face than the mystery that can be found in a tide pool. It is even more interesting and also educational if the child knows a little about the creature he is viewing or trying to catch. An excellent place for gaining this kind of background and information is at the Mark O. Hatfield Marine Science Center in Newport. The center has tanks with over 100 sea creatures that inhabit the Oregon coast. Perhaps even more important to parents is that the Marine Center can provide answers to the countless questions that youngsters ask about the ocean and its inhabitants, their habits and habitats. The center offers many tours that are a fascination for both young and old. Admission to the Marine Science Center is absolutely free; it is supported by the State of Oregon, the National Science Foundation and other agencies. The faculty exists to provide answers to questions about the sea from children and adults.

RESEARCH VESSEL WECOMA
Located in Yaquina Bay on the south side
near the Marine Science Center
Newport, Oregon

Near the Marine Science Center, moored next to fishing and work boats, a work boat of a different kind awaits her next assignment. The research vessel *Wecoma* works for science. Manned by a specially trained operating crew of 13, with up to 16 researchers, she cruises the oceans of the world on voyages of inquiry. The *Wecoma* is owned by the National Science Foundation and operating under charter by Oregon State University. Her home base is Newport, but she spends much of her time at sea and is one of the few research vessels built especially for that purpose. She is a clean, modern, comfortable craft capable of performing all kinds of oceanographic research. The *Wecoma* functions as a seagoing laboratory and classroom for the College of Oceanography at OSU. Graduate students serve as assistants in research and learn the methods to become researchers and scientists in their own right. This vessel is vital to the oceanography program at OSU and contributes valuable data to oceanography research around the world and to Oregon.

RIPLEY'S BELIEVE IT OR NOT
Mariner Square on the bay front
Newport, Oregon
503-265-2206

I can't give you very much information about Ripley's. It opened in May of 1986, which was after we went to press. I have visited Ripley's in California and this promises to be better. It has the advantages of high technology and a better location. This place is run by the same folks as The Wax Works and from the briefing they gave me, it sounds like a very complimentary addition to The Wax Works and to Mariner Square in general. They are making use of animated, state-of-the-art displays with holographic projections and laser beams. They also have a display plan like the mermaid that was shown for years by Barnum & Bailey Circus during the 1930s. I regret that I cannot tell you personally what is inside. It wasn't finished when I visited Newport, but I can tell you that Chris Waugh, general manager, told me with a sparkle in her eye that this will be one of the most up-to-date attractions on the West Coast. Ripley's Believe It or Not is located in Mariner Square and it is a very lively place, similar to Fisherman's Wharf in San Francisco. It has interesting sidewalk entertainment like the Bay Area, but many times you'll find families standing around watching the free entertainment outside of Mariner Square. The Square also offers a nice family-style restaurant where you can dine or snack and watch the show go on around you. For a surprise and a best choice, don't miss Ripley's Believe It or Not on the bay front in Newport.

(See special invitation in Appendix.)

SUNRISE AVIATION
Located at the airport, four miles
south of Yaquina Bay Bridge on Hwy 101
Newport, Oregon
503-867-7767

For the past ten years, Sunrise Aviation has been providing a full range of services to the flight happy among us. Owner Jim York and chief pilot Barbara Bonds specialize in offering visitors breath-taking scenic flights. Imagine relaxing comfortably as you wing your way over boat jetties, pristine beaches, tide pools and Yaquina Head Lighthouse. Or perhaps you would like a half hour scenic flight that glides over Depoe Bay, the Devil's Punchbowl and huge spouting grey whales as they migrate close to shore. If you have the time, why not try the one hour flight which whisks you to Florence and the majestic Oregon sand dunes, then past the Sea Lion Caves, up over gorgeous Heceta Lighthouse, then above the rushing waters of the Alsea River. Be sure to bring your cameras along because you are in for a photographer's paradise from on high. Sunrise Aviation also offers air taxi service that will land you just about anywhere your heart desires, plus car rental arrangements, flight instruction, aircraft rentals and sales, and the fuel to do it all. Call ahead for reservations. When you want to soar like an eagle and view our Oregon beauty from up high, Sunrise Aviation is a best choice in our book.

UNDERSEA GARDENS
On the bay front
Newport, Oregon
503-265-7541

A trip to the Undersea Gardens of Newport is like going to a large aquarium, only in this case, the fish are swimming freely and the people are inside an air-filled tank. With this reverse perspective in mind, it is interesting to wonder what the fish think of the human faces peering at them from the other side of the glass walls. Do they wonder about the variety of the millions of people they have seen on the other side of the glass over the years? Do they marvel that some of the air breathers are much larger than others, of different colors, or seem to be much more evident at certain times of the year and more active at certain times of the day? Do the Pacific salmon on the other side study the lives and migration patterns of humans who swarm pass the glass windows in countless numbers during the summer months? Who can say what the inhabitants of this water world think of ours, but thanks to the Undersea Gardens, we can fantasize. Here the salt water world of the King salmon, octopus and moray eel coexist with that of you and me, separated by a plexiglass boundary which allows us to see the forbidden beauty of a world we can only touch and visit for a time. The Undersea Garden has a gift shop, The Treasure Chest, to provide mementos of this visit to the strange and exciting world below the waves. To make this visit even more of a bargain, they offer group rates for schools, clubs and organizations with eight or more members.

(See special invitation in Appendix.)

THE WAX WORKS
Mariner Square on the bay front
Newport, Oregon
503-265-2206

Summer hours: 9-8 daily
Winter hours: 10:30-4:30 Wed-Fri
10-5 Sat & Sun

One of the newest attractions in Newport reminded me of the wharf area of San Francisco. The Wax Works offers a still life slice of history and fantasy for the whole family. One thing I have never been able to get over in a wax museum or department store with realistic mannequins, is a momentary feeling of unease when you wonder if the figure you are standing next to is real or not. That feeling is not so evident here because many of the figures are not human at all, but rather robots and mermaids that you wish were real as well as monsters that you are just as glad that they are make believe. There is a realistic erruption of Mt. St. Helens, a sea battle of the past, and a space battle of the future. The Wax Works offers far more than the same usual wax replicas of famous and infamous people which populate wax museums across the country. The entertainment is well worth the low admission, especially if you have children along. Chris Waugh is the general manager. She likes to think of herself as the host or master of ceremonies for your trip through what is, what has been, what might have been and what may yet be. The short journey takes about an hour and ends when you find yourself outside in the Mariner Square gift shop area. There are over 3000 square feet of souvenirs to help you remember your trip to the Oregon Coast and to Newport.

(See special invitation in Appendix.)

YAQUINA BAY LIGHTHOUSE
Newport, Oregon

This proud lighthouse perched over Yaquina Bay stands as a reminder of a bygone era when safe seafaring often depended on a trustworthy light keeper and his light. This lighthouse provided a harbor entrance light for ships coming into Yaquina Bay. Its beam was operational for the first time to guide coastal navigation on Nov. 3, 1871. Today the lighthouse has been restored by public funds and attracts many visitors interested in exploring a remarkable remnant of our marine history and heritage. The Yaquina Bay Lighthouse is the only one of its kind on the Oregon Coast to provide a combined keeper's dwelling and light tower. It is listed on the *National Register of Historic Places* and remains the oldest existing building in the town of Newport.

BAKERY

BRIDGE BAKERY
1006 South Coast Highway
(just before you go over Yaquina Bridge on Highway 101)
Newport, Oregon
503-265-8607

Hours: 6-6 Mon-Sat, closed Sun

Remember the days when there was a neighborhood bakery and you could smell the delicious bread, rolls and cakes as you went in or walked by? Well, you can definitely relive that memory at the Bridge Bakery, run for 13 years (50 years in the business) by Margorie and Maurice Merrill, two of the friendliest people you'll ever meet. You can just about taste everything in their bakery by taking a deep breath. There are delicious coffee cakes, tarts, cream puffs, creme eclairs, custard eclairs, and doughnuts as well as bread, sourdough and French. All their goodies are the freshest and made from scratch with eggs and real butter. You'll go crazy over their delicious cookies, handmade croissants and cream pies. As a matter of fact, Maurice has been baking since he was nine years old. This is truly a favorite bakery. The people in the community love this place and also enjoy the soup and hot coffee that are served. So if you have a hunger pang and you can't quite decide what you want, stop at Bridge Bakery — you'll probably make a number of tasty decisions.

(See special invitation in Appendix.)

CHARTER FISHING

NEWPORT SPORT FISHING
Embarcadero Marina
Newport, Oregon
503-265-7558 for reservations

For a thrill that just can't be beat, there is nothing like deep sea fishing on a charter boat. Here is a chance to go out on the blue water where the big ones hide. A well-equipped Coast Guard licensed boat and skipper take you there and furnish all gear and tackle, and it doesn't cost as much as you would think. Art and Terri Burk operate Newport Sport Fishing. They are well informed about local fishing conditions and can maximize your chances of landing trophy size game fish or bottom fish. During the salmon season, their boats leave the docks twice a day, weather permitting, for four, five or eight hour trips. A combination salmon and bottom fishing trip is also offered. The excellent Oregon bottom fishing is available all year long with a variety of destinations from the five hour inner reef trip to the 12 hour Heceta Banks halibut expedition, 32 miles offshore. Whatever your pleasure, fighting King Salmon, bathtub size bottom fish, or a day of whale watching, Art and Terri can provide a boat and a skipper to make it safe and exciting.

GIFTS

LAND'S END GIFTS
Seatowne Shopping Center
1610 North Coast Highway
Newport, Oregon
503-265-7526

Gifted with the reputation for being "a store beyond the ordinary", set one foot inside the door and it is easy to see why. The gifts chosen by local owners Morrie Hauge and Scott Martin are sure to delight your eyes and ignite your imagination. You'll love the fine collection of professional grade wind and weather instruments set in brass cases, the nostalgic "snow village" collection of hand-painted ceramic houses, and the limited edition figurines inspired by artist Frances Hook. Scott and Maurie feature sculpture by Bijan, historic scrimshaw reproductions, a huge selection of fascinating shell creations, and the central coast's largest array of fine crystal giftware.

So whether your taste runs to hand-painted porcelain depicting the history of Santa Claus, delicate bud vases, colorfully designed wind socks or unique paper weights, you'll find plenty of original items waiting to inspire you right here at Land's End Gifts. Special orders and daily UPS mail service is available.

(See special invitation in Appendix.)

SWAFFORD'S OREGON
Seatowne Mall
1630 North Coast Highway
Newport, Oregon
503-265-3044

Hours: 10-6 Mon-Sat, noon-5 Sun

Here is the perfect place to stock up on many of the gourmet food items native to Oregon. Owners Joe and Christina Swafford and son, Johan, have been lining their baskets with a super array of local, coastal delectables for over four years now. Choose from fruit and berry syrups, hearty bread mixes, hazelnuts, Tillamook cheeses, prime quality packed seafood, specialty herbs, and cranberry sweets. They also stock folding tables and service accessories, cookbooks, ceramic trivets, fine stoneware and lots of shelves brimming with a great selection of local, Northwest wines mostly from Oregon and vintage imported varieties. The fancy pack gift boxes are a great way to bring the tasty culinary morsels of native Oregon back home to your dinner table. A shop full of the best Oregon has to offer has to be a best choice and Swafford's Oregon is definitely one of Oregon's best choices.

GOLF

AGATE BEACH GOLF COURSE
4100 Golf Course Drive
(on Highway 101, north end of Newport)
Newport, Oregon
503-265-7331

Golfers in the Newport area are very fortunate. They have one of the nicest courses in the Central Oregon coast to play on. It lies among the trees overlooking the Pacific Ocean like an emerald on display. The dazzling greens are made possible by year- round irrigation from the underground sprinkling system. If you happen to be taken in by the beauty of the course like I was, and you don't have clubs or the vaguest idea of what to do with them, no sweat. PGA pro Bill Martin, who, with his wife Ramona own the course, can outfit you with rental clubs and equipment and teach you the game. The clubhouse also sells new clubs and all the other equipment necessary for playing golf. They carry warm weather clothing and something you'll need sooner or later in Oregon, rain gear. They have a nice, informal restaurant at the clubhouse which serves breakfast and lunch with beer, wine or soft drinks. For the late risers, breakfast is served all day. If you eat lunch there, I recommend the Double Bogey Burger with ham and cheese. Even if it is the only double bogey you get all day, you will be well satisfied. As I mentioned, the course is outstanding for its greenness. Terry Martin, who maintains the course, deserves thanks for this. The course itself is a regulation par 36, nine hole golf course. Along with the nine hole playing field, it has a driving range as well as chipping and putting greens. It also offers a nicely distracting view while playing. The ocean is visible on the east side of the course, a creek runs the fairway on hole number 7, and there are sand traps along the trees. For an added bonus, it is a great place for wildlife and bird watching. Deer are a common site and bears are not unusual. An occasional cougar passes through, no doubt wondering why the grass is so suddenly smooth and green. There is not a great deal of difference between winter and summer here. The course is playable year 'round. However, they do advise you to call a day ahead in the summer for a starting time, but you can usually get to play even if you don't call ahead.

OYSTER FARM

OREGON OYSTER FARM
6878 Yaquina Bay Road
(Seven miles up Yaquina Bay Road)
Newport, Oregon
503-265-5078

The story of the Oregon Oyster Company, the parent company of the Oregon Oyster Farm at Newport and the Dan and Louis Oyster Bar in Portland, is an interesting one, part of the history of Oregon. The Wachsmuth family, starting with Meinert who was shipwrecked in Yaquina Bay in 1865, has had a long involvement with Oregon's oyster industry. In those days, the bay produced native oysters for the California gold fields. The demand from the protein hungry miners was so great that the native varieties were harvested to the point that they could not reproduce and nearly became extinct. That would not be a problem now because oysters are farmed and not just harvested. However, two Japanese varieties, the Pacific and Kumamoto, have replaced most native oysters farmed for commercial use.

The Oregon Oyster Farm, like several similar operations in the state, has been in the hands of the family for several generations and is largely a family enterprise. In some respects, including the family involvement, oyster farming is like growing wine grapes. The environment they are grown in is almost totally responsible for the taste of the product, and the quality and quantity varies from year to year. Yaquina Bay is considered one of the best environments in Oregon for growing oysters and, due to the 12 decades of experience the family has had with oyster cultivation, they seldom have bad years. They grow oysters of all shapes and sizes, but they specialize in exquisite miniature cocktail sizes. Their products, including the shells, are in constant demand all over Oregon. Over 20% of their harvest goes into their own restaurant in Portland. Part of the reason for the high demand is superb quality of the product. Their oysters are grown in an excellent natural environment. They are kept out of the bay's mud on plastic trays or are strung on wires from floating rafts. Either method ensures pure flavor. To ensure freshness, the mature mollusks are pulled daily to fill orders for fresh roe oysters. Make your trip to the Newport area complete with a visit to the Oregon Oyster Farm. The current generation of Wachmuths would like you to sample their product.

PARKS

SOUTH BEACH STATE PARK

Located two miles south of Newport on Highway 101, South Beach State Park has 254 improved campsites. Each site features drinking water, electricity, picnic tables and a fireplace. Picnic areas are located at the western end of the park, a short distance from the beach. Trails provide easy access to the broad, sandy ocean stretches. Rock hunting near the north jetty is a popular pasttime for finding agates, jasper and petrified wood. The park has a central utility building containing flush toilets, hot showers and laundry facilities. Firewood is available for a small fee.

RESTAURANTS

BRIDGE COMPANY RESTAURANT
Located in Bay Bridge Mall
North end of Yaquina Bay Bridge
(Highway 101)
Newport, Oregon
503-265-9551

Hours: Mon-Sat 7am-9pm, Sun 9-9

Some people are truly naturals at what they do. Even though Kent and Deborah Jeppesen had no past experience in operting a restaurant, they are one of the best teams anywhere in the business. Kent and Deborah own and operate the Bridge Company Restaurant in Newport and, to this date, I have heard no one make a derogatory comment about the food served here. Kent explained to me that he really loves the restaurant business because, in preparing and presenting food, he finds his creativeness is in full gear. You see, Kent was an art teacher before getting into the restaurant business and his wife was in the medical profession. This might be why the restaurant is so spotless. The Bridge Company is open for breakfast, lunch and dinner, and I asked them to recommend what they enjoy serving the most. The top of the list for Deborah was her secret recipe bran muffins. I tried them and they are a meal in themselves made with coarse, stoneground wheat and all natural ingredients. Kent's suggestions, since he is one of the chefs, included omelettes for breakfast that the customer creates (a combination of meats, cheeses and other goodies so you can have what you enjoy the most). For lunch, try the fish and chips. The fish is flash frozen Arctic cod, the most delicate, light fish you can eat. The chips are called "Walk the Plank Fries", large steak fries cooked to perfection. If you are a burger nut, you'll love the one million combinations of burgers you can create on the lunch menu. For dinner, try any seafood dish and you will be pleased by its fresh taste. For the light eaters, the menu also offers light courses and a good selection of salads. One thing I know for a fact after wandering through the kitchen, is that all the soups and pastries are made from scratch with top quality ingredients. A best choice team makes a best choice eatery — the Bridge Company Restaurant, don't miss it!

CHRISTINA'S CHAMPAGNE PATIO RESTAURANT
Seatowne Mall
1639 North Coast Highway
Newport, Oregon
503-265-3044

Hours: 11-4 Tues-Sat, closed Sun & Mon

The good life and the best food begin at this special resurant in Newport. Enjoy a bubbly glass of champagne or Oregon wine and let Christina serve you a great quality lunch. The highlights here are hearty deli-style sandwiches with a choice of fine meats and cheeses, fresh leafy green salads, scrumptious razor clam chowder, and specialty entrees which change daily. Christina recommended the "Executive Sandwich" with layers of ham, roast beef and turkey piled high and topped with lettuce, ripe tomatos and all the fixings. Another favorite is the "Gourmet Salad" with fresh turkey, ham and roast beef spread on a bed of tossed green salad and garnished with crispy sun flower seeds, Parmesan cheese and the tangy house dressing. The chef is Swedish and comes up with some wonderful international specialty entrees as well as delicious homeade breads, pastries and desserts. Christina's is a great place to relax and enjoy the good life, your favorite bubbly and some of the best food anywhere.

THE WHALE'S TALE
Corner of Bay Blvd. and Hubert
On the bay front
Newport, Oregon
503-265-8669

Hours: 7am-9pm Mon-Fri
9am-11pm Sat & Sun, closed Wed

In the ten years that The Whale's Tale has been in business in Newport, it has become the standard that others imitate. It has been reviewed in many magazines and newspapers, and it rates as high as seeing a real migrating whale off the Oregon coast for the first time. And no wonder! The food is good, wholesome and flavorful. Since most menus begin with breakast, we shall also. Many people like the poppyseed pancakes made from stoneground whole wheat flour; likewise, I love them. But I also tried another famous dish The Whale's Tale serves — Eggs Newport. It is like Eggs Benedict, only fresh Oregon shrimp is used instead of Canadian bacon. They also have a nice selection of omelettes with some interesting local variations including an oyster topped fisherman's model which oyster lovers will relish. For lunch, the locals recommend the seafood sandwich with oysters or whatever seafood is being brought in off the fishing boats. There is also an intriguing Greek salad with feta cheese and Greek olives. They have a wide variety of dinners including a list of specials they start serving after 5pm. For those who love fresh seafood, I recommend the Ciappino. It gives you a chance to taste everything with a combination of fish, prawns, oysters, scallops, clams and shellfish in a tomato base. It is served with The Whale's Tale's own freshly made bread and salad. To enter The Whale's Tale is like entering a rustic fishing village with brass, whale bones and lots of interesting things to see. For consistency, try a whale of a place and a best choice on the Oregon coast — The Whale's Tale restaurant on the bay front in Newport.

(See special invitation in Appendix.)

FRESH SEAFOOD/DELI

GINO'S SEAFOOD AND DELI
808 S.W. Bay Blvd.
(at the Coast Guard end of the bay front)
Newport, Oregon
503-265-2424

Hours: 8-7 seven days a week

If you like hearty deli sandwiches, fish and chips, smoked salmon and other high quality seafoods and cheeses, Gino's is the place to go. For over 45 years, Gino and Maxine have been in the deli business serving delicious food for all comers. For the last three years, they have been at this bay front location, quietly enjoying the sea and the locals who whisper how gret and fresh the food really is. Now that you are in on this secret, try some fish and chips or one of their numerous deli sandwiches like roast beef, turkey, or salami served on San

Francisco's Boudine bread that is flown in daily, with cheese from Oregon's dairy farmers. Again, sandwiches are not the only thing available in their deli. You can find smoked tuna, salmon and ling cod jerky, as well as pickled cod, herring and salmon. Gino gets the best of seafood from the local fishermen and he has his own boat bring in fresh Dungeness crab, rock fish, sole and cod. Oysters from the Oregon Oyster Farm are sold in the store, fresh picked daily. There are scallops, prawns, steamer clams, smelt and more. You'll always find a good selection of sauces, bread mixes and expert advice on how to prepare any fresh seafood dish. This seafood market has it all — good deli sandwiches, the freshest of seafood, and a very friendly staff. A definite best choice in Newport — Gino's Seafood and Deli on the bay front.

WOMEN'S APPAREL

CATHY'S APPAREL
716 N.W. Beach Drive
(of Nye Beach)
Newport, Oregon
503-265-5671

Hours: 9:30-5:30 Mon-Sat
Sun, July-Sept only, noon-3

Imagine a classic sportswear shop which has built such a strong reputation over the past 31 years that customers return regularly from all over the United States. Owner Betty Giles, who began her career in fashion years ago as a model, believes in providing great service and a quality line of misses and women's apparel. Let your fingers roam along the racks of brand label casual wear. There is Koret of California, Jantzen, Catalina, Joyce, La Roy — things we all need when we are on the Oregon coast like sweaters, all weather coats, shorts, shirts, beachwear, and sweatshirts, along with great gift items like lingerie, leather handbags, coordinated jewelry and scarves. When you want name brand, quality clothes items in a rainbow of tempting colors and styles at a price that is very fair, Cathy's Apparel in Newport is the place to treat yourself stylishly.

(See special invitation in Appendix.)

MAXI'S
Located in Seatowne Shopping Center
1654 North Coast Highway
Newport, Oregon
503-265-6113

Hours: 10-6 Mon-Sat, noon-5 Sun

When you are looking for unique, quality women's clothing, everything from casual to classy, Maxi's is definitely the place to go. Shirley Williams opened this stylish boutique seven years ago with the goal "to provide updated, contemporary apparel for the fashion conscious woman." Thanks to Shirley's tasteful fashion buying sense and strong emphasis on friendly, personal service, the store today is frequented by many loyal repeat customers and has more than doubled in floor size. Maxi's has become synonymous with style, from the cotton casual look of Gloria Vanderbilt to the elegance of Ned Gould Originals. There is a dazzling array of clothing options for the fashion conscious woman in sizes 3 through 16 — comfortable sports slacks, denim jeans, natural fiber sweaters, lingerie, elegant evening wear, slick rain gear, and a complete collection of accessories to add the finishing touch for any outfit. While you are here, don't forget to head upstairs and around the corner to Maxi's Sale Attic where you'll find racks of her classic clothing at unbeatable marked down prices. Shirley tells shoppers that in her Sale Attic, you'll find "a bargain in every corner" and she's not kidding because saleprices and quality are great. The newest addition to Maxi's boutique is Maxi's Upper Class which extends the high fashion Maxi's look to the full figured woman. Here is the place where top name apparel begins at size 18, offering coordinate groups and separates for all seasons. Maxi's — the best choice for the style and quality of a major city boutique, located right here, away from the crowds, on our beautiful Oregon Coast.

YARN/GIFTS

PACIFIC STITCH
Seatowne Shopping Center
1620 North Coast Highway
Newport, Oregon
503-265-8988

Pacific Stitch is definitely a paradise for the stitching and knitting enthusiast. It features what is probably Oregon's largest collection of stitching supplies and fine quality yarns for knitting and crocheting in a variety of weights, textures and colors, as well as patterns and stitch chart books for beginners or old pros. If you have any questions or problems with a project you are working on, just ask Vera Lund or Velma Freudenthal. They have over a half century of needlework experience and will gladly help you with any problem. They teach knitting and crochet classes by VCR tapes, with free instruction and private assistance. They display and sell some of the fine work of locals such as sweaters and stitchery samplers. So if you need supplies, want help with a project, want to take a class or just do a little browsing for gifts, you'll love Pacific Stitch where you'll find the finest materials and the best in professional, friendly help.

(See special invitation in Appendix.)

NEWPORT TOUR

While walking on Nye Beach in the morning, you can look south toward Yaquina Head Lighthouse and see a breathtaking view. Then you can eat breakfast at one of the best restaurants on the Oregon Coast, known for their quality food and bay-front atmosphere. You can make your stay in Newport very memorable by following this tour.

TIME	PLACE	DESCRIPTION	HOW TO FIND IN BOOK
Dawn	Walk on Nye Beach	Best beach	Newport/Beach
Breakfast	The Whale's Tale	Best breakfast	Newport/Restaurant
A.M.	The Oceanic Art Gallery	Best art	Newport/Art Gallery
A.M.	The Wax Works	Best fun	Newport/Attractions
A.M.	Undersea Gardens	Best fun	Newport/Attractions
A.M.	Ripley's Believe It or Not	Best fun	Newport/Attractions
A.M.	Wood Gallery	Best art	Newport/Art Gallery
Lunch	Gino's Seafood and Deli	Best deli	Newport/Fresh Seafood/Deli
P.M.	Pacific Stitch	Best stitchery	Newport/Yarn/Gifts
P.M.	Land's End Gifts	Best crafts/collectibles	Newport/Gifts
P.M.	Swafford's Oregon	Best Oregon gifts	Newport/Gifts
P.M.	Maxi's at Sea Towne	Best apparel	Newport/Women's Apparel
Snack	Bridge Bakery	Best bakery	Newport/Bakery
Fun Drive	Oregon Oyster Farm	Best oysters	Newport/Oyster Farm
Dinner	Bridge Company Restaurant	Best dinner	Newport/Restaurant

SEAL ROCK

ATTRACTIONS

SEA GULCH
North end of Seal Rock,
Highway 101
Seal Rock, Oregon

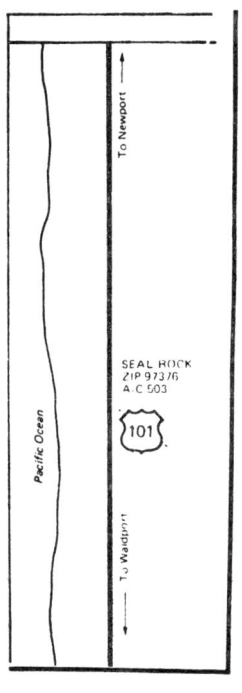

Whoa, Pardner! You don't want to miss the best of the old west on the entire Oregon coast! The place is Sea Gulch and, by golly, it's just as much fun for adults as it is for kids. Outside the Gulch you see a pile of wood shavings and a live, authentic cowboy busy turning large Oregon logs into recognizable lifesize forms with a big chain saw. The real cowboy is Ray Kawalski, and he knows how to take a hunk of wood and turn it into forty-niner miners, Indians, cowboys and bears. The work is great, even though canvas and brush are log and chain saw. Once you pass by Ray as he works with his "roaring paint brush", head to the gift shop full of Old West memorabilia. Here you'll find a secret passage into Sea Gulch City full of Ray's figures and lots of fun things to see. For a few bucks or a speck of gold dust, you can find over 400 of Ray's characters waiting to say "Howdy" as you walk through this mythical town of yesteryear. You'll wander along a three-quarter mile path and discover the Mile High Saloon with real donkeys tied up out front, a glistening pond teeming with catchable trout, and just around the next bend, you'll see Big Foot and his whole family. Be careful not to scream too loudly when Big Foot attacks you, because you might end up in the Gulch City jail for disturbing the peace. Bring your camera and have a "best time in the Old West!" It's fun and you won't find anything like it anywhere else on the Oregon Coast.

GIFTS

SEA GULCH GIFT SHOP
North end of Seal Rock on Hwy 101
Seal Rock, Oregon
503-563-4274

Winter hours: 9-5 seven days a week
Summer hours: 8-7 seven days a week

Take a walk into the Old West, complete with cowboys, Indians, bears and gift shops! But this isn't one of your ordinary gift shops. The theme here is definitely that of the good old pioneer days. You'll find turquoise jewelry, Indian belts, moccasins, authentic replicas of bows and arrows, and beaded leather pouches and wallets. Owner Opal Frye also offers you a nice selection of myrtlewood and Black Hills gold jewelry, shell jewelry, Oregon coast mugs, ceramic seals and sea gulls, T-shirts and other gifts and souvenir items. But wait, there's more loot to be had! How about some wind chimes, a Greek fisherman's cap made of leather and wool, or forever yummy salt water taffy. Located in the Sea Gulch Western Theme Park where there are many lifelike wooden carvings by artist Ray Kowalski of cowboys, Indians and wildlife, as well as saloons, Indian villages and jails. You'll find that perfect gift that will remind you of your journey into the Old West.

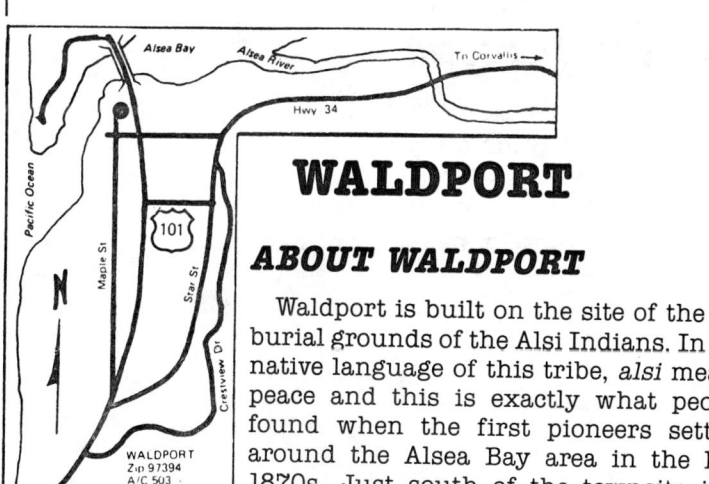

WALDPORT

ABOUT WALDPORT

Waldport is built on the site of the old burial grounds of the Alsi Indians. In the native language of this tribe, *alsi* means peace and this is exactly what people found when the first pioneers settled around the Alsea Bay area in the late 1870s. Just south of the townsite is a point that bears the name of Chief Yaquina John, one of the last of the Alsi tribe. The peace founded just over 100 years ago still reigns in Waldport.

Located 134 miles southwest of Portland, this community of about 1550 people on the south bank of the Alsea River (right on Alsea Bay), offers a variety of outdoor activities like salmon, steelhead and blue back (searun cutthroat trout) fishing as well as Dungeness crab in the bay and clamming for cockles, clams, horsenecks and razor clams on the shores. Beachcombers will love the miles of beaches with agates, jaspar and Japanese glass floats washed ashore after winter storms. For another kind of hunter, the outdoors offers a sportsman's dream of blacktailed deer, black bear and Roosevelt elk, the largest elk in the world. If you would rather hunt for a lower handicap, a year 'round golf course is located in the hills near the town.

The weather in Waldport is moderate. Temperatures rarely drop far below freezing even in the coldest of winters, and summer days are usually in the 70s. The average temperature is a comfortable 51 degrees with about 61 inches of rainfall annually. So visit the comfortable sea village teeming with outdoor activities, friendly people and interesting history, and find what the Alsi Indians and pioneers have found and inhabitants enjoy to this day, *alsi* — peace.

ACCOMMODATIONS

BAYSHORE INN
500 Bayshore Drive
Waldport, Oregon
503-563-3202

Pool, restaurant/lounge, view of bay.

ANTIQUES/GIFTS

TRIDENT ANTIQUES AND COUNTRY STORE
(center of downtown)
Waldport, Oregon
503-563-3631

Winter hours: 9:30-5:30 seven days a week
Summer hours: 9-6 seven days a week

There is nothing like the good, old-fashioned family feeling you get when you walk into this store. It is different from most antique stores because there is a great sense of fun-filled life here, not old dust covered memories and furniture. For over 14 years, Maren and Mike Taylor and their daughter, Jennifer, and son, Marc, have been helping visitors to find everything from things you weren't allowed to touch as a child to imported English oak furniture or antique silver flatware. Well, you can touch now and there is plenty of that to be done here. You can find Phoenix glassware, Blue Willow and Doulton pottery, collector coins, interesting old books, gold and silver jewelry, and lots of antique furniture. For more contemporary taste, there are fine baskets made in the Philippines, local pottery, locally sewn teddy bears, and local, delicious salt water taffy. They also offer a full wine shop with plenty of Oregon wine and even special tastings. So for a good, old-fashioned gift finding expedition with lots of smiles and courteous service, stop by the Taylor's place. You'll feel welcome and find that special gift for that special someone.

(See special invitation in Appendix.)

EVENTS

ALSEA BAY BRIDGE

Completed in 1936, spanning Alsea Bay and joining two sections of what was then known as the Roosevelt Highway, the Alsea Bay Bridge is a huge 3028 foot, 9/16 of a mile structure that cost $778,260.73 to build at that time. If it were built today, the cost would be a staggering $35,000,000 and it does have to be replaced. So make sure you get a picture of this historic structure on Highway 101 in Waldport.

ANNUAL SALMON DERBY

When the salmon run, you better believe the fishermen run — they do to test their skills at Waldport's Annual Salmon Derby. Started in 1983, the Derby is held on the Alsea River right in Waldport. This is an event where fishermen young and old and in between go after those prize salmon. There are cash prizes for a great catch. Besides good old fishy fun, you will enjoy a hometown salmon barbecue with all the fixings prepared by the Beachcomber's Club. For exact Derby dates, depending on the salmon of course, contact the Visitor's Center and watch those salmon and fishermen run. The Waldport Visitor's Center is located south of Alsea Bay Bridge on the west side of Hwy 101, 503-563-2133.

BEACHCOMBER DAYS
503-563-2133 for more information

Beachcomber Days happens every June when the community rolls up their sleeves and celebrates the treasures of the seas. You will enjoy a grand parade down Main Street, the coronation of a Festival Queen and her court, dances for young and old, special exhibitions, a flea market, sandcastle building contest, slug races, a cake toss, beach run and hydroplane races. Join in the wonderful tradition of this three day festival that has become part of the folklore of the Oregon Coast.

PARKS

BEACHSIDE STATE PARK

Situated four miles south of Waldport on Highway 101 and almost halfway between Newport and Florence, Beachside is a good coastal base location for sightseeing. There are 80 campsites; 20 are improved sites with drinking water, electricity, picnic tables and fireplaces. The other 60 are tent sites with a picnic table at each and drinking water nearby. A utility building houses flush toilets, hot showers and laundry facilities. Firewood is available for a small fee. The picnic area is at the northern end of the park with a short trail to the beach where you can enjoy beachcombing, clamming and sunbathing. Fishing and crabbing are also available north at Alsea Bay, Waldport.

RESTAURANTS

THE EXPERIENCE
3¼ miles east of the signal on Hwy 101
Waldport, Oregon
503-563-4555 (reservations only)

For the ultimate in fine dining and cozy atmosphere, this small, out-of-the-way restaurant is an experience you don't dare miss. Seafood extraordinaire is the bill of fare as Betty Hoffmaster and Janice Willinger prepare from scratch some of the finest in seafood delicacies to be found anywhere. For over 11 years, these two talented chefs have served up dinner dishes like the mouth-watering Escargots baked in their shells with seasoned butter and served on hot sourdough bread. Another fantastic meal is Betty and Janice's tender Australian Lobster Tail, a very large lobster steamed over wine and served with drawn butter. There are hot and cold soups such as Hungarian Tomato, and salad or marinated artichoke hearts or, perhaps, Tabouleh. Only fresh seafood is served at this fine restaurant (absolutely no frozen fish or products are allowed). Another dish recommended by the chefs is the 12 to 14 ounce stuffed, boned trout cooked to order. The fresh Dungeness crab dish is also beyond belief. I tried the shrimp in black bean sauce with scallions and fresh garlic, a specialty you will not find anywhere else. For dessert, the homemade Cashew-Kumquat Pie is delicious and an original you will long remember. Reservations are an absolute must to ensure the freshness of your seafood. After enjoying the food here, you will truly see why the restaurant is called The Experience.

ROCK SHOP

BILL'S AGATE SHOP
Milepost 153, Highway 101
(three miles north of Waldport)
Waldport, Oregon
503-563-3920

Beautiful agate knickknacks are the fun specialty in this shop with fine butterflies, flowers and stained glass sliced from agates lighting up your eyes. For about nine years, Patty and MaryJo, sisters, have been collecting rare and curious rocks, petrified wood, sea shells, myrtlewood and other washed up treasures of the sea to be transformed in their shop into the beautiful handcrafted jewelry, mobiles and doo-dads just perfect for gifts. If you are looking for thunder eggs, you don't have to find an ostrich, but you can find them right here as well as onyx eggs, sea shell planters, rock specimens, beachcomber guides and more. Beachcombers and rockhounds will find more treasure here in a few minutes than they could in a lifetime of beachcombing. This is a great shop for browsing, so don't forget to stop three miles north of Waldport on Highway 101 for a rockhounder, beachcomber paradise, and a best choice for the whole family on the Oregon coast.

SEAFOOD

MOBY DICK'S WALDPORT SEAFOODS MARKET
Highway 101, downtown
Waldport, Oregon
503-563-HOOK

Instead of "thar she blows", it is "this is the place to go" for some of the freshest seafood to be found on the Oregon coast at Moby Dick's Seafood Market. And who is there to greet you landlubbers but ol' Cap'n Ahab himself! As great as Melville's classic *Moby Dick* is this market's fine seafood selection of oysters, snapper, cod, alder smoked salmon, scallops, Oregon shrimp, pickled herring, whole and cracked crabs and fish jerky, just to name a few. Also featured is a rich, creamy Oregon-style clam chowder with lots of chopped clams and potato chunks you can recognize, available hot in carryout cups for a walk-around lunch, or in cook-at-home quantities of chowder base (all you add is milk). Made with care — from scratch — right there! Dick Brouillette, owner, will make sure you find what you need as he's been doing for seafood lovers since 1984. If special recipes are what you are looking for, you'll find a good selection of cook books and down-to-earth, friendly, fishy advice. So enjoy some of the finest selection of seafood anywhere and say hello to the statue of Cap'n Ahab who would be happy to be in a picture with you.

YACHATS

ABOUT YACHATS

Yachats is a quiet, unhurried little village of about 500 souls, nestled between lush green forests and rolling sea near the middle of the beautiful Oregon Coast. In this small area you'll find some uniquely picturesque spots of coastline. You'll also find uncrowded beaches, and activities that would satisfy the interests of any beachcomber, fisherman or clam digger. In town, you'll enjoy gift shops, kite shops, fine motels with swimming pools and excellent restaurants. The mild climate (average temperatures range from the 40s to the 70s), the unspoiled natural beauty and the friendly people make Yachats an excellent place to spend a quiet and peaceful vacation.

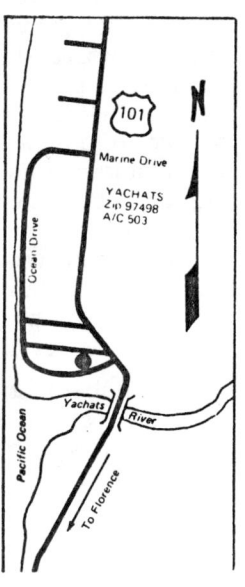

ACCOMMODATIONS

THE ADOBE RESORT/MOTEL
½ mile from Yachats Bridge on Hwy 101
Yachats, Oregon
503-547-3141 for reservations

Breakfast: 8am-11am Mon-Sat
Dinner: 6pm-9pm daily
Sunday: Champagne Brunch, 9am-12:30pm

Perched on the ocean's edge just a few short steps from the Pacific and a long way from hectic cares, sits a resort carved from the spell of the sea. It was the native American tribes who lived along this Oregon coast and originally bestowed the name to this area of natural beauty, "Yachats". According to legend, it means "dark waters of the foot of the mountain". You'll understand as you gaze from your room's picture window to the surging ocean as it washes the shore out to the wild, unspoiled sandy beaches, tide pools alive with anemones and starfish, past agate beds and even to the spawning grounds of the silver smelt. There is a special seasonal occurrence here the second week in September marked by a huge Smelt Festival. Father and son, Bob and Ed Pfannmuller, and Ed's wife, Karen, have been handing out Oregon hospitality at this resort for the past nine years. The atmosphere is handsomely rustic, warm lights, earthen adobe brick, antique knotty woods and beam ceilings accentuate the spell of the sea. There are 47 very comfortable, furnished ocean-view rooms, each accommodating two to four people, fitted with queen or king-sized beds, coffee makers plus chair, color cable TVs and luxuriously appointed bathrooms. Some of the rooms have fireplaces brimming with logs ready for your special touch. There are also north and south two-story units and four-person apartments. For the romantically inclined, we suggest the "love nest" which features king-sized bed, oversized tub and shower, wet bar, fireplace and terrific view.

The Adobe features conference facilities, jacuzzis and saunas, separate lounge area for cocktails, and a delightful dining room which boasts plenty of panoramic glass, natural wood and rustic ambience. For breakfast, we suggest the scrumptious Gingerbread Pancakes topped with hot applesauce and sour cream; or try one of their three-egg omelettes, like the Spanish Virgin — three whipped eggs filled with cooked onions, green chiles, tomatoes, cheddar cheese and topped with a tangy Spanish sauce. For lunch, the Reuben sandwich was not only bountiful but yummy and comes with soup plus a choice of potato or a salad. The dinner entrees at The Adobe are outstanding. Everything from delicious seafood fettucini to grilled scallops and ribeye steak cut to order. Dinner is complete with rice and vegetable, the Adobe special baked bread and the chef's unique salad bar, or a cup of soup d'jour. If you are a chocolate lover, be sure to save room for one of their famous homemade desserts. The chocolate chocolate cake — you'll love it. The Adobe, a place to relax, enjoy the sunset and rolling surf, sample great cuisine and watch the rapture of the mighty Pacific.

THE FIRESIDE MOTEL
One mile north of Yachats city center
on Highway 101
Yachats, Oregon
503-547-3636 for reservations

Picture your vacation among shore pines bordering the thundering surf, as you watch fishing boats at work or enjoy the frolicking antics of migrating whales just off shore. If this sounds to your liking, you'll certainly enjoy the emphasis on comfort and atmosphere at The Fireside Motel, owned by Fireside Hospitality, Inc. and managed by two warm people, Leighton and Judy Taylor. This fine motel offers vacationers meticulously clean and spacious rooms with beautiful views of the ocean, as well as warm, woodburning stoves and fireplaces in many of their units. There are also three comfortable beach houses available that accommodate small groups or families. Another wonderful feature of The Fireside is its proximity to lots of fun. You can surf fish right off the rocks in front of the motel or in the nearby river, take a charter out for some deep sea fishing, dig for clams, hike at Cape Perpetua, beachcomb for little treasures, or explore the life that can be found in tide pools. It is also close to some of Oregon's finest restaurants, gift shops, the Sea Lion Caves, Newport Bay front, and the lighthouses at Heceta and Yaquina Heads. So comfortable, so close to fun and so affordable, people love it at The Fireside.

(See special invitation in Appendix.)

SHAMROCK LODGETTES
1/4 mile south of Yachats off Hwy 101
Yachats, Oregon
503-547-3312 for reservations

Imagine a quiet, park-like estate setting on four beautiful acres overlooking the Pacific Ocean, a place were you can cozy up in the evening to a toasty fire glowing from the hearth of your own log cabin and meet the sunrise with a view of ocean and river from across your open air breakfast table. Why not enjoy a leisurely stroll of only 50 feet to a clear, sandy beach just waiting to welcome you. The Shamrock Lodgettes is such a place and it has been owned and operated by Bob and Mary Oxley for the past 15 years. They run this resort/spa with the belief that hospitality and good service make for happy guests. Shamrock Lodgettes offers several lodging options—everything from motel units with king sized beds, fireplaces, jacuzzis, tubs, kitchenettes and front ocean views, to rustic log cabins that will sleep up to nine. The grounds are gorgeous and special guest touches include daily newspaper deliveries, firewood restocking, color cable TV and in-room movies. There are units featuring covered carports, stone fireplaces, private ocean view decks and bathroom jacuzzis. The resort features a health spa with sauna and hydrotherapy tub which is available for use by all guests. A licensed massage therapist is also available by appointment. Well-behaved pets are welcome in cabins at a small extra charge. The Shamrock offers a 10% discount for seven nights' stay or more, plus a 15% for all fourteen nights' stay or more. So when you are looking for fine accommodations amid the tranquil beauty of four acres of Oregon coastline, we suggest the Shamrock Lodgettes in Yachats. Rates are moderate, particularly considering all the fine amenities. MasterCard, Visa, Diners and American Express accepted.

(See special invitation in Appendix.)

ART GALLERY

GALERIE DE CHEVRIER
430 Highway 101 North
(across from the school)
Yachats, Oregon
503-547-3988

Capture gentle wings, the winds of Oregon fields, mythical creatures, ocean storms, majestic mountain splendor and innocent spirits of children — all in the various media of art to be found at the Galerie de Chevrier. You'll find beautiful works from the Northwest's finest artists who work in media as diverse as watercolors, pastel, oils, acrylics, terracotta and bronze. In addition to the watercolors and oils of prize-winning Vernon Nye, the bronzes of Keith Jameson from England bring an international flavor to the Galerie. The prices at the Galerie range from under $100 to over $10,000, but that's not all! Owners Harold and Charlotte Chevrier also deal extensively in stamps. Indeed, this is a dream store. Here you can see the first U.S. stamps ever minted in 1847. Harold and Charlotte traveled the entire Oregon coast before selecting Yachats as the place to live. Having been art collectors for several years they decided to open the "serious gallery for the discriminating art collector" over three years ago. When you come to the Galerie, you may meet the present mayor of Yachats; yes, it is Harold Chevrier!

CRAFTS/GIFTS

THE TOLE TREE
One mile north of Yachats on Hwy 101
Yachats, Oregon
503-547-3608

Do you need a splash of color, a touch of country charm to brighten your home, or a gift for someone special? The Tole Tree will have that special something and more. Not only is there a wide selection of beautiful Oregon handcrafted gifts, but if you are an artist at heart, there is a room full of canvasses, paints and new craft ideas for your creative projects. For over ten years, Kay and Al Ludlow have been providing visitors with original gifts made from myrtlewood, as well as tole and art supplies, craft classes and seminars, art books, and packet patterns for your every creative need. The Tole Tree is indeed three shops in one — a gift shop, an art room for do-it-yourselfers, and a studio for classes and instruction. So if you are combing the coast for gifts like tole painted pieces, Old World folk art, cutting boards, lazy susans, or jewelry, creative craft ideas and seminars, comb The Tole Tree, an art lovers' paradise.

(See special invitation in Appendix.)

EVENTS

COMMUNITY SMELT FRY

Between April and October, you can witness a rare wonder of nature. During the mating season of the mysterious silver smelt, hundreds of these fascinating, delicious, sardine-like fish come to the sandy shores of Yachats. These fish are also the guests of honor at the Yachats Community Smelt Fry in July. Yachats residents celebrate being in one of the few places in the world where the sea smelt come to shore.

KITE FESTIVAL

During October winds, children and those who are children at heart will be out flying their kites. On a wonderful day in October, you'll love watching the hundreds of beautiful handmade kites and wind socks flash their colors in the Oregon ski at this fun festival in Yachats. Don't miss it.

MYRTLEWOOD FACTORY/GIFTS

THE MYRTLETREE FACTORY
One mile north of Yachats on Hwy 101
Yachats, Oregon
503-547-3930

Winter hours: 9-5
Summer hours: 9-6

The natural beauty of Myrtlewood, a rare and colorful hardwood found in Oregon, is only surpassed when it is crafted into fine works of art. You will find a variety of unique items such as lovely vases, original handpainted plaques, covered candy dishes, salad bowls, trivets, candlestands and plates, all in durable mat, satin or high gloss finish, designed and manufactured as the Myrtletree. Ken and Herta have dedicated nine years to creating some of the most beautifully crafted Myrtlewood pieces of the Oregon coast. If you are looking for a gift or that perfect piece, this is the place to find it. Ken and Herta will give you special attention and gladly help you with any questions. For outstanding quality, reasonable prices and friendly, knowledgeable service, try the Myrtletree for a best choice in gifts on the Oregon Coast.

(See special invitation in Appendix.)

NATURAL WONDERS

CAPE PERPETUA
Located just two miles south of Yachats
on Highway 101 in Suislaw National Forest
Yachats, Oregon

Rising abruptly out of the cold Pacific, the volcanic Oregon coastal range meets the sea. This massive headland of volcanic basalt that spewed from deep in the earth's crust as molten lava, is now teeming with plant and animal life from the sea and land. It is constantly changing. Each succeeding wave takes piece after piece of rock back into the sea in the never ending cycle of change. Just as the earth is forever evolving in cycles, history proved it does the same with the disappearance of the coastal Indian culture that once inhabited this region. Evidence of their simple lives dot the coastline in the form of shell mounds, all that is left of what was once taken as food from shellfish beds along this part of the coastline. These mounds are all that remain of this peaceful tribe's presence. First sighted by European explorer Captain James Cook on March 7, 1778, he named the cape for Saint Perpetua who was martyred for professing her faith in Carthage on March 7, 203 A.D. Cape Perpetua is a nature lover's playground of fun. You'll find wildlife like deer, elk, black bear, bobcat, sea lions and harbor seals. You'll also enjoy marine gardens, sandy coves, the old Indian shell mounds, and great hiking trails. Cape Perpetua is not a place for you to miss when visiting the Oregon coast. You and your family will enjoy experiencing the many beautiful and complex cities of nature as well as the history and geology of these unique spots on the Oregon coast.

RESTAURANTS

LA SERRE RESTAURANT
Second and Beach Streets
(look for state sign, turn west
off Hwy 101 in Yachats)
Yachats, Oregon
503-547-3420

Winter hours: 9-8 seven days a week
Summer hours: 9-9 seven days a week

Imagine a French country inn set on the Oregon coast. Relax amid lush greenery with the sun filtering through pebbled skylights, the scent of natural wood beams and freshly cut flowers, antique oil lamps sending a warm glow across oak furnishing, and knotty floor planks. Owner Joanne Lambert, with the help of her manager, Beverly Potts, have been bringing the warmth of their personality to La Serre for the past 9½ years. Meals here are prepared lovingly with a special emphasis on fresh, seasonal ingredients, simply cooked and beautifully presented. The seafood and beef specialties are fresh, never frozen. Breakfast features homemade breads, freshly squeezed juices and specialty tea and gourmet coffees. There is a fine, fresh pastry selection including a great Danish or bran and currant muffins. We highly recommend the omelette here as the best we've tasted anywhere on the Oregon coast — light, perfectly cooked with a choice of delicious fillings (combos like crab and shrimp). Another breakfast favorite is the whole wheat Poppyseed Griddlecakes. They are scrumptious. For lunch, start with a cup of homemade soup. The light French Onion or heartier clam chowder are both good bets. To follow, we suggest the shrimp sandwich on sourdough, a tangy mix of shrimp, dill and gherkins, blended with mayo and served with green salad, jack cheese and tomato. For lighter palates, the Spanish salad with poppyseed dressing is a very tasty mix of greens, eggs, mushrooms, red onions and croutons. For dinner, check the specialty board for daily fresh fish offerings. We loved the dover sole fillets served over a bed of Pacific shrimp, then topped with bearnaise sauce and freshly grated parmesan. Dinners are served with soup of the day or tossed green salad, steamed fresh vegetables, table sized, fresh whole wheat bread loaves with herb butter, and your choice of brown rice or steamed red potatoes. The filet mignon is another favorite here. To round off your gourmet dining at La Sere, save room for the dessert trolley of tempting, homemade delectables. There is full bar service featuring a selection of Northwest wines, cocktails, and warm spirits. La Serre, a best choice when you want finely prepared fresh meals, served in the comfort of an elegant French greenhouse style eatery — bon apetite!

SOUTH LINCOLN COUNTY TOUR

This rural and beautiful area starts out with a fantastic view and breakfast you won't soon forget. You can enjoy a dinner that's definitely the most gourmet you could find between Seattle and San Francisco. With this tour, there is variety and enough sightseeing for anyone.

TIME	PLACE	DESCRIPTION	HOW TO FIND IN BOOK
Dawn	Yachats Beach	Best beach	Yachats/Beach
Breakfast	The Adobe Resort/Motel and Restaurant	Best breakfast	Yachats/Accommodations
A.M.	The Myrtletree Factory	Best myrtlewood/gifts	Yachats/Myrtlewood Factory/Gifts
A.M.	The Tole Tree	Best tole supplies/gifts/crafts	Yachats/Crafts/Gifts
A.M.	Galerie De Chevrier	Best art gallery	Yachats/Art Gallery
Lunch	La Serre Restaurant	Best lunch	Yachats/Restaurant
P.M.	Trident Antiques and Country Store	Best antiques/gifts	Waldport/Antiques/Gifts
P.M.	Bill's Agate Shop	Best rock shop	Waldport/Rock Shop
P.M.	Sea Gulch Gift Shop	Best gifts	Seal Rock/Gifts
P.M.	Sea Gulch	Best attraction	Seal Rock/Attractions
P.M.	Moby Dick's Waldport Seafoods Market	Best seafood	Waldport/Seafood
P.M.	Port of Waldport	Best crabbing	Waldport/Port
Dinner	The Experience	Best dinner	Waldport/Restaurant

152 Lincoln County

Chapter Four

LANE COUNTY

ABOUT LANE COUNTY AND FLORENCE

Florence, located in Lane County, has the reputation of being a special place where colorful rhododendrons and azaleas grow wild along the roadside and decorate the lush landscape. Imagine a serene coastal village flanked by pristine, fresh water lakes, miles of scenic ocean beaches, babbling mountain brooks, dramatic sand dunes and the Siuslaw River estuary. Florence is situated mid-state on coastal Highway 101; the region is rich in history, going back to the days when the Siuslaw Indians inhabited the banks of the Siuslaw River. In the year 1870, the area was opened up to settlement and by the early 1900s, Florence boasted a population of 300. One of the original store buildings remains intact and is recognized as a National Historic Landmark. Today that pioneer heritage lives on in the restored historic buildings of Old Town Florence. Stroll along the quaint Old Town lanes and experience the charm of a bygone era in the interesting collection of restaurants, curio shops and boutiques. Catch the sun dipping gold behind Florence's picturesque bayside harbor where colorful fishing boats and sailing craft lay swaying to the ripple of gentle sea breezes. The outdoor rests at your fingertips.

There are more than 2000 campsites overlooking the Pacific Ocean, tucked away in woods or along creeks and lakes. Within seven miles of Florence you'll find 17 fresh water lakes including Siltcoos Lake which is Oregon's largest coastal lake, boasting outstanding fishing all year. There are rivers, creeks, bountiful beaches, waterskiing, scuba diving, golfing, sailing, canoeing, river rafting, horseback rides along the shores, bicycling, miles of hiking trails, seaplane rides, three-wheelers and dune buggies, and even good old-fashioned swimming holes. Along the mud flats of the Siuslaw River, roll up your sleeves to enjoy some of the best clamming you are likely to find. The local docks and jetties are perfect for catching your own bounty of fresh Dungeness crab. As for fishing, the lakes have a reputation for yielding some of the best bass and trout catches in the state. Challenge your skill by casting a line into the Siuslaw River for the seasonal runs of mighty salmon, steelhead and cutthroat trout. Deep sea charters are available for world famous Chinook and Coho salmon, bottom fishing and halibut. Wildlife also take kindly to the area around Florence. There are brown bears, deer, raccoons, Roosevelt elk, mighty bald eagles, Canadian geese, seals and sea otters, plus a rich array of coastal marine life.

The area surrounding Florence is abundant with natural wonders awaiting your exploration. The Oregon Dunes National Recreation Area begins in Florence and extends south 41 miles along the Coast. The famous Sea Lion Caves lay just 12 miles north of the town. Heceta Head and Lighthouse, also north of Florence, is renowned as the most photographed, scenic spot on the Oregon Coast. Between November and May, you can spot the grey whales migrating through the coastal waters. Darlingtonia Botanical Wayside features a profusion of rare carnivores — cobra lily plants. Harbor Vista Park and the North Jetty offer outstanding views of the Siuslaw River mouth and the Pacific beyond. At Indian Forest, you can wander through a village of recreated Indian tribal dwellings plus live buffalo herds and deer.

Yes, Florence is a special place where a wealth of outdoor pursuits and great guest amenities await you. But it is special for another reason, and that is the natural warmth of the local people. Residents take real civic pride in protecting and enhancing the gorgeous scenery and quality of life they love. Community in-

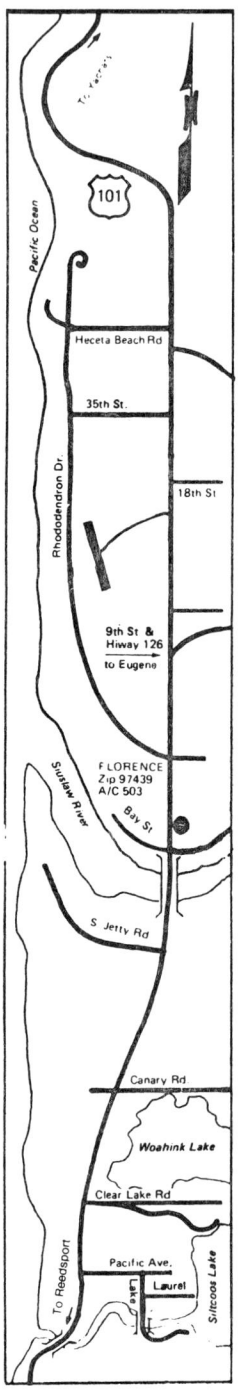

volvement and volunteerism is so high that the Florence library is run by approximately 100 volunteers and one of the town's eleven parks, Miller Park, was recently constructed entirely by Florence volunteers. In Florence, you can bet visitors can look forward to a friendly welcome by neighborly people high on the good life.

CHAMBER OF COMMERCE
P.O. Box 712
Florence, Oregon 97439
503-997-3128
Toll free in Oregon 1-800-292-6278
Outside Oregon 1-800-982-6287

For further information on lodging, attractions, places to dine and special events, contact the friendly Florence area Chamber of Commerce.

ACCOMMODATIONS

DRIFTWOOD SHORES SURFSIDE RESORT
88416 First Avenue (turn west on
Heceta Beach Rd. off Hwy 101)
Florence, Oregon
503-997-8263
or toll free in Oregon 1-800-422-5091
outside Oregon 1-800-824-8774

A relaxing oceanside atmosphere—Pacific beaches drenched in weather-worn driftwood—cool sea breezes that mingle serenely with the comforts of luxurious, ocean view suites—it's all here at the Driftwood. This 137 unit complex is brilliantly run by expert general manager Terry Coleman. Choices range from studio, queen unit accommodating one to two people, up to three bedroom suites for up to eight persons. All suites overlook the ocean or are tastefully appointed. Junior and Executive suites feature fully appointed kitchens with a private balcony overlooking the sea. The three bedroom suites boast large living rooms, fireplaces, kitchens, formal dining rooms, very large master bedrooms with private bath, and two queen rooms with an adjoining bath, plus a private balcony overlooking the Pacific. Full resort facilities here include an attractive restaurant featuring fresh seafood and steak entrees served right by the shoreline, a full wine list, evening entertainment in the lounge, indoor pool, saunas and jacuzzis.

Reservations are recommended 60 days in advance for the peak summer period of July and August. A family plan for children under 12 years old and complimentary cribs for the toddlers are available. Driftwood Shores is the only accommodation located directly on the beach for miles. It is a best choice for homestyle comfort and beach views in the Florence area.

(See special invitation in Appendix.)

ADDITIONAL ACCOMMODATIONS

THE MONEY SAVER
170 Highway 101
Florence, Oregon
503-997-7131

New, close to bay, TV, phones.

PIER POINT INN
85625 Highway 101 South
Florence, Oregon
1-800-452-8328 or 503-997-7191

Restaurant/lounge, bay view, TV, phones, gift shop.

ATTRACTIONS

INDIAN FOREST
(4 miles north of Florence on Hwy 101)
Florence, Oregon
503-997-3677

Hours: 8-8 June 1-Sept 1
10am-4pm May, Sept & Oct

An adventure awaits you and the whole family as you enter Indian Forest and pass from today's modern society into America's native beginnings from long before the arrival of European explorers. The winding forest path weaves through coastal pines, rhododendrons, wild huckleberries and into a cluster of full-sized, authentically recreated Indian dwellings from all over North America. Each tribal structure has its own unique character reflecting the different Indian lifestyles and climate conditions of its origin. Robert Manseth has owned and operated this exciting, educational exhibit for over twenty years. The whole family will be fascinated with the intricate structures of the hogans, teepees and earth lodges. As part of this tribute to our great native American ancestors, you will meet some of the real animals that formed the lifeblood of their way of living such as deer and buffalo. At the entrance to this adventure forest, you'll find an A-frame Indian Trading Post offering a selection of handmake Indian artwork and crafts. Enjoy and look at Hopi pottery, handsome Navajo rugs, native dolls, baskets, jewelry, beadwork, sand paintings, toys, moccasins, and an array of informative books. Indian Forest — a best choice you'll want to explore in the spirit of our original ancestors.

OREGON DUNES NATIONAL RECREATIONAL AREA

The dunes area begins in Florence and spreads south along the coast for 41 miles. These large, magnificent sand dunes, some reaching as high as 500 feet, rival the dunes of the Sahara in size and grandeur. The National Recreation Area covers over 32,000 acres. Within the dunes are individual pockets of evergreen forests, fresh water lakes and streams which support complete habitats and natural wildlife. There is something for everyone here — hiking, camping, fishing, riding dune buggies, picnicking and bird watching. The Recreation Area falls into seven geographic areas: (1) South Jetty to South Jetty Road; closed to vehicles; narrow strip of land bordered by the Foredune to the west and the Siuslaw River to the east. This area is a wetland plain and is fairly heavily vegetated; habitat for several species of migratory and resident waterfowl including whistling swans. Parking lot along South Jetty Road provides access to the beach and dock for fishing and crabbing. (2) South Jetty Road to Siltcoos River; open to vehicles; second largest area of open sand in National Recreation Area and the second highest dunes contain popular off-road vehicle access. (3) Siltcoos River to Three Mile Creek; closed to vehicles; northwest part of Recreational Area; mostly vegetated and contains a variety of wetlands, ecosystems that provide nesting sites and forage for many wildlife species; hiking trails connect campgrounds with nearby rivers, lakes and beaches. Oregon Dunes Overlook offers visitor information on the dunes with a scenic view and trail to the beach. (4) Three Mile Creek to Umpqua River; closed to vehicles; contains some open sand areas with smaller, traverse dunes; mostly freshwater marsh habitat for birds, waterfowl and several species of sensitive plants and animals; maintenance by the Forest Service as an undisturbed, back country location to preserve this section's high natural value. (5) Umpqua Lighthouse State Park to Douglas/Coos County Line; open to vehicles; contains some of highest dunes and 25% of open sand; very popular area; access via County Road 251 which begins in Winchester Bay or via access road that joins Highway 101. Two parking lots for RVs and beach access. Also, access to the Umpqua River Jetties for some excellent fishing. (6) Douglas/Coos County Line to Ten Mile Creek; closed to vehicles; known as Umpqua Dunes Scenic Area; third largest area of open sand and some of the highest dunes; left in an undisturbed condition; several campgrounds located in an area along Eel Creek. (7) Ten Mile Creek to National Recreation Area boundary. Contains the most open sand, diverse land forms and largest non-vegetated area. Large areas of lakes, marshes and old cranberry bogs on both private and public land within NRA. Visitors urged to respect private land boundaries; vehicle access via Spinreel Campground, south of Ten Mile Creek and Horsefall Road at southern NRA boundary.

DUNES OUTSIDE NATIONAL RECREATION AREA

Lily Lake to Siuslaw River; closed to vehicles from Heceta Head to Sutton Creek; open to vehicles south of Sutton Creek; Forest Service currently developing management plan for the area to address vehicle use and protected sensitive species which inhabit marshlands just in from the beach; access to vehicle closed area north of Sutton Creek is via Baker Beach Road; popular area for hikers and horseback riding; vehicle accessed area south of Sutton Creek is via Joshua Lane.

SAND DUNES FRONTIER
(4 miles south of Florence on Hwy 101)
Florence, Oregon
503-997-3544

Hours: open March-Oct
By appointment in winter

Imagine roaming across Oregon's coastal dunes amid 32,000 acres of national recreation area which contains some of the most outstanding and beautiful sand dunes in the nation. These amazing expanses of ever moving, silently shifting hills of golden sand rise up in places to some 400 feet. From the comfortable seat of your dune buggy, you'll explore ocean, lakes, mysterious ghost islands of lush, evergreen trees and remnant forests, and miles of spectacular sand dunes. Owner Ruel Chapman and son, Galen, have been personally sharing their love for the Oregon Dunes for more than 28 years. In the summer, they offer terrific commercial dune buggy rides for parties of three or more with no reservations necessary. These scenic buggy tours accommodate up to 30 people at one time. Skilled drivers highlight all points of interest for visitors. Private tours are also available for special sand dune and beach excursions. Try one for an hour, half day, or a day. The vehicles used are especially equipped with roll bars and reinforced to ensure total passenger safety and comfort. My ride was an absolutely fantastic experience as I relaxed and zigzagged across breathtaking dunes scattered with deer everywhere.

The Chapmans invite you to witness firsthand this unique landscape dotted with gravestone forests, bird sanctuaries, and marooned lakes. Visitors have a choice of the commercial buggy rides or a "you drive yourself" (Honda Odysseys). The Chapmans provide some other fun amenities, too, with an 18-hole miniature golf course, a gift shop brimming with unique, around-the-world import items, and game room and snack bar for the kids, plus trout fishing for rainbow in their own lake. Incidentally, the fishing here is rather different — no license, no limit, tackle and bait furnished. Fish to your heart's desire, catch as many as you can, and then simply pay by the inch. Be sure to stroll through the special flower gardens while you're here. Two acres of beautiful coastal blooms are waiting to welcome you. A best choice at the Frontier awaits to amaze the whole family with a great day of fun on the Oregon Sand Dunes.

(See special invitation in Appendix.)

SEA LION CAVES
Highway 101 (11 miles north of Florence
and 14 miles south of Yachats)
Florence, Oregon
503-547-3111

Summer hours: 8am to one hour before dusk
Winter hours: 9am to one hour before dusk

On any given day, you may witness just a few or over 600 wild Stellar and California sea lions in their natural habitat. Not only is this America's largest sea cave, but also the only place known where wild sea lions make their home on the mainland year 'round. Three families, the Sauberts, Jacobsens and Houghtons, originally purchased the 95 plus acres here back in 1928. Some 54 years ago, in 1932, the caves were opened to visitors. Today, third generation family members Steve Saubert (general manager) and Clifton Saubert (director) ensure that the great devotion here to preserve and protect this natural experience lives on. (In all other places, sea lions live on rocky islands located from a few hundred yards to several miles offshore.) The basic goal at the caves is to preserve the sea lions, the pigeons, cormorants and gull seabirds, the rich variety of marine life and natural wonders of the area, while making it easily accessible for everyone. This is an exhilarating experience and I know your whole family will love it as much as I did.

A walkway with gorgeous views of Oregon's rugged coastline leads you down 208 feet to one of the largest sea caves you'll find anywhere in the world. The cave itself covers the length of a football field, spanning 300 feet across. Volcanic rock walls, multi-colored by minerals and lichens, reach up to a vaulted dome 12 stories high. You'll marvel as the rock walls echoes the roar of both mighty sea and sea lions. From the mouth entrance of the caves, you'll have a breathtaking view of the handsome Heceta Head lighthouse. Look southward to see miles of shimmering sandy beaches and distant headlands. Take time to enjoy the wonderful bronze sculpture "Stellar Sea Lion Family" which was dedicated in 1982 to commemorate the 50th anniversary of the Sea Lion Caves. There is a very attractive gift shop featuring a fine collection of original art, collectibles, and novelty items ranging from 25 cents to $25,000. An interesting note: the sea lion breeding season begins in the spring and they continue their mating ritual until early summer. From April until about mid-July, the family structure is fairly evident with the young pups born on the rocky ledges outside the caves. Once breeding season is completed, sea lions return to the inside of the cave itself which they occupy as their principle home during fall and winter. Whatever the season, the Sea Lion Caves by coastal Florence offers you a best choice chance of a lifetime to witness the magic of these lovable creatures and the panoramic vistas of the surrounding coastline. Open all year 'round.

THREE WHEELING DUNES NATIONAL RECREATION AREA

The dunes offer a natural playground for the newest breed of offroad vehicles, namely three-wheeled motorcycles. About 48% of the park is open to offroad machines and the long, rolling acres of dunes makes the recreation area here one of the most popular spots for offroading in the Northwest. South Jetty Road, just south of Siuslaw River Bridge, provides access to about 7000 acres of dunes and beaches. The area to the south of the road is one of the most popular offroad sections and includes the imposing, steep sand of South Jetty Hill. Another popular section is the Driftwood 2 campround area near the Sitcoos River, almost five miles south of Florence. A Forest Service map outlining which areas and beaches in the Dunes Recreation Area are open to offroad vehicles can be obtained at the Mapleton Ranger District Office, the Dunes NRA headquarters in Reedsport, the Florence Chamber of Commerce and many sporting goods stores.

EVENTS

March — Boat Show
May — Rhododendron Days Celebration
July — Fourth of July Celebration
August — Blueback Fishing Derby
October — Carnival
December — Christmas Parade & Celebration

RHODODENDRON FESTIVAL

In mid-May when the beautiful wild rhododendrons and scotch broom are at their most glorious, Florence boasts the second oldest flower festival in Oregon. It has been an annual occurrence for almost 80 years. It is a festival, pageant, carnival, sand sculpture competition, rowboat races on the river, children's contests, a fireman's tug-of-war, art shows and musical presentations. The festival normally gets under way on Friday evening and culminates with a grand parade on Sunday afternoon. As part of the festivities, the town hosts the popular Rhody Run which features 5000 and 10,000 fun runs. Best of all, you'll marvel at the gorgeous blooms of azaleas and rhododendrons everywhere.

Lane County

GIFTS

INCREDIBLE-EDIBLE OREGON
1336 Bay Street (on the bay front, Old Town)
Florence, Oregon
503-997-7018

Summer hours: 10-6 seven days a week
Winter hours: 10-5 Wed-Mon

Whether your fancy runs to delectible Oregon edibles, interesting books on the Pacific Northwest, assortments of gourmet cheeses, smoked meats and seafoods, or local myrtlewood creations you'll cherish, it's all here at Incredible-Edible Oregon. Locals Bob and Les Freeman and daughter, Andi, are rightly fond of the spirit of the people and spectacular natural beauty of their state; so much so that they opened this shop to share with you their love affair for Oregon. There are shelves stacked high with local honey, wild berry jams, cranberry sweets, gourmet mustards, yummy brandied cranberries, local wild salal berry jam, and chocolate covered Oregon hazelnuts. Bob and Les feature a huge supply of Oregon wines plus locally crafted wooden toys, "Florence fuzzies" stuffed animals, plus specialty gift items — sculptures, wood creations, and local Oregon stoneware. Bob and Les have a delightful selection to choose from, all homegrown a la Oregon style, definitely a best choice in our book. Mail order shipping is available. Ask for one of their free catalogs.

(See special invitation in Appendix.)

THE QUEST FOR GIFTS
1383 Bay Street (Old Town Florence)
P.O. Box 2013
Florence, Oregon
503-997-9681

Owners Ruth and Kermit Butler have worked hard to make their Oregon dream come true. A gift emporium featuring unique creations by artisans and craft persons local to the Pacific Northwest and afar. Roam amid the ceramic gifts of stoneware, porcelain and raku; watch the lights dazzle through intricate stained and art glass pieces; run your fingers along the silky, hand-finished myrtlewood and handsome wood sculptures; check out the array of stone carvings, brass creations and imaginative cement and metal sculptures. This place is a paradise of artistic creations, many of them locally crafted with plenty of Oregon love. There are gifts from the Oregon sea — seafood, smoked salmon, fresh packed Albacore tuna and shrimp, gifts which offer you a special taste of the Oregon coast including Florence's own, Joann's Pure Honey, wild berry jams and jellies. Your choice continues with gifts of aromatic enchantment like potpourri and scented candles, Mount St. Helens glass ornaments, whimsical hand-blown pyrex oil candles mounted on ocean driftwood, whale's tale and ship mugs, myrtlewood stamp boxes and crafted-by-hand soap dispensers, pewter fantasies in the way of adorable miniature figurines, country French butter crocks with myrtlewood butter spreaders, crystal hummingbirds and ceramic feeders, kangaroo tea mugs, Oregon klip-klop rocking horses, and a stuffed family of cuddly Bare Bears. There is a courtesy gift wrap service plus free color brochures for convenient mail order shopping. UPS shipping is available throughout the United States. MasterCard and Visa accepted. Discounts available for senior citizens. Your quest has ended — The Quest for Gifts is a best choice for wonderful local Oregon creations available right here in Florence or by mail.

(See special invitation in Appendix.)

GOLF

FLORENCE GOLF CLUB
(3 miles north of Florence off Hwy 101
turn east on Munsel Lake Road)
Florence, Oregon
503-997-3232 for start time & directions

Uniquely nestled among 75-foot sand dunes in a nature sanctuary area of deer, bear, raccoon and birds sits a golf club of a special order. Managers have meticulously maintained their club for over 25 years, to the public's delight. Local manager, Mark Shepherd, and golf pro, Mike Dwyer, are personally on hand to ensure that your golfing here goes like a pro. The club offers a 9-hole, par 34, 2700 yard golf course plus driving range, power carts and club rentals, full pro shop, snack bar and practice putting green. As you tee off on the course, make a note of number four — it is a rather unique, short par 4 since a sand dune cuts right through the middle, dogleg fashion. The greens are fantastically maintained. Built on a sand base, the course provides golfers with dry, firm play conditions for year 'round use. An automatic underground sprinkler system ensures exquisite green turf even during the driest summers. Classes include group and private lessons, tournament groups are warmly welcomes, and special group, junior and senior rates are available. During the Rhododendron Days Festival, a crazy four-man scramble is held right here at the club where any group teams of four players can try their best shots. The club is open all year. A great time to hit the greens is early morning, when the summer temperatures are a delightful 65-70 degrees. During summer weekends, it is advised that you call in advance to ensure start times. A pristine golf club, set amid the dramatic coastal sand dunes — a best choice in our book for teeing off, Oregon style.

(See special invitation in Appendix.)

ICE CREAM

B.J.'S ICE CREAM PARLOUR
48 flavors
2930 Highway 101 North
Florence, Oregon
503-997-7286

Or find **B.J.'s Bay Street Annex** in Old Town Florence, Oregon

Winter hours: 11-10 Mon-Sat, noon-9 Sun
Summer hours: 11-11 Mon-Sat, 11-10 Sun

By now we reckon word has spread so wide that you've probably already heard of B.J.'s in Florence; but if you haven't, you are in for an unforgettable treat. The homemade batches of superb gourmet ice cream here are the result of master chef owners Brian and Jodie Cole. For the past eight years, the Coles have been personally whipping up scrumptious ice creams from an exclusive recipe which they tell us leaves blissful customers convinced that "it is better ice cream than they've ever tried anywhere." It is not surprising, since Brian and Jodie prefer to use natural flavorings in their ice cream. That means real chocolate, real strawberries, and real delicious! Try some bittersweet nugget made with real rich chocolate and lots of semisweet flakes running through it, some red raspberry cheesecake, or a yummy scoop of white licorice. B.J.'s serves up fountain-style, old-fashioned sarsaparillas, custom sundaes, thick shakes, ice cream floats, sodas and terrific banana splits. The cones are waffle-style sugar cones made right here from scratch. Try a double header cone which holds up to six heavenly scoops for the true ice cream connoisseur. Brian and Jodie also feature decorated ice cream cakes, frozen chocolate-dipped bananas, old fashioned "nutty butty" cones and ice cream to go. Some good news is that prices are remarkably moderate for this kind of quality. B.J.'s Ice Cream is famous once you've tried it, and it is definitely a best choice in Florence.

(See special invitation in Appendix.)

MYRTLEWOOD FACTORY/GIFTS

LAKESHORE MYRTLEWOOD
6 miles south of Florence on Hwy 101
on Wohink Lake shore
Florence, Oregon
503-997-2753

Minimum summer hours: 8-5 Mon-Sat, 10-5 Sun

Oregon myrtlewood is a rarity that grows in a short, narrow band along the rugged southern Oregon coast right in the heart of beautiful Coquille Valley. Dick and Pat Stanfill, inspired by the beauty of this richly colored, native Oregon wood, opened Lakeshore Myrtlewood in a retail gift shop, a manufacturer's outlet, some ten years ago. They also bring splendid wood creations to life at their table factory location in Tillamook. Myrtlewood logs chosen for use at Lakeshore are graded for color and quality, custom turned and sanded to a silky smooth finish. Pieces are hand-rubbed with Danish oils and protective coatings so that items can be used for warm or cold foods, washed in soapy water and dried. All pieces displayed at Lakeshore are hand-crafted from original designs which means that, while each piece is unique, all share the common bond of high quality workmanship. The range of myrtlewood pieces here is incredible — 42 different myrtlewood bowl styles ranging from 6 inch salad bowls to bountiful 24 inch ones. There is an assortment of stylish myrtlewood pedestals, fruit bowls, covered dishes, candy servers, vases, condiment sets, trays, plaques, clocks ornaments plus 60 to 70 specialty items boasting the intricate, rich pearl markings that myrtlewood trees are famous for. Dick and Pat's table factory features bargain, redwood burl-topped tables, myrtlewood tables of all kinds, pine tree clocks, handcrafted dolls, wooden toys, soft sculpture, a year 'round Halloween and Christmas craft session, and lots of original wood carvings native to this coastal area. Prices at both locations are quite reasonable. This is a best choice for capturing the skilled craftsmanship of our native Oregon wood creations.

PARKS

GALLAGHER'S PARK
940 Spruce Street by Munsel Creek
Florence, Oregon

3½ acres featuring picnic areas, short trails and plentiful rhododendrons.

JESSIE M. HONEYMAN STATE PARK
3 miles south of Florence on Hwy 101

The campground has 241 tent sites, 75 electrical campsites, and 66 with full hookups. Firewood is available. Hot showers, supplies and food concession, plus public telephones are provided. There are also six group campsites accommodating 25 people each. This is a popular park with a sparkling, fresh water lake, towering sand dunes which provide shelter from wind, and a profusion of colorful rhododendrons. Day use picnic facilites at Clearwox Lake and on Woahink Lake which also provide boat launching ramps, bath houses and swimming beaches. Park activities include boating, waterskiing, fishing, swimming, lakeside trail hikes and nature study.

MINIPARK
1290 Bay Street
Florence, Oregon

Featured is an historic gazebo within an attractively landscaped area plus a popular fishing dock on the Siuslaw River.

MUNSEL CREEK GREENWAY PARK
Near 24th & Willow Streets
Florence, Oregon

18 acre park with seasonal lake; forest, sand dunes and stream. Parking available. There are paths and restrooms; playground/picnic facilities are planned.

SINGING PINES PARK
1295 Airport Road
Florence, Oregon

7 acres of heavily forested area with picnic tables, hiking paths and parking.

CARL WASHBURNE STATE PARK
13 miles north of Florence &
14 miles south of Yachats

The campground is open year 'round; there are 58 full hookup sites, six walk in tent sites and two regular tent sites. Firewood is for sale at a nominal fee. Two utility buildings with hot showers and restrooms with flush toilets are available. A picnic area is next to the beach. Beachcombing is popular along the coastline and there is lots of marine life in tidal pools formed in the rocky cliffs. Fishing and clamming are favorite activities.

RESTAURANTS

BRIDGEWATER RESTAURANT
1297 Bay Street (Old Town)
Florence, Oregon
503-997-9405 for reservations

Winter hours: 9-9 Mon-Sat, 10-8 Sun
Summer hours: 7am-11pm seven days a week

Imagine a tropical 1940s atmosphere set in one of Florence's oldest buildings. Step inside the Bridgewater and be transported back to the feel of Rick's Cafe in *Casablanca*, replete with cool, comfortable wicker and cane furnishings, overflowing greenery and a background of big band style music. The Kezar family, Larry, Mary and son, Wayne, have built up quite a reputation over the past three years of business and it is no wonder since the Bridgewater serves up the freshest and some of the most fantastically prepared seafood we've tasted anywhere. An added bonus that will keep you coming back for more is that prices are very moderate indeed. For lunch, we recommend the popular shrimp and avocado sandwich, a large open face featuring the freshest Oregon Bay shrimp on French bread with a special dressing and plenty of sliced avocados, served up with French fries, clam chowder or salad. Another specialty is the pan- fried oysters (directly from Coos Bay), lightly battered, seasoned and pan-fried gently in pure olive oil and served with a choice of side dishes. The Oregon shrimp salad, stuffed croissants and tostadas are always popular. The restaurant features a full-service lounge specializing in tropical blended libations made from the freshest fruits and juices. An extensive Oregon wine list is also offered. For dinner, entrees include a trip through the Kezar's famous soup (usually clam chowder) and salad bar plus hot, fresh bread and butter. The dinner menu is extensive and entrees are prepared beautifully. Begin with an appetizer of Oysters Rockefeller, the Cajun Creole Jubilee or their specialty, nachos. Then perhaps a steaming bowl of homemade clam chowder. The Kezars are so confident that their chowder is the world's best that they say, "If you don't like it, we'll buy it." Be sure to check the "catch of the day" for the freshest crab, salmon, trout, etc., that come right out of the water that very same morning. The Caribbean Cabob dinner is a favorite of mine — chicken, sirloin and shrimp charbroiled with pineapples, mushrooms and green bell peppers. Another best bet is the delicious Seafood Saute featuring a gorgeous assortment of seafood sauteed gently in wine, mushrooms and oil. The charbroiled rib- eye will leave steak lovers in culinary bliss. There is a delicious assortment of desserts prepared by Mary Kezar, plus a full-service oyster bar featuring clams, oysters and crab prepared a dozen different ways. Sundays from 10am-2pm, there is a delectable 32 item buffet brunch that has become a real local favorite. On Sunday afternoons you may spot a light jazz band playing on the outdoor dining deck. During summer, breakfast is added to the menu. Enjoy it either inside or out on the deck. The Bridgewater — definitely a mouth-watering best choice right here in Florence. In fact, the reputation here is so good that we strongly recommend dinner reservations in the summer.

WINDWARD INN
(north end of Florence, Hwy 101)
Florence, Oregon
503-997-8243 (reservations accepted)

Winter hours: 8am-9pm Tues-Sun
Summer hours: open 7 days a week

Dine amid country-style, rich, wood furnishings, book-lined shelves and warm, log fireplaces right here on the Oregon coast. Owners Lynnette Wikstrom and David Haskell have been in the business of serving up great culinary experiences for the past seven years and are proud of the friendly welcome the staff likes to bestow to guests. Specialties include local seafood, broiled steaks, Oregon veal, fresh vegetables, homemade desserts, breads and pastries, all featuring high quality and fresh ingredients. Breakfast, lunch, dinner and light suppers are offered at the Windward Inn and all share the emphasis of homemade goodness and creative preparation. For lunch, try the Boudin Blanc, which is a chicken and veal sausage, a blend of subtle spices served with fresh vegetables and steamed, new potatoes. The fresh seafood entrees are real favorites here along with great French onion soup and clam chowder made from scratch daily. Try the quiche of the day or a fluffy omelette served with soup or a tender salad of mixed greens. For dinner, you'll have some tempting entree decisions to make. There is everything from the scrumptious Captain's Plate brimming with fresh oysters, steamed clams, crab legs, mussels and scallops, to Mussels Mariner sauteed in white wine and onions. All steaks are choice 6 oz. or 8 oz. center cuts of top sirloin and prime filet, charbroiled and served with fresh sauteed mushrooms. The Veal Maderia and seafood sausage entrees are additional favorites. Dinners include either homemade soup or mixed green salad, baked or steamed new potatoes, wild rice pilaf or special Saratoga chips cooked to order, plus a loaf of the Windward's hearty seven-grain bread. There is an excellent selection of good Oregon wines to enjoy along with the fine dining and friendly service — the Windward Inn, a best choice for great Oregon dining along the Pacific coast.

SPORTING GOODS

THE SPORTSMAN
On Highway 101 (one block from the bridge)
Florence, Oregon
503-997-3336

Winter hours: 9-7 Mon-Sat, 11-4 Sun
Summer hours: 7am-9pm seven days a week

When you're after fine outdoor gear and expert sporting tips, here's the place to come. Local owners Warner and Jolene Pinkney, with the help of son, Bill, have been running this business for some 39 years and have been doing such a good job of it that The Sportsman now boasts the reputation of being the largest sporting goods store up and down the Oregon coast. The huge outdoor selection includes a full line of guns and ammunition, fishing gear and bait, warm and cold-blooded clothing, athletic equipment, archery supplies, and bird and game hunting gear. The store can outfit you for backpacking, camping, jogging, and both team sport and gym needs. They stock durable work clothes, hiking and recreational shoes and boots, information books, swim gear, trophy items, and even a great selection of gift items and women's apparel. The Sportsman has a complete line of boats, 18 to 26 foot Starfire, bass boats, canoes, rubber rafts, outboard motors, plus three and four wheel all terrain vehicles, minibikes, Honda motor scooters, and scuba gear. The store is a complete Honda dealership with a full- fledged service department available. The Sportsman is definitely a best choice when you want the biggest sporting goods assortment anywhere along the coast with a most knowledgeable and friendly staff.

(See special invitation in Appendix.)

FLORENCE TOUR

From the Sea Lion Caves to the best ice cream you've ever tasted, a day's tour in the Florence area is exuberating. You'll enjoy great food, fun shops, friendly people and striking scenery. This is one tour you won't want to miss.

TIME	PLACE	DESCRIPTION	HOW TO FIND IN BOOK
Breakfast	Windward Inn	Best breakfast	Florence/Restaurants
A.M.	Sea Lion Caves	Best attraction	Florence/Attractions
A.M.	Indian Forest	Best attraction	Florence/Attractions
A.M.	The Sportsman	Best sporting goods	Florence/Sporting Goods
Lunch	Bridgewater Restaurant	Best lunch	Florence/Restaurants
P.M.	Incredible-Edible Oregon	Best Oregon gifts	Florence/Gifts
P.M.	The Quest for Gifts	Best gifts	Florence/Gifts
Snack	B.J.'s Ice Cream Parlour	Best ice cream	Florence/Ice Cream
P.M.	Sand Dunes Frontier	Best ride	Florence/Attractions
Dinner	Windward Inn	Best dinner	Florence/Restaurants

Chapter Five

DOUGLAS COUNTY

ABOUT REEDSPORT/WINCHESTER BAY

When people hear of Winchester Bay, they think of the towering sand dunes, the home of salmon harbor fishing, the Umpqua River, friendly, down home people and toes wiggling in the sand at surf's edge. Winchester Bay, located about midway down the Oregon Coast on Highway 101, is the perfect place to break out of those weary winter doldrums and enjoy a moderate coastal climate with the diverse, beautiful scenery of the bay, the rolling dunes of the Oregon Dunes National Recreation area, rugged cliffs and sandy beaches. There is no better place in which to breathe in the salt air, listen to the surf and see an abundance of wildlife like deer and bear. At Winchester Bay, there is one of the best moorages on the coast for boat launching, boats for hire and modern deep sea fishing trips. Whale watching, cruises, crabbing, clamming and jetty fishing are all available in or near Winchester Bay. Then go right into Reedsport and enjoy many more fine restaurants and accommodations.

Recorded history in this region began in 1578 when Sir Francis Drake noted this beautiful bay in his log as he sailed north, searching for the mythical Strait of Amin. In 1850, Winchester Payne & Co. of San Francisco sailed up the Umpqua River and planted the early settlements that were later to become Winchester Bay in 1856. A lighthouse was built but was washed away in the flood of 1861. In 1892, it was replaced and that lighthouse, the Umpqua River Lighthouse, still stands today, guiding vessels entering the Umpqua waters. It is the only lighthouse which beams a red light to all seafarers for almost 100 years. In 1950, development of Salmon Harbor began and it is now the largest sports fishing marina on the Oregon Coast.

In either Reedsport or Winchester Bay, you can leave the crowds behind and truly experience the beautiful days of winter, summer, spring or fall.

ATTRACTIONS

FISHING / BOATING

There are literally 1001 ways to enjoy fresh and salt water near Reedsport/Winchester Bay, and that includes sailing, kayaking, canoeing and water skiing. Salmon Harbor and several private marinas have modern moorages and launching facilities for boats of all sizes. Boating on the Umpqua and Smith Rivers is also available.

CAMPING

Don't forget your sleeping bags for the numerous private, county, state and federal campgrounds, most with beautiful waterfront settings. There are accommodations for those who really like to rough it in tents or rough it in the comfort of full service hookups.

FISHING

Fishing of all kinds is done in Umpqua country. You can either slip on your fresh water rubber waders to do a little Umpqua River fishing for trout, striped bass and sturgeon (year 'round), do some winter steelhead fishing, or hook up with Chinook in the spring. For the sea fisherman, ocean salmon fishing usually starts in June and lasts until late September. If you are not looking for salmon, you can fish year 'round. There is plenty of smelt, crabbing and clam digging for everyone.

HUNTING

Whether you are armed with a gun or camera, it is entirely possible you may run into deer, elk or even bear, and all closer than you think. There is also a wild pigeon season in the late summer. Guiding services are available in either Reedsport or Winchester Bay.

WATER SPORTS

You'll enjoy swimming, water skiing, scuba diving and spear fishing.

WHALE WATCHING

Watch grey whales frolic and spout as they are on their semi-annual migration. Oct-Nov and Feb-March are the best months for watching these fascinating sea creatures.

EVENTS

FLEET DAYS OCEAN FESTIVAL
In late July, join Winchester Bay and Reedsport citizens for all the fun and festivities of a real hometown ocean festival. Join in on the festival parade, tug-of-war, salmon dinners, dancing, art exhibits, a photo contest, an anchor throw, a quilt show, carnival booths, old time fiddlers and much more. The Fleet Days Ocean Festival Queen and her court reign over festivities to make sure everyone has great fun.

REEDSPORT

ACCOMMODATIONS

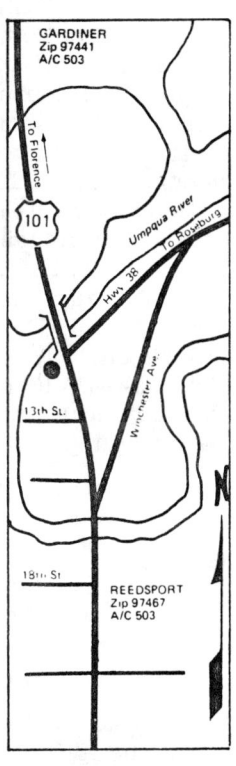

TROPICANA MOTEL
1593 Highway 101
Reedsport, Oregon
503-271-3671

Restaurant/lounge, kitchens, pool.

ATTRACTIONS

OREGON DUNES NATIONAL RECREATION OFFICES

I was lucky when I went to this particular office to find out more about the Oregon Dunes because I met a special person by the name of Wilma A. Shouse who, at 75 years old, is truly in love with the Oregon Sand Dunes. She told me some very fascinating things which helped me love them too. Wilma is knowledgeable about dune history, geology, wildlife and the unique dune ecosystem. She also knows where the recreational opportunities exist, current developments and updates. You can meet Wilma at the Federal Sand Dune Office and learn about how the dunes developed and how, at 47 feet high, they are taller than the dunes of the Sahara Desert. Wilma can also direct you to the best hiking and offroad vehicle spots, as well as tell you what unique birds to watch for — with Wilma to guide you, you can't go wrong.

GIFTS

J.R.'S FOR GIFTS
417 Fir Avenue
Reedsport, Oregon
503-271-3321

J.R.'s is the first place to stop in Reedsport if you are looking for artistic and classic collectibles for your home. The owner, Joan Dunn, prides herself on the quality of the pieces on her shelves. There are solid brass sculptures and castings that keep good company with stoneware and glassware, a large selection of pottery with some made in Oregon, as well as the etched glass souvenir items. This is probably the only place on the Oregon coast where you can find a truffle bowl. A large section of the store is devoted to wicker items, famous Oregon myrtlewood, and lots of items to help you remember your visit to this beautiful area of Oregon's coast. The wine glasses and crystal sets are tasteful patterns that would lend grace to any dinner table. The punch and salad bowls make excellent gifts and, after all, it doesn't hurt to have an extra punch or salad bowl around. The Blue Mountain Arts card collection from J.R.'s is unique and interesting. They have the kind of art work that makes you keep the card long after the occasion is past. The only other thing you could want from a gift shop would be wrapping, and J.R.'s has that, of course — free.

(See special invitation in Appendix.)

GOLF

FOREST HILLS COUNTRY CLUB
Reedsport, Oregon
503-271-2626

Every avid golfer has probably dreamed of putting for birdie on the 18th hole of the PGA Championship against the likes of Jack Nicklaus, Arnold Palmer or Gary Player. But for most golfers, nine holes against a friend who has bet you a lunch, or serious golfers who just want to lower their scores and enjoy the outdoors, is all the glamour and pressure needed.

Reedsport's Forest Hills Golf Course, one of the finest nine-holers on the south Oregon coast, offers beginners, the very good, and professionals plenty of challenges on its beautiful 9-hole, par 72, 6,108 yard course. Play nine or eighteen holes amongst pines and an occasional deer, sand traps, water hazards and beautiful greens. Practice your game on an excellent driving range. For the golfer who wonders whether to use a six or seven iron, or needs some putting or driving refinement, there are classes and lessons offered by the friendly club pro, Jeff Rosenow. As for equipment, there is everything from clubs, shoes and clothing to rental golf carts, clubs and club storage. If you plan on staying for awhile, there are also memberships available and, who knows... with a little practice at Forest Hills, you may someday be putting for "the big one".

RESTAURANTS

FOREST HILLS RESTAURANT AND LOUNGE
(on the golf course just off Hwy 101)
Reedsport, Oregon
503-271-3414 for reservations

Even though the Forest Hills Restaurant is located on a golf course, it isn't necessary to be a golfer, or to even known one, to eat there. The steak and seafood meals prepared by the staff of Jim and Bobbi Unger will please the palate of even the most discriminating non-golfer. This is one of the best places in Reedsport. As an alternative to the usual steak and seafood, they have prime rib dinners Tuesday, Wednesday and Thursday, and interesting seafood dishes, prawns cooked in beer batter, and scallops are delicious sauteed or deep fried in buttermilk batter. They have a nice selection of desserts including an eye-catcher called Grasshopper Pie — it is worth ordering just to find out what's inside. (I can't tell you because I was sidetracked by the carrot cake and my wife is fiercely loyal to cheesecake, both of which were superb. Perhaps a reader would try the Grasshopper Pie and send a report to us for the next edition.)

The Ungers also own a restaurant on the waterfront in downtown Reedsport — **Jim's Waterfront Restaurant and Lounge**. It is mostly a local watering hole, but it is an interesting place for people-watchers who want to get an insight to the local community and eat great food. The clientele consists of fishermen, boaters and employees of downtown businesses. If you believe in eating like the locals, you will probably want the broasted chicken; They also serve pan fried local oysters from Qualman's, fish and chips in buttermilk batter, and beer batter prawns.

(See special invitation in Appendix.)

PIZZA RAY'S AND SUZY'S
2165 Winchester Avenue
(On Highway 101)
Reedsport, Oregon
503-271-4100

Hours: Pizza Ray's, 11-11 Sun-Thurs
   11:30am-midnight Fri & Sat
Suzy's, summer, 6am-10pm seven days a week
   winter, 7am-10pm seven days a week

It is not always desirable or necessary to dine out in expensive restaurants surrounded by atmosphere. Sometimes you just want to eat a good tasty meal and get on about your business. Ray and Suzy Wasson recognized the need for good quality, low priced food in 1975 when they opened their first pizza parlor in Reedsport. Since then, their ever expanding business has grown to include a fast food restaurant next door to the pizza parlor, and pizza parlor/fast food combinations at locations in Coos Bay and Winchester Bay. Meals at Suzy's are satisfying and priced so that eating out need not be a special event. A good breakfast can be had for around $1.50, and one of their most filling lunch specials is the Super Suzy, a half-pound of hamburger on a bun with all the trimmings and fries. You can also eat dinner at Suzy's, but I recommend slipping next door to Pizza Ray's and having their smoked salmon pizza. It's the only fish pizza I would ever eat. They make their own crust dough daily and it is thick, soft and juicy, but solid enough that you can eat it by the slice and not get messy. As I mentioned before, Pizza Ray's and Suzy's have two other locations — Coos Bay, across from Fred Meyer (267-5839); and at Winchester Bay located on Beach Blvd. (271-2431). Try them for fine fast food at low prices.

(See special invitation in Appendix.)

WINCHESTER BAY

ATTRACTIONS

UMPQUA RIVER LIGHTHOUSE

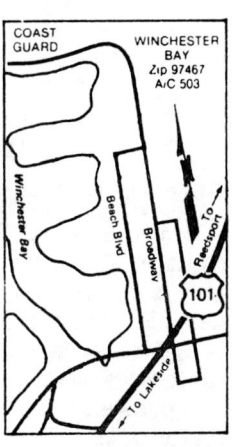

Two white flashes of two seconds, three eclipses of three seconds, followed by a red flash of two seconds — this is the unique beacon flashed to all seafarers approaching the mouth of the Umpqua River. For years, upon seeing this unique signal, sailors have known that they are approaching Winchester Bay and the old Umpqua River Lighthouse. Built in 1892 at a "huge" cost of $50,000, the Umpqua Lighthouse has been a key guide not only to sailors but to the development of the lower Umpqua areas as it safely guided ships, people, products and dreams. The 67 foot tower is at an elevation of 165 feet with its hollow lens 5 feet in diameter, 10 feet high and weighing 2 tons. The almost 1000 prisms in the lens were handcut in Paris, France, in 1890. It revolves around a stationary lamp that has 2100 candle power with 12 separate beams that can be seen almost 20 miles out to sea. The unique red beams are created by red glass on acrylic placed in front of the lens. Visit the visual presentation of rich history of the area that was placed on the National Register of Historic Places in 1978. You'll be glad you did. The lighthouse is located a short distance from Highway 101 south of Winchester Bay and overlooks the mouth of the Umpqua River and Oregon Dunes National Recreation Area.

FRESH SEAFOOD/CANNERY

SPORTSMEN'S CANNERY
(located on Beach Blvd.
between docks B & C)
P.O. Box 11 (for mail order information)
Winchester Bay, OR 97467
503-271-3293

Hours: open seven days a week

Um-m-m, good! Taste the freshest delicacies of the sea from right off the Oregon coast — salmon, tuna, shad, Pacific snapper, crab, and so much more, courtesy of Sportsmen's Cannery. For over six years, R.A. and Jeanne Armstrong and their son, James, have been selecting the finest quality seafood from their fleet of fishing boats to smoke, kipper and can for you in a process which ensures that the distinctive freshness and flavor of the sea is captured. All of the Armstrong's products are handpacked with no preservatives or artificial additives, and you can taste the difference. For tuna and salmon lovers, the Armstrongs have a delicious selection of salmon and tuna treats to dizzy your tastebuds — Chinook, silver and pink salmon. For those who like the smoked taste, Indian-style smoked salmon in rich-flavored recipes smoked with alder in the original manner used by Oregon's coastal Indians. For you tuna lovers, the Armstrongs offer top-of-the-line Albacore tuna caught right off shore and canned in their own natural juices. All of these Oregon-fresh delicacies, along with ling cod, sole and sturgeon, can be found in the Armstrong's gift shop which features gift packs of all your favorites, or can be ordered by mail in prearranged gift assortments which include trimmings, gift wrapping and gift cards — all for very reasonable prices. So enjoy the delicacies from the Oregon sea, prepared with a little history and tender loving care in mind.

RESTAURANTS

SEAFOOD GROTTO RESTAURANT
Corner of 8th & Broadway
Winchester Bay, Oregon
503-271-4250

One of my favorite places on the Oregon Coast is, without a doubt, Winchester Bay. Its clean, rustic buildings and picturesque dock area are a delight to the eye. Even though the town is populated by hard-working fishermen, there is a kind of relaxed atmosphere that makes me feel as if my watch runs a little slower. I don't need much of a reason to stop and prowl around, but one of my best excuses for stopping is to eat a crab sandwich for lunch at the Seafood Grotto Restaurant. Now I realize there are hundreds of places on the coast in which you can get a crab sandwich (I have probably eaten dozens of them up and down the coast of Oregon), but I don't believe any compare with the taste of those served at the Grotto. I'm not sure exactly what it is that keeps bringing me back to the Grotto — it could be the smell of fresh baked bread; it could be the wholesome, lived-in feeling of the restaurant, clean and neat but not sterile and lifeless like so many places are these days. Not everyone has a craving for crab sandwiches. (That's all right, though I think it's a terrible shame.) For lunch, they also have fillet of sole sandwiches and excellent clam chowder. It is worth visiting the Seafood Grotto for their dinners, also. Fresh Winchester Bay salmon cut into thick fillets with shrimp or oyster cocktail, choice of potato, rice or fresh vegetables, and soup or salad bar. As I mentioned, the bread is fresh baked. Steak that compares with the excellent quality of the seafood is also available. During weekends and summer months, they also serve breakfast. Pancake eaters will appreciate the Swedish pancakes; I prefer the Spanish omelette myself, but I tend to be conservative as far as breakfast goes. I think you'll like the Seafood Grotto Restaurant in Winchester Bay.

DOUGLAS COUNTY TOUR

Reedsport and Winchester Bay are beautiful places with friendly people. There are alluring lighthouses, plentiful sand dunes, and excellent salmon fishing as well as the shops and restaurants. You won't want to miss any of this tour or its residents.

TIME	PLACE	DESCRIPTION	HOW TO FIND IN BOOK
Breakfast	Suzy's	Best breakfast	Reedsport/Restaurants
A.M.	Forest Hills Country Club	Best golfing	Reedsport/Golf
Lunch	Forest Hills Restaurant	Best lunch	Reedsport/Restaurants
P.M.	J.R.'s For Gifts	Best gifts	Reedsport/Gifts
Snack	Sportsmen's Cannery	Best fresh seafood	Winchester Bay/Fresh Seafood/Cannery
P.M.	Umpqua Lighthouse	Best lighthouse	Winchester Bay/Attractions
Dinner	Seafood Grotto	Best dinner	Winchester Bay/Restaurants

Chapter Six

COOS COUNTY

ABOUT COOS COUNTY/THE BAY AREA

Although Hudson Bay trappers were the first white men to explore the Coos Bay area from the early to mid 1800s. The native Indian population saw few white explorers. In 1828, the legendary Jedediah Smith passed through the land and was one of four survivors from an Indian confrontation.

The city of North Bend was first settled in 1853. Three years later Captain Asa Simpson acquired the land and it became a lumber and shipbuilding village. After 1900 the area was sold to Simpson's son, Louis, who became the first mayor of North Bend in 1903.

The city of Coos Bay, called Marchfield until 1944, was originally founded in 1854 by J.C. Tolman. Pioneers found Coos to be a land rich in wildlife, minerals, rugged, fertile landscape, moderate climate and inhabited by friendly Indians of the Coos and Coquille tribes. The Indians had established permanent dwellings along the shores of Coos Bay and found ample food resources available here — ocean shellfish, eel, trout and salmon catches from the bay and nearby streams. They fished, caught crabs and feasted on clams, mussels and other rock shellfish. After the first arrival of white settlers, Coos Bay rapidly became the shipping center between San Francisco and Seattle.

North Bend grew to become a major shipbuilding location on the West Coast and in 1874, a native-built Clipper ship, *Western Shore*, gained reputation as the fastest ship of her time sailing from Oregon to Liverpool in 97 days. Then in the 1850s, gold and coal were discovered in the region, bringing large numbers of prospectors, farmers and tradesmen. It wasn't long before the Bay area became the hub of Coos County. Today Coos Bay is the world's largest lumber shipping port. The area holds the traditional reputation of being "the lumber supplier to the nation." Coos holds a mighty 20 billion board feet of standing saw timber.

The Coos Bay area makes a great vacation headquarters, offering everything from luxury accommodations to camping, gourmet dining to snacks on the run, live theater to nine movie houses, antiques to arts and crafts, festivals to tranquil walks on the beach. Visit the experimental wind farm at Whiskey Run, check out the museums and take an historic walking tour of Coos Bay. There are over 47 miles of National Dunes Area and you can cast your lines for some great deep sea fishing out of the charming fishing village of Charleston. View the sea lions and lighthouse of Cape Arago, or enjoy seal watching and sun bathing at Bastendorf Beach. There is so much outdoors to enjoy. Gorgeous botanical gardens and fishing at Shore Acres, beachcombing and camping at Sunset Bay, fresh water swimming, boating and great bass fishing at Lakeside, the picturesque sights of small tugs chugging up the Coos River, spectacular waterfalls and hiking trails at Silver Falls — it's no wonder the friendly people of the Coos Bay area invite you to discover their country. They tell me they live in a place that has it all where coastal wildlife abound and fishermen feel sure they have reached paradise.

ATTRACTIONS

SOUTH SLOUGH NATIONAL ESTUARY SANCTUARY

Hours: 8:30-4:30 June-Aug, 7 days/week
8:30-4:30 Sept-May, Mon-Fri except holidays

In 1974/75, Oregonians created the first estuarine sanctuary in the nation, a place where vital questions for man's future by the sea may be answered. Located near the fishing village of Charleston, the estuary boasts 600 acres of water and tide flats which contain organisms from bacteria, clams and sand shrimp to salmon and striped bass, native of the region. The sanctuary offers 3800 acres of upland forest including 100 acres of fresh water wetlands. Mixed connifer and broad leaf forested slopes surround the drowned river mouth which forms the estuary. Here among the trees you may spot raccoons, bobcat, bear and deer.

A number of recreational opportunities are offered as a way to educate the public about the ecological value of estuaries. Enjoy hiking trails that weave through stands of Sitka Spruce, over open meadows with blooming wildflowers, past beaver dams, tide flats and even the site of a late 1800s dike and pioneer homestead. Two separate entry areas are provided for launching canoes, and the south slough offers good fishing grounds for trout, salmon steelhead, perch and sea bass. Staff at the slough conduct workshops for visitors on such topics as wildflowers, animals, plants and local birds. The Visitor's Center features displays and literature about the ecology and history of the estuary. Lectures, special programs and guided trail walks are available for groups on request. For more information, call 503-888-5558.

McCULLOUGH BRIDGE

The bridge, opened in 1936 as the span across Coos Bay, is known as the most beautiful bridge along the Pacific Coast. Except for the steel, virtually all the materials used in the construction of the bridge are native Oregon products. The total length measures more than one mile.

TEN MILE LAKE

Just off Highway 101, 12 miles north of North Bend, you'll find the largest coastal lake in Oregon. There is fishing, food, lodging, camping, picnicking and fishing tackle available, plus a free boat launching ramp, boat rentals and water skiing. This is the home of Camp Easter Seals and Coos Bay Yacht Club.

TIDEPOOLS

To glimpse some abundant intra-tidal areas, head for Cape Arago. Located just 11 miles south of Coos Bay, the Cape is broken up by three coves. The north cove is the largest with an immense intra-tidal area that extends to Shell Island and beyond. Enjoy the sandy beach, the scattered boulders and shells found here. The middle cove is the smallest and most exposed with a trail leading down the steep banks. You'll spy many animal varieties — purple sea urchins and even solitary coral have been spotted. The south cove has a steep trail leading down a sandy beach where you can check out algae bed of bull kelp, sea urchins, starfish and crabs. The north side of Sunset Bay Cove has a uniformly wide shelf area with several tide shelves cutting into it. Offshore are numerous vertical cliffs and reefs.

WHISKEY RUN COASTAL WIND FARM

Fifteen miles south of Coos Bay just off Highway 101 sits Oregon's first commercial experimental wind park. Twenty-five 60 foot tall wind generators have been built on this 800 acre site on the beach. Coastal wind speeds average 13-17 mph and the park is expected to produce energy 75% of the time. This is a fascinating sight to see. You can also do some gold panning while you are here for a visit.

EVENTS

THE ANNUAL NORTH BEND AIR SHOW

Late June marks an aerial event you won't want to miss. Started in commemoration of annual Armed Forces Day in 1981, this air show has grown to become a real tradition on the Oregon Coast. Today it not only hosts the largest display of military aircraft of any show in Oregon, but also features one of the finest displays of aerobatic performances in the state. The show draws a full program of aerial celebrities who demonstrate their daring and expertise to the delight of spectators. You'll be able to inspect full civilian and military aircraft displays, witness military flybys and parachute demonstrations, and enjoy a tempting array of food booths, pancake breakfasts, and even a beer garden. For more information, call 503-269-0215.

OREGON COAST MUSIC FESTIVAL

Mid-July marks a very special festival. Imagine the charms of small-town Oregon matched by the unrivaled beauty of our splendid coastline and the added attraction of some of the finest musical offerings you are likely to find in any major city. The result is a real winner you won't want to miss. Superbly performed music ranges from chamber and symphonic to folk, jazz, concert band and dance compositions. Concerts are held both inside and outside against the scenic backdrop of Shore Acres State Park. A number of cultural events support the festival happenings during the week. There are art exhibits, free park concerts, nature walks, seminars and even a music camp for young people. So whether your taste runs to Blue Grass, Bach, ballet, music of India, brass bands or an all star group of Western jazz musicians, you won't want to miss this highly acclaimed music treat. For a free brochure and more information, write to: Music Enrichment Association, P.O. Box 663, Coos Bay, Oregon 97420.

MUSEUMS

COOS COUNTY HISTORIC MUSEUM
Hours: 11-4 Tues-Sat, 1-4 Sun
Open Memorial Day-October 1, closed Mondays

Locomotive No. 104, a logging railroad engine built in 1922, marks the entrance to the museum which is located on beautiful, pocket-sized Simpson Park at the north portal to North Bend. The museum treasury of artifacts includes exhibits on local Indian culture, historic shipwrecks, early logging and transportation. Visitors can enjoy wandering through the library collection of books, manuscripts, photographs and other antique materials that highlight local history. Don't miss the newly acquired circa 1930s Klamath Indian basketry dolls featured as part of an exhibit on the art of basketry.

COOS ART MUSEUM
235 Anderson Avenue
Coos Bay, Oregon

Gallery hours: Tues-Sun, noon-4

Visit the Art Museum's new home in Coos Bay. Doors officially opened to the public in January, 1985. There is an active exhibition scheduled which changes approximately every six weeks with one-week intervals between each new show. Lectures, public events and fund raisers are held in the handsome second floor brick atrium featuring five arched skylights over a beamed ceiling. The museum sponsors a colorful children's art program and has exciting plans for a permanent Prefontaine Gallery to house awards and memorabilia by the late Steve Prefontaine — a sculpture gallery, weaving room and classrooms to encourage the perfection of skills in various art media.

THE MARSHFIELD SUN PRINTING MUSEUM
1st and Fir Streets
(Hwy 101 north of Coos Bay)
Coos Bay, Oregon
503-269-1363

Hours: 1-4 Mon, Wed, Fri, Jun-Aug

The museum preserves *The Sun* (from 1891-1944) historic newspaper's printing office in its original layout complete with original printing presses, typecases and cables and tools of the trade. *The Sun* is reputed to have been one of the last surviving handset papers in Oregon. The museum houses a Washington hand press, a Chandler and Price platen press and nearly 200 typecases and fonts. The downstairs has been preserved in the original condition of *The Sun* newspaper and printing show. Upstairs, you'll enjoy exhibits on the history of printing, early Marshfield and American newspapers, and Oregon Hall of Fame exhibit features photographs and sketches of distinguished publishers and editors from out state. Telephone for more information.

PARKS

BASTENDORFF BEACH COUNTY PARK

This park is located two miles west of Charleston, with camping, picnicking and a playground for children. It overlooks the bar.

CAPE ARAGO STATE PARK

Located six miles west of Charleston, this park offers spectacular ocean views, picnicking, rugged headland, Simpson reef, tidepools, beach, and sea lions, with a viewpoint nearby. The park is just ½ mile south of Shore Acres.

HORSE FALL BEACH PARK

5½ miles northwest of North Bend, the park offers beachcombing, surf fishing and the south entrance to Dunes Recreation Area.

SHORE ACRES STATE PARK

4½ miles west of Charleston is this gorgeous 743 acre park nestled on ocean shoreline. So lovely is the scenery that seacoast photographers have nicknamed this popular park "the Rembrandt of the sea". Originally the estate mansion of Louis J. Simpson stood here. The mansion had an indoor swimming pool 26 feet wide and 52 feet long, and a third floor ballroom measuring 2736 square feet. In 1921, the original house burned to the ground; a glass enclosed observatory shelter marks the original spot where the mansion stood. The glass shelter offers a 180 degree view of the coast. A highlight of the park is the botanical garden including a 100 foot lily pond and sculptured arrays of flowers blooming forth in all colors of the rainbow. There are lots of trails here for strolling, dramatic ocean vistas from the top, sandstone bluffs and a snug little protected bay far below for serene sea musing.

SIMPSON PARK

The North Bend Chamber of Commerce is located here with azaleas, rhododendrons, picnic areas, tennis courts nearby, museums and playgrounds for children. It is a great park in a beautiful setting.

SUNSET BAY STATE PARK

Just 3½ miles west of Charleston, Sunset Bay State Park offers lots of recreation opportunities. There is a campground with 108 tent sites and 29 full hook-up spaces; utility buildings provide hot showers and flush toilets. Picnic facilities are south of the beach along Big Creek. Enjoy a day of fishing, swimming, boating, skin diving and surfing. There is a broad sandy beach plus a boat launching area. The bay is surrounded by steep, sandstone cliffs and tidepool areas.

TUGMAN STATE PARK

Thirteen miles north of North Bend, the park offers swimming, fishing, boat ramps, picnicking, bathhouse and camping in summer.

TOURIST INFORMATION CENTERS

CHAMBER OF COMMERCE

Available in Coos Bay and North Bend

For lots of helpful visitor brochures and tips on restaurants, attractions, lodging and special events, contact Bay Area Chamber of Commerce, Southeast Central, P.O. Box 210, Coos Bay, Oregon 97420, or call toll free in Oregon, 1-800-762-6278 or out of state, 1-800-824-8486.

LAKESIDE

ATTRACTIONS

SPINREEL DUNE BUGGY RENTALS
9122 Wildwood Drive
(Just south of Lakeside
exit off Hwy 101)
North Bend, Oregon
503-759-3313

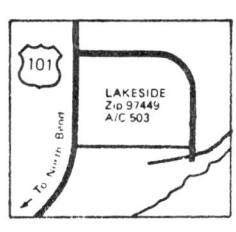

Hours: 8am-sunset, seven days a week

Rain or shine, just hop into a buggy and take off for the dunes aboard the safe, all terrain buggies. You and your family will feel the excitement of racing up and over towering dunes or along the beautiful sandy beaches of Spinreel Park at the Dunes National Recreation Area. If you enjoy a slower pace, ride along at your own leisure to listen to the sound of the surf and observe wildlife or the expansive beauty of the beaches. Terry and Betty Trost, along with their daughter, Karen, and their son-in-law, Tony, have been providing these fun and easy-to-drive buggies for over three years. Terry is eager to point out to all visitors the safety features of these vehicles, and told us that "... even mothers love us for our safety." Vehicles come with helmets, goggles, gloves and rain jackets at no extra charge. You have a choice of either three or four-wheel vehicles and you can enjoy the dunes while paying by the hour or by the day. You can also visit George, the parrot, in the rental shop, who has tales to tell about the dunes. So head for the dunes and enjoy the natural beauty and wildlife to be found in a Spinreel buggy.

(See special invitation in Appendix.)

NORTH BEND

ABOUT NORTH BEND

North Bend is ideally situated for exploring lots of interesting attractions and outdoor pursuits. Check out the Coos County Historical Museum located at Simpson Park, a favorite local picnic and playground area. Shoppers will enjoy the largest covered shopping center on the Oregon Coast. Take a dip in the town's award winning swimming pool, then head over to the municipal airport for a flight over the panoramic bay and get an aerial view of McCullough Bridge. You'll be able to explore the 40 plus miles of Oregon Dunes Recreation Area which begins just across the bay from North Bend. There is plenty to keep the whole family active. There are botanical gardens planted beside spectacular sandstone cliffs at Shore Acres State Park, sea lions basking in the sun at Simpson's Reef, ships from all around the world cruising the waterfront of the international port of Coos Bay, beachcombing at Horse Fall or any number of fine sandy beaches; enjoy fishing, golf, camping, art museums, live theater, harbor excursions, Bluebill Lake, an air show each June — North Bend, a place of many exciting options.

ANTIQUES

WAGON WHEEL ANTIQUES AND COLLECTIBLES
(look for yellow barn front)
1984 Sherman Ave. (Hwy 101 South)
North Bend, Oregon 97459
503-756-7023

Imagine feasting your eyes on an assortment of vintage 1920 comic books, checking out baseball cards that date back over 100 years, or rubbing milk bottles and intricate glassware once owned by our pioneer forefathers. There is something for everyone at the Wagon Wheel. Al and Linda Irish, with the help of their two boys, have over 30 years of knowledgeable experience in collecting and preserving the unusual relics of the past. Their emporium is loaded with memorabilia that will fascinate and delight the whole family. There are items covering W.W. I and II, an impressive collection of rare coins and stamps, well-preserved mechanical and wooden toys, colorful tins, medicine jars, tokens, dolls, and an adorable assortment of miniature collectibles. As part of their honest, helpful approach to serving people, Al and Linda offer a layaway plan for purchases and will be happy to put you on their "want" list in case they do not have a particular antique you are after; in this way they can assist you in finding it. A shipping service is also available for mailing purchases anywhere in the United States or worldwide. So when you hanker after a nostalgic glimpse of the past, complete with antique comics, ornate tin canisters, dancing mechanical bears and other relics of yesterday, the Wagon Wheel is just the place to indulge your fantasy.

(See special invitation in Appendix.)

ART GALLERY

SEABORNE GALLERY
Highway 101, downtown
(three blocks south of the bridge)
1656 Sherman Ave.
North Bend, Oregon
503-756-3451

The Seaborne Gallery is more than a showcase for the works of its artist/owners Beverly Jansen-Cooper and Sandy Kretzschmar. It is also a marketplace for the best of local and Northwest artists and craftsmen. It features works of art from artists in several mediums including pottery, bronze, glass, wood and water color paintings. But more than being an art gallery, the Seaborne is also a working studio where visitors can watch the process of producing the finished works on display around them. At the Seaborne Gallery, water colors, pottery, jewelry, stained glass, weaving, woodworking, baskestry, prints, sculpture and fiber work are on display and are for sale. You can spend a lot of money or a little at the Seaborne — there are beautiful baskets starting at just a few dollars, and rainbow windsocks are very reasonable. The Seaborne Gallery is a good place to visit just to get a picture of the quality of the art from North Bend and the Northwest. There are interesting local variations on standard themes and an assortment of diverse art expressions evident at the gallery. Ask about the seafood platters designed and made by Beverly and Sandy. You'll find them in fine galleries and gift shops up and down the Oregon coast. Shaped like Oregon's coastal fish, they are great for gift giving or decorating your own kitchen. The Seaborne Gallery — a best choice for art that appeals to everyone.

CRAFTS/GIFTS

THE CALICO COTTAGE
2674 Broadway
North Bend, Oregon
503-756-1722

The Calico Cottage is a delightful shop where many women will enjoy spending time and meeting Doris Andrews, the knowledgeable and friendly owner. The store carries all kinds of soft crafts to make your own beautiful, decorative items. You will find the supplies you need and classes so you will know how to begin. If you have always wanted to make a quilt but were afraid to start because you didn't know how, this place is for you. There are quilt classes, lamp shade classes, soft craft classes and many others. They carry patterns, sewing supplies, knitting supplies, books, fabric and Bernina sewing machines which they believe is the best sewing machine on the market. Doris started The Calico Cottage in North Bend five years ago because there was a need for it. Her daughter, Nancy, helps out and both women are knowledgeable and glad to answer your questions.

They also sell quality gift items. The gifts are unique and priced very reasonably, as is everything in the store. This is just the place to shop for the person on your list who has everything. The Calico Cottage is the only business of its kind in the Coos Bay area. It is a good place to get help or advice for the projects you have always wanted to try. Doris and Nancy have turned The Calico Cottage into a best choice for the creative who live in Oregon's bay area.

GIFTS

MYRTLEWOOD CHALET
Home of "The Real Oregon Gift"
Five miles north of North Bend Bridge
on Highway 101
North Bend, Oregon
503-756-2220

Another name for Roger Clark, owner of Myrtlewood Chalet, could appropriately be Mr. Myrtlewood. From his five retail outlets he sells a large percentage of the myrtlewood produced products sold in Oregon. His 40,000 square foot factory in North Bend supplies the products for his stores in Ashland,

Eugene, Tigard, Newport and North Bend. Clark, a former Oregon State Trooper, is involved in all aspects of the myrtlewood business including retail and wholesale marketing in the five stores he owns, the production of stock in his factory, and supplying the raw material for the factory from his own mill. Clark's factory, the Bayview Myrtlewood Factory, is the oldest and largest myrtlewood factory in Oregon. Clark is only the third owner of the business in the last 75 years, although he has changed the business more than any of the previous owners. The factory makes everything from bowls to furniture items including chests and coffee tables. They also do custom work, designing and producing specially requested items. Prices in all five stores are the same and are 10-15% less than any other retail myrtlewood store on the Oregon coast. Myrtlewood Chalet also carries gourmet food items and gift packs. Tours of the factory are available from June through October during business hours; tours can be arranged at any other time of year with reservations.

(See special invitation in Appendix.)

GOLF

KENTUCK GOLF COURSE
(Turn east off Hwy 101
at north end of North Bend Bridge over bay.
Travel approximately three miles;
Look for Golf Course Lane.)
North Bend, Oregon
503-756-4464

Open 365 days a year, daylight to dusk

For many people, a vacation without golf is pure purgatory. However, there is no reason to torture yourself when visiting the Oregon bay area. North Bend has a golf course, the Kentuck Golf Course, an attractive 18-hole course with a 70-par average. It is a peaceful place built on reclaimed tidelands. In the early morning and late afternoon, deer graze the same grounds over which fish once swam. The only water there now is the water flowing through the course. The Wickett family, Wallace and Joanne, have owned the golf course for over 25 years. They rent golf carts, clubs and other equipment, and also sell a complete line of golf equipment. It is a good idea to bring raingear when you play in this area, but don't panic if yours is somewhere else. The good people at Kentuck will see that you are covered. Martin Culp is the local pro and he gives individual or group lessons year 'round. He is equally adept at teaching the game of golf to rank beginners or helping advanced players refine their techniques or correct bad habits. The Kentuck Golf Course has a nice picnic area that has been planted in fruit trees (mostly cherry and apple). They have parking for RVs but they advise you to call ahead first since the spaces are limited. The next time you head over to the coast for a weekend, throw your golf clubs in the trunk and try a few rounds at the Kentuck. As a golfer you owe it to yourself to play on as many different courses as you can and this course is pleasant but challenging.

(See special invitation in Appendix.)

RESTAURANTS

PANCAKE MILL RESTAURANT
On Highway 101 between
Coos Bay and North Bend
North Bend, Oregon
503-756-2751

Hours: 6am-9pm daily
All major credit cards accepted

This restaurant has what it takes to keep the people who live in the area coming back because of the quality of food served here. There is more to eat at the Pancake Mill than pancakes. For breakfast, Gary Goodson and Beverly Rice, owners, suggest their prize-winning three-egg omelettes. They use real ham and cheddar cheese, not some nameless processed mixture. If you prefer an Old World recipe from Denmark, try oven-baked apple pancakes that take up a whole plate and then some, and are delicious! Lunches in this place are interesting. The "Generator" is an appropriately named hamburger which is guaranteed to charge your batteries. It is a quarter-pound burger with two slices of ham or bacon covered with cheddar cheese. You may choose between homemade soup, potato salad or a crisp vegetable salad. When the shadows are long and the sun is creating a sunset for which the bay area is famous, it is time to select a dinner. I recommend the Chicken Kiev. You will have plenty to eat and will not destroy your budget. If you are a light eater for one reason or another, the Pancake Mill offers dinners which are wholesome, good-tasting and recommended by the diet center. There is an excellent staff providing friendly, fast service. So for delicious food, good service and quality, dine at the Pancake Mill on Highway 101 between North Bend and Coos Bay. It is a best choice for breakfast, lunch or dinner.

(See special invitation in Appendix.)

HILLTOP HOUSE
166 North Bay Drive
(north end of Bay Bridge just off Hwy 101
on North Bay Drive)
North Bend, Oregon
503-756-4169 or 756-6525

Hours: 11:30-10
Lounge open 'til 11:30pm seven days a week

I can promise you a rose garden if you eat at the Hilltop House. I can also promise you a fine, relaxing place to eat, drink and watch the setting sun. Doug and Joanne Fennell have owned this restaurant for the last eight years and many of the waitresses and cooks have been there almost as long. The restaurant itself has been a landmark in the North Bend area for over 25 years. Once you are inside, or even outside on the landscaped grounds, you can see the reason for the long lasting continuity of this establishment. It is a comfortable, pleasant setting in which to work and dine. The chef at the Hilltop House prepared all items on the menu from fresh, local products. Seafood is cooked in butter, broiled or sauteed, or even deep fried if you prefer it that way. If you have any other way you would like to have your food prepared, the kitchen staff will fix it the way you want. The lounge is the kind of cozy, quiet place where you can visit with a friend, have a relaxing afternoon drink, or celebrate an especially sweet success with one of Oregon's excellent wines. For lunch, we recommend a fish dish, cottage fries or baked potato and a small green salad with choice of dressing. There is also local, fresh baked French bread. If you prefer to eat lightly during lunch, they have soup and a well-equipped salad bar. There are more than a dozen seafood dinners to choose from, depending on the season, but almost anyone would be impressed by the broiled Australian lobster tails. These tails are between 16 and 20 ounces and are prepared and served in the shell. With dinner, you have a choice of potato or rice, fresh baked bread, and Boston clam chowder or salad. For dessert, try the Amorano Mousse Cake.

(See special invitation in Appendix.)

COOS BAY

ACCOMMODATIONS

THUNDERBIRD MOTOR INN
1313 N. Bay Shore Drive
Coos Bay, Oregon
503-267-4141 for reservations

Situated on the banks of the largest bay in Oregon where the Coos River meets the Pacific, the Thunderbird boasts a stylish decor, soft woods, plush furnishings, wrought iron chandeliers and warm, friendly service. The Thunderbird Motor Inn features 115 very comfortable, spacious guest rooms, each featuring color TV, queen size beds, phones and full room service. There is a great, indoor heated swimming pool, perfect for feeling refreshed after a day's exploring along our rugged, beautiful Oregon coastline. In the evening, sit back and enjoy an intimate dinner in the Thunderbird Restaurant where the chef prepares a delicious selection of tempting entrees — everything from same day fresh seafood to prime cuts of steak with all the trimmings. A wine list is available, plus the Thunderbird features a separate lounge where you may sip after dinner specialty cocktails to the sounds of some great, live entertainment. It is all here: very comfortable accommodations, full service amenities, and just a short block from the colorful, bustling waterfront of Coos Bay.

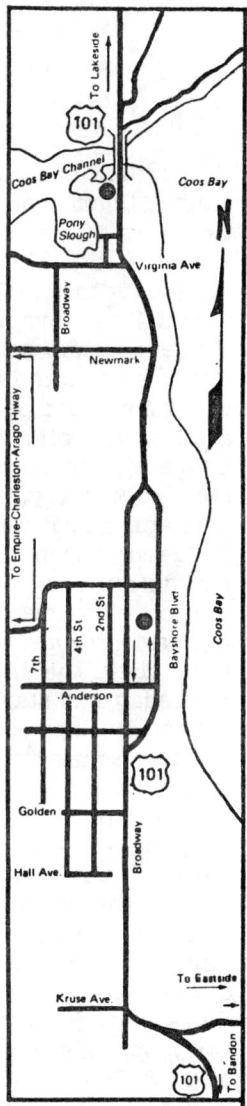

TIMBER INN—TIMBER LODGE
1001 Bay Shore Drive (downtown)
Coos Bay, Oregon
503-267-7066 for motel reservations
267-4622 for restaurant

Restaurant hours: 5am-12pm Mon-Thurs
open 24 hrs weekends, 5am-9pm Sun
All major credit cards accepted.

In order to do justice to all the sights in Coos Bay area (including Charleston and North Bend), you should spend at least two days there. An excellent choice for home base is the Timber Lodge. Gordon and Elaine Joelson, owners, are glad to help visitors to the lodge plan their tour of bay area. Elaine especially enjoys meeting people and talking with travelers. These travelers will find that the Timber Lodge is convenient and has the familiar comfort of home without astronomical rates. A covered pool, sauna, racquetball and other recreation are available off the premises to anyone staying at the Timber Lodge. For those who just want to relax, they have well appointed rooms with satellite and cable TV. Free coffee is available and direct dial 24-hour telephone callout. The Timber Lodge can accommodate a variety of needs with family units, a bridal suite and single rooms. For the traveling professional, they offer commercial rates year 'round. Even in summer, the regular rates are amazingly low. For the convenience of the early riser, the dining room opens at 5am Monday through Thursday and stays open 24 hours on Friday and Saturday. It is not really necessary to get up at 5am for breakfast, and you won't miss it if you sleep until noon — breakfast is served all day. When you do finally get ready to eat, try the Belgian Waffle or one of their traditional omelettes. They also have a daily breakfast special. Lunch at the Timber Inn is always pleasant, but if you want to be surprised, just close your eyes and ask the waitress to bring on the daily special. If you prefer a sure thing, the Timber Burger is rumored to be the best burger in town and is very popular with onion rings. The best dinner here is the fresh seafood from the local fishermen. For those who are not on an expense account, they have daily and early specials to save you money without any decrease in quality. There is a banquet room which seats 175 people. The lounge is equipped with a full bar and one of the best dance floors in this part Oregon with live entertainment six nights a week. This, combined with first class food and service in the dining room and the excellent accommodations in the motel will make your stay at the Timber Lodge a reason in itself to linger in the area.

ART GALLERY

THE VELVET TEASEL
172 Anderson Street
(corner of 2nd Street)
Coos Bay, Oregon
503-267-5321

Hours: 10-5:30 Mon-Fri, 10-5 Sat

When you are looking for some functional stoneware pottery made by native Oregon artisans, The Velvet Teasel in the place to go. Resident potter, Keith Garnett, prefers to use only local raw materials to make his unique glazes. You will be welcome to tour Keith's studio and watch him at work on the wheel. The large selection of distinctive pottery lines the shelves — one-of-a-kind plates, covered casseroles, bowls of different sizes and shapes, quiche dishes, mugs, honey pots, jars and much more. The shop also carries useful, attractive kitchenware, cookbooks, basketry, cards, teas, delicately scented silks and potpourri. The Velvet Teasel — a best choice for fine, original stoneware made by local Oregon potters.

CLOCKS/ANTIQUES

ENGLEWOOD CLOCK AND GIFT SHOP
355 Anderson
Coos Bay, Oregon
503-267-6615

Hours: 9:30-5 Mon-Fri

Literally turn back time with antique clocks, phonographs, furniture, sewing machines and more in this charming shop with one of the best inventories of antique knickknacks, time pieces and precious collectibles in the bay area. For over seven years, Norm and Eileen Bjarnson have been helping browsers find that special antique as well as repairing by hand those attic-found treasures that are in a little need of restoration. You can feel history overflowing in every nook and cranny in this special shop. Their collection of sewing machines that date from the 1890s to the 1950s is very unusual, as are their collectible glassware, bells, plates and music boxes. As well as being born and raised in Oregon, antique-collector Norm shares a bit of old Oregon's history in his blood. Kaiser, Oregon, is named after his own pioneer grandfather. So turn back time a little with Norm, Eileen and family, and come to the clock shop that still knows how to repair them. It is a little like going back home.

(See special invitation in Appendix.)

MYRTLEWOOD FACTORY/GIFTS

THE HOUSE OF MYRTLEWOOD
Highway 101 (South Coos Bay)
P.O. Box 457
Coos Bay, Oregon 07420
503-267-7804

Hours: 8:30-5:30 Oct-May 1
8-6 May-Sept 31

Visit the factory and gift shop here in Coos Bay and watch firsthand as master artisans turn myrtlewood into unique creations you'll want for yourself. The company was established in 1929 and visitors are offered a complimentary tour through the production process from log to finished product. Myrtlewood's characteristic fine grain, its durability and the rich coloring variations of each piece make it an excellent choice for the finely crafted gift items produced here. Run your fingers along the silky smooth bowls, platters, goblets, boxes, clocks, and handsome candle holders. The assortment of myrtlewood creations seems to be as big as your imagination. There is one thing you can be sure of and that is the high quality craftsmanship of the wood creations. It extends equally to an extensive, careful selection of other gift items offered in the shop. The wine room features an excellent selection of local Northwest wines. Try the candy kitchen for some truly mouthwatering cream and butter fudge as well as a scrumptious assortment of gourmet food items. Local hand-crafted gift items are the emphasis here, and inventory changes often to reflect the ever new talents of native Oregonians. Ask about the free catalog which describes the range of handmade products currently available.

RESTAURANTS

HURRY BACK
Hwy 101 south (downtown Coos Bay at turnoff to Charleston)
Coos Bay, Oregon
503-267-3933

Hours: 7am-10pm, Sun 9-3
All major credit cards accepted.

This is going to be one more of several books listing the Hurry Back restaurant — not that I am climbing on the same bandwagon with *Oregon Magazine, Bon Appetit, The Best Places* and the *Mobil Travel Guide*, but I will say that we are in good company in our appreciation for natural, wholesome food. The Hurry Back is one of the few survivors of the natural food movement of the early 1970s. Most restaurants found the effort of preparing wholegrain breads, slicing avocadoes, mushrooms, and searching for best products to be uneconomical and too much trouble. Fortunately, Wim and Karen deVriend, the proprietors, feel that it is worth the trouble. After all, this is the kind of food they prepare for themselves; why not go to the same trouble for their customers. For the sprout crowd, they have several vegetarian sandwich choices. They serve lots of fresh fruits for breakfast, lunch and dinner. They bake seven different kinds of bread on the premises, plus quiches, croissants, danish and fancy desserts — oh, the desserts. They may not be straight out of a health food book but they are so tempting, so luscious looking, and only real ingredients are used. No shortening, no mixes, no margarine, no artificial flavors or colors.

Breakfast at the Hurry Back Cafe will start your day off right with a big omelet with home fries and whole wheat toast. You can have freshly squeezed orange juice with that, or one of the ten varieties of coffee they carry, including decaf espresso. The place is busiest at noon, with a lively mixture of local businessmen, students and travelers. The seafood quiche is highly recommended for lunch, as is the homemade lasagna. Or try one of the 60-some sandwiches. Dinner entrees are mainly homemade pasta dishes (fettucine, ravioli) and fresh local seafood, including locally grown mussels in a secret sauce. There is a nice selection of Oregon wines and about 40 beers, ales and stouts from which to choose.

On Friday and Saturday nights, they have live music, usually a mix of light classical, ragtime and singalong tunes.

(See special invitation in Appendix.)

KUM-YON'S RESTAURANT
835 South Broadway (on Hwy 101)
Coos Bay, Oregon
503-269-2662

With the best recipes from around the world amid fresh flowers, candlelight and crisp, linen tablecloths, a place where tantalizing aromas lure you with the likes of great Japanese, Chinese, Korean and American specialties — Kum-Yon's is the place. This is definitely a personalized family operation. Jerry and his wife, Kum Yon Pratt, are assisted by brothers, sisters and in-laws, to ensure that their extensive selection of dining entrees are all prepared to the highest standards. The prices are very reasonable and lunch and dinner menus offer a range to suit the choice of hamburger lovers or culinary connoisseurs of the Orient. For lunch, we enjoyed the Shrimp Tempura served with a choice of steamed or fried rice, plus fresh vegetable. For dinner, try the Szechuan Mongolian Beef — tender, sliced beef sauteed with green onions and real peppers in a special hot sauce. A favorite house specialty in Pul-Koki which is thinly sliced, prine sirloin charcoal-broiled in a delicious marinade of honey and exotic spices. From the American menu, we suggest the 12 oz. T-bone prepared to your liking with a choice of soup or salad, bread and baked potato, French fries or fried rice. For appetizers, try the deep fried dumplings and vegetable tempura. The hot and sour soup is distinctive and very tasty. Beer is served, plus wine by the glass or carafe, various teas, cocoa, soft drinks and coffee. Be sure to leave room for dessert because Kum Yon's homemade cheesecake and chocolate cake have to be some of the best I've tasted anywhere. Kum Yon's is definitely a best choice in pleasing the palate in the bay area with a wide range of the best recipes from all over the world.

(See special invitation in Appendix.)

SCUBA/SKIING

NORTHWEST DIVERS SUPPLY
Highway 101, south end of Coos Bay
(look for a red building)
Coos Bay, Oregon
503-267-3723

Hours: 10-6 Mon-Sat

The steel-like toughness and quiet confidence of Sheryl Carmichal would make almost anyone willing to follow her to the bottom of the ocean or the top of a snow-crested summit, and she is quite willing (even anxious) to show you the beauty and excitement of these two extremely different worlds. For the last eight years, Sheryl has made a profitable business from her two favorite hobbies — scuba diving and snow skiing. Her store, Northwest Divers Supply, carries (as you would expect) a full line of diving equipment, rentals and tank refills. What takes you by surprise when you walk into the red building on Highway 101 is the skiing gear at one end of the building, with racks of downhill and cross country skis, boots, poles and clothing. She rents both Nordic and Alpine equipment for children and adults at a price far less than that of Willamette Pass or HooDoo. She also handles the rare Burton snow board for those diehard surfers who are more at home on a board than skiis. Sheryl does not expect scuba divers to abandon their pleasure when the waters chill and snow covers the mountains. "We have cold water gear for year 'round diving," she says. They also have classes to qualify prospective divers for their certification cards. They teach underwater photography and sell much of the equipment necessary to take excellent underwater pictures. If you are not satisfied with the diving in the area, ask Sheryl. She knows where to find the best. She also leads charters down to La Paz, Mexico, twice a year. Make a predive stop at Northwest Divers Supply to fill your tanks or get information about locations and conditions. Or if you prefer your water sports of a colder and more solid variety, make a preski stop for equipment and information before that long drive to the mountains.

(See special invitation in Appendix.)

SEAFOODS

OCEAN BOULEVARD SEAFOODS
12855 Ocean Boulevard
Coos Bay, Oregon
503-269-7720

There are sections in this book where we talk about how you can win the bounty of the sea by fishing or by gathering mussels. However, don't feel you are obligated to get your seafood in this manner — on the hoof, so to speak. Carl and Sherri Bock have one of the best seafood markets on the Oregon coast. They carry everything that swims or crawls in the ocean that you would want to eat — at least everything that comes from the lines, nets and pots of Oregon fishermen. The Bocks are committed to supporting the area fishermen by buying everything locally that they don't catch themselves in their own 76-foot boat. In their store, you can almost always find cod, rockfish, snapper, sole, shark or shrimp. They have fresh salmon during the season, as well as crab and squid. They have their own smokehouse to produce their own excellent smoked salmon. If you are driving a long distance and want to bring a quantity of seafood home, an icepack ensures freshness no matter how far away you live. All products are fully guaranteed. Whether you fish or not, you can get an excellent variety of quality, fresh seafood at Ocean Boulevard Seafoods. On the days that you fail to catch anything, a trip there can save you from returning home empty-handed.

(See special invitation in Appendix.)

SPORTING GOODS

SURPLUS CENTER
310 South Broadway
Coos Bay, Oregon
503-267-6711

Hours: 9-6 Mon-Sat, open 'til 9 Fri

Owners Alice and Harry Hakanson believe in making beautiful Oregon outdoors affordable for everyone. Starting back in 1969, they began offering brand name camping, fishing and hunting gear at bargain prices. This is a family-run, service oriented business. Let Ken Grove, manager of the Coos Bay store, or Roseburg manager Bob Cline, fill you in on some of the inside tips that make for great fishing trips and well-equipped camping expeditions. You will want to allow time to roam through the center since it is packed with goodies. There is a full line of Coleman stoves, pup tents to family-sized tents from White Stag, backpacks for children to adults, sleeping bags, ground pads, knives, wallets and great campsite accessories. The Hakansons stock a full range of fishing rods and reels, offer a repair service, and are loaded with inside info on the favorite spots of local fishermen. A gunsmith is on duty to assist you in checking out the rifles, shotguns and handguns in stock, or you can bring your own in for repair. By now, I imagine you are getting the feeling that this is not a small operation — well, you are right, for the selection here is extensive and all at very affordable prices. Marine supplies include rubber rafts, canoes, small fishing craft, crab pots and live bait. Surplus outdoor clothing covers the gambit from wool pants to natural cotton shirts. There are lines of full rain gear, boots, fleece wear and fun beach wear. A handy shipping service is available, too. So take the "rough" out of "roughing it" at the Surplus Center. You'll find that exploring the great outdoors really is affordable.

TOYS/GIFTS

FIDDLESTICKS TOYS AND JOYS
Downtown, across from theater
Coos Bay, Oregon
503-267-3713

Hours: 10-5:30 Mon-Fri, 10-5 Sat

In all of us, no matter how old we are, a little of the child remains. There is that urge to build castles in the sand, race the laughing waves, laugh or make someone else laugh. In general, we still want to have fun. To help children and adults have fun, Karla and Gary Rifkin opened Fiddlesticks, a fun place to shop. They sell toys, cards, kites, stationery and novelties. In the novelty department, there are funny and unusual cards, practical jokes like whoopee cushions and cigarette loads, and other items you may have always wanted to try as a kid but never did. There is an electric horse named Fiddles that gives free rides to the kids, which is something you won't find everywhere. They have collectible dolls, jewelry kits and books on making things. This is the kind of place to go when your life becomes too serious and you want to put some fun back into it. The atmosphere is more like "come on in and join the party" rather than "Will that be cash or charge?" There is a sign visible when you first walk in that explains it all... "Caution! Adults at play."

(See special invitation in Appendix.)

BAY AREA TOUR

This tour is a sample of what Oregon's Bay Area has to offer — great food, the best scenery, and something fun for everyone. The kids will love to watch the little tug boats and the big ships near the waterfront, and the adults will appreciate the beauty of the surrounding area. You are sure to have a fun day with this Bay Area tour.

TIME	PLACE	DESCRIPTION	HOW TO FIND IN BOOK
Breakfast	Pancake Mill	Best breakfast	North Bend/Restaurants
A.M.	Myrtlewood Chalet	Best myrtlewood	North Bend/Gifts
A.M.	Seaborne Gallery	Best art gallery	N. Bend/Art Gallery
A.M.	Wagon Wheel Antiques and Collectibles	Best antiques	North Bend/Antiques
A.M.	Surplus Center	Best sporting goods	Coos Bay/Sporting Goods
A.M.	Northwest Divers Supply	Best diving & skiing	Coos Bay/Scuba/Skiing
Lunch	Hurry Back	Best lunch	Coos Bay/Restaurants
P.M.	Fiddlesticks	Best toys	Coos Bay/Toys/Gifts
P.M.	Englewood Clock and Gift Shop	Best antique clocks	Coos Bay/Clocks/Antiques
P.M.	House of Myrtlewood	Best myrtlewood	Coos Bay/Myrtlewood Factory/Gifts
P.M.	Qualman's Oyster Farm	Best fresh oysters	Charleston/Oysters
Dinner	The Portside Restaurant	Best dinner	Charleston/Restaurants

CHARLESTON

OYSTER FARM

QUALMAN'S OYSTER FARM
Joe-ney Slough, near Charleston
Charleston, Oregon
503-888-3145 for directions

Hours: Mon-Sat 8:30-5:30

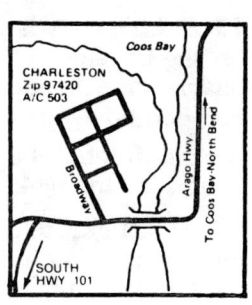

No trip to the Oregon Coast is complete without the taste of oysters. Wherever you decide to buy your oysters, restaurant or store, it's a good bet that they come from Qualman's Oyster Farm if you are in the Coos Bay area. The Qualmans produce from 3000-6000 gallons of oysters per year from 145 acres of beds in the South Slough of Coos Bay. The Qualman family has been farming oysters in the South Slough for over 50 years, with second generation Larry and Sandy running the operation now, and the third generation working their way up. Over the years, the Qualmans have pioneered several oyster farming techniques including the stake method. By attaching their seed oysters to stakes in the shallow bay, they can grow a larger crop in the same body of water. The oysters grow up out of the mud and silt and have a fresher, cleaner taste. The taste of any oyster depends on the water in which it was grown. According to Larry, South Slough produces the finest oysters on the entire coast. Oyster lovers recognize this he says, because he can never grow enough to keep up with the expanding demand of 10% or more a year. More than anything else, the clean, unpolluted water where they are grown accounts for the sweet taste of the south slough oysters from the Qualman farms. The Qualmans can supply oysters in the shell, or shelled and in pints, quarts, half gallon or six pound containers. They have all the sizes from large to extra small, although they do not conduct tours, they will answer questions and explain some of the details of oyster farming when you visit. Their beds are visible at low tide from Joe-ney Bridge. If you look down and see thousands of stakes in the shallow water, you are looking at Qualman's Oyster Farm.

RESTAURANT

THE PORTSIDE RESTAURANT
On the harbor
Charleston, Oregon
503-888-5544 for reservations

Hours: lunch 11:30-3
Open for dinner 4:30pm seven days a week

It is difficult to tell whether Joe Tang is happier being the master of a fishing boat of the master of one of the finest restaurants in the Coos Bay area. His own fishing boat supplies the restaurant fresh seafood daily and you can tell this is the finest you'll get on the Oregon Coast. Guests can pick out their own fresh lobster or crab dinners from the dozens of excellent specimens swimming in tanks at the front of the restaurant.

Joe and his wife, Bonnie, have been in the hotel and restaurant business for over fifteen years. For several years now, their business has been one of the most successful on the Oregon Coast. They often have as many as 180 reservations for Sunday brunch alone. The main reason for their fantastic success is their extensive menu and the atmosphere of quiet quality that pervades the Portside Restaurant.

It is very difficult to choose items from the menu. For lunch, you might want to try sauteed culamari with fresh fillet of fish or Dungeness crab. On Friday nights they have a seafood buffet with over 30 main course items including sushi, shrimp, prawns, fish and scallops. Oysters are eigher baked, sauteed or raw. There are smoked and pickled lox prrepared Norwegian style, steamed and deep fried oysters are on the half-shell.

There is also live entertainment on Friday and Saturday nights. In keeping with the atmosphere of the restaurant, it is usually folk or easy listening. This is one of the best restaurants on the Oregon Coast — a lot of people know it, so better make a reservation.

BANDON

ABOUT BANDON

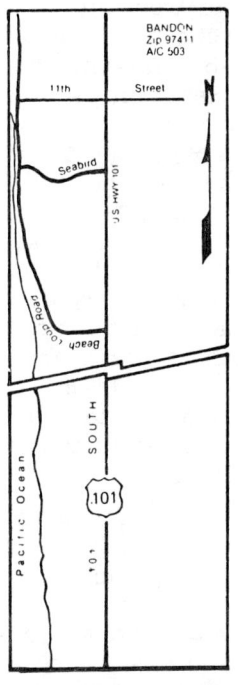

Bandon, so easy to find, so hard to forget. Located on Highway 101 on the beautiful south Oregon coast about 233 miles southwest of Portland, Bandon is a fun-filled little community where you and your family can enjoy captivating beaches, picturesque ocean vistas and historical Old Town, with countless activities for every kind of taste. Once you've arrived at this interesting village, it is not hard to tell that you've come to some of the most beautiful beach country on the West Coast. It was enjoyed by the first known people in this area, the Na-so-mah Indians, and the first pioneers who came years ago. You, too, can still see the dramatic stretches of sand with huge rock formations and hear the pounding surf. Often these views are accented by billowing clouds, legendary faces in the rock, white surf and glowing sunsets.

But beaches are not all you will find. Bandon's history is also the history of the Coquille River which empties its peaceful waters into the sea nearby and is teeming with salmon, steelhead, perch, smelt, crabs and clams. With a little imagination, you can see the Na-so-mah, as they did 130 years ago, watching at the meeting of the ocean and the Coquille. Whales and seals frolic just offshore and there are many fascinating aquatic birds like pelicans and herons that visit the estuary. Now there is an old-fashioned sternwheeler that ties this rich past to the present. The first Euro-Americans settled in the Bandon area in the late 1850s, drawn by rich deposits of black sand gold, the fertile soil of the lower Coquille valley, huge runs of salmon and stands of oak, fir and cedar that cover the surrounding hills. Unfortunately, the native population was displaced and after several destructive wars against the new settlers to regain their lands failed, many of these honorable people were then wiped out by epidemics.

Bandon then exploded economically in the late 19th century with the growth of San Francisco and northern California. With rapid growth came a large demand for natural resources which Bandon could provide. Bandon was a busy marketplace for wool, lumber and coal to be shipped south on sailing schooners and steamships. The town grew rapidly from 1870-1914; in 1914, a disastrous fire totally destroyed Bandon. Rebuilding soon after, the emphasis from industry to resort forever changed the face of Bandon. In the 1920s, it became a resort center for people attempting to escape the blistering summer heat of the American West. In the '20s, cranberry farming became an important industry and continues to this day. Bandon is known as the "Cranberry Capitol of Oregon". Just as Bandon began to recover from the fire of 1914, another struck and completely destroyed the town again in 1936. Once again, Bandon rebuilt and has become the summer resort for those looking for respite from the summer heat. Bandon's unconquerable and friendly spirit can be seen today in Old Town. Here you can enjoy a vast array of shops, restaurants, activities and friendly people which make for lots of fun day or night.

It hasn't always been this way. Four years ago, this area was in shambles. A visitor could find nothing but dilapidated buildings, potholed streets and empty storefronts. But thanks to a grant procured by the City of Bandon and efforts of local volunteers and business people, Bandon has become rebuilt and has earned recognition as one of the nation's best examples of community development. Their successful project has also won top honors in Oregon State Competitions. The Old Town arches, also paid for with a government grant, were made by local crartspeople and welcome all visitors to this example of civic, spirit and pride.

CHAMBER OF COMMERCE

Open seven days a week, visit the Bandon Chamber of Commerce visitors' information center located in Old Town at the corner of Second and Chicago Streets. People there can answer all your questions concerning Bandon and other points of interest throughout Oregon. Built and staffed by volunteers, the center is open from 10am-5pm Mondays through Saturdays, 1-4pm on Sundays. Inside are pamphlets about Bandon, accommodations, restaurants and myrtlewood shops, as well as maps of the area. The number to call to reach the center is 503-347- 9616.

ACCOMMODATIONS

THE HARBOR VIEW INN MOTEL
(above Old Town on Highway 101)
Bandon, Oregon
503-347-4417 for reservations

Now that you've fallen in love with charming Bandon, you may just want to snuggle into comfortable lodging within walking distance of the historic Old Town. The Harbor View Inn with its panoramic views of the ocean and river from each of the rooms is just the place. The motel has 25 comfortably furnished rooms, all equipped with telephone, cable TV with Showtime, and a choice of queen, double queen, or king size beds. Take in the view of Bandon's historic lighthouse, mingle amid salt air and fishing boats, enjoy a stroll along gorgeous beaches, wander in the unique Old Town shops and fine eateries, then settle back, relax and enjoy your stay at the friendly Harbor View Inn. Prices are very reasonable; reservations recommended during the summer season.

THE INN AT FACE ROCK
3225 Beach Loop Drive
Bandon, Oregon 97411
503-347-9441 for reservations

Indian legend has it that Face Rock is the beautiful visage of an Indian princess once captured by a sea spirit while wading in the surf and gazing at the beauty of a full moon. Just like the princess gazing into the sky, you too will be enchanted by this fine inn and restaurant nestled against a beautiful backdrop of Oregon coast. The Inn at Face Rock has been in business for five years and is managed by local Jackie McNeil for Unical Financial Corporation. The inn offers just about everything — fine dining, serenity, lodging, golf, and some of the most beautiful beaches in the world. The suites overlook the beaches and golf course, and are just the right touch of romance and luxury. Each suite can accommodate up to four persons and includes queen sized beds, two baths, color cable TV, and telephone. In the dining room, enjoy some of the finest in fresh seafood and meat entrees, as well as Oregon, California and French wines. Some menu suggestions: Eggs Benedict with Canadian bacon and a toasted English muffin for breakfast; try the California Supreme with ham, avocado, cream cheese and sprouts for lunch; at dinnertime, try the Ling Fling, fresh ling cod sauteed in garlic butter (it is fantastic!). All steaks are charbroiled, and for dessert, save room for the chef's own almond Amaretto pie or "Bananas Old Crow" with whipped cream. Make sure you book reservations ahead; in July and August, give 60 days advance notice; 30 days for the rest of the year. Rates are moderately priced, especially for a beautiful location and gorgeous suites.

(See special invitation in Appendix.)

PROSPER VILLAGE
(Vacation home rentals)
Route 2, Box 1080
Bandon, Oregon 97411
503-347-4314

Open year 'round

Tucked away in the sleepy, picturesque hamlet of Prosper sits this rather special vacation village. Imagine just five minutes down the road from Bandon rests a cozy home away from home waiting tranquilly to welcome you. Hosts Arlene and David Kappos know how to lay on the hospitality for guests. The tastefully appointed rentals here rest in a peaceful setting just steps from the rhythm of the gentle Coquille River. Little touches, like a bouquet of fresh flowers ready to welcome your arrival, seasonal vegetables ripe for picking in the garden and wild blackberries that are overflowing here in late summer. Units like the comfortable Captain's House come equipped with washer, dryer, full fenced yard for kids, sun deck, gorgeous river view, firewood, all linens and kitchen utensils, cable TV and sparkling spring water. Enjoy a fisherman's cottage for a long weekend or whole summer. Everything but the food is included, even boat docks. The location is great — just minutes from coastline, tall forests, great crabbing, fishing and beachcombing. Water taxi trips, fishing charters, plus relaxed cruises up the Coquille River are planned to be in operation by mid-summer 1986. Prices are very reasonable.

(See special invitation in Appendix.)

ATTRACTIONS

ART GALLERIES

Artists and craftspeople abound in the Bandon area and you will see their work as well as the work of prominent artists from around the Pacific Northwest in wonderful galleries throughout the Old Town district. Enjoy water colors, oils and pastels as well as ceramics, sculptures and fiber art.

BANDON BEACH

You'll find unsurpassed beauty at Bandon Beach where you can enjoy the thundering surf, fresh salt air, tide pools teeming with aquatic life, legendary rocks and smooth sand. This is truly a beachcomber/rock hound/nature lover's paradise. In winter, you can experience the power and fury of a winter storm with galelike winds that pound the rocks and beach with cascading ocean spray. In its wake, you'll find treasures on the shore just waiting for you to find.

BOLD DUCK RIVERBOAT TRIPS
Ticket office on the waterfront,
Old Town Bandon, one block north of Hwy 101
Bandon, Oregon
503-347-3942

You can feel much of southern Oregon's history unfold as the old sternwheeler, Bold Duck, makes its way up the Coquille River, passing the natural beauty of the river valley as well as places of historic and cultural interest. Step back in time as the stern wheeler's guide narrates the history of the river from the beginning when the Indians depended on the river for survival, to its becoming the largest agricultural valley north of San Francisco. The Bold Duck, a U.S. Coastguard licensed, authentic stern wheeler, accommodates up to 48 passengers on its mid-day cruise. The lower deck is enclosed and has a snack bar. The upper deck offers a beautiful, open air view and plenty of room in which to walk around and enjoy the two hour, six mile cruise past Ballard State Park (where the ghosts of the Na-sho-ma tribe haunts old shipyards), a 200 acre bird sanctuary, Old Bill's Creek railroad log dump, and many other interesting sites. There is also a three-hour informal dinner cruise on weekends with special group rates.

COQUILLE RIVER LIGHTHOUSE

One of Bandon's most popular attractions is the Coquille River Lighthouse which, in days of old, guided schooners and steamboats to Bandon. Although no longer in opertion, visitors can enjoy the restored lighthouse that was built in 1896. During the summer months, you can see one of the few buildings that survived the catastrophic fire of 1936.

CRANBERRY COUNTRY

Known as the cranberry capital of Oregon, Bandon invites visitors to experience the bog country. Farmers have carved out bogs throughout this area to fill truckload after truckload of this wonderful fruit to produce some of the best cranberry juice found anywhere. While many of the bogs are hidden away, several can be seen on the east side of Highway 101 south of town, and on Prosper Road just west of Bandon. Most of the growers in the region use the wet harvest method. At harvest time, a machine with special wheels that cause little damage to the cranberry vines, loosens the berries which then float to the top of the flooded bog. Then it is a matter of corraling the "little critters" and shipping them to the Ocean Spray plant in south Bandon.

FRANK'S FLIGHT SERVICE
Highway 101 (2 miles south of Bandon;
look for airport sign; on Kehl Rd.,
turn north into parking lot;
look for yellow hanger)
Bandon, Oregon
503-347-2022
Hours: 8-6, seven days a week

Whether you hanker after capable flight instruction, instruments up to commercial, the purchase of a new or rebuilt aircraft, or simply want to sit back and comfortably enjoy winging across a splendid, panoramic view high above our breathtaking Oregon coastline, here's the place. Frank Crook, with the help of sons Brady and Wayne, and sister-in-law Fran, has been passionately taking to the air for over 32 years. The business here is based on service and that means complete maintenance, inspection and engine overhauls are available on everything from light aircraft up to twin engine. They offer total rebuilts here. In fact, Frank will pick up and deliver anywhere in the U.S. at very low prices. His complete line of aircraft sales range from orders on sleek, new planes to offering competitive prices on pampered, more vintage models. We especially recommend the scenic flights that leave from here. You'll be absolutely awestruck over the incredible, beautiful ocean views. Fly over the white water magic of the Rogue River; glide and soar above the lush Coquille River Valley, botanical gardens and rushing waterfalls; glimpse whales spouting out beyond the majestic, rockhewn coastline; take in the unrivaled, tall stands of native woodlands; sit back and enjoy the flight as your pilot guides you over the scenic wonders and explains all the special points of interest. A bonus! The price per person is very reasonable indeed!

(See special invitation in Appendix.)

OLD TOWN

This is a unique waterfront section of Bandon that retains the flavor of years gone by, complete with charming gift shops, art galleries, restaurants with live entertainment, fresh markets and so much more. Totally destroyed in the fire of 1936, this unique waterfront area has recently undergone extensive renovation. You will love shopping and browsing in this old-fashioned village atmosphere. The new Harbor Hall located in Old Town district seats 300 people and features a variety of excellent entertainment.

WEST COAST GAME PARK
(On U.S. Highway 101, seven miles south of Bandon, or 18 miles north of Port Orford; signs posted.)
Route 1 Box 1330
Bandon, Oregon 97411
503-347-3106

Open summer and winter, closed December

Imagine, just down the road from Bandon, the largest exotic animal petting adventure in America awaits you and the whole family. Experience the thrill of roaming over 21 natural wooded acres across a real wildlife safari where over 400 friendly exotic birds and animals wait to greet you. It is a gem of a place where visitors can mingle, touch, hand feed and be entertained by creatures from around the world. Local owners Bob and Mary Tenney are really beautiful people who, over the past 18 years, have been dedicating themselves to the goal of bringing people and wildlife closer together in harmony and gentle warmth. The Tenneys hand raise every animal themselves, bestowing them with personal names and a humanized environment in which to live and grow up. Pristine cleanliness, loving care and helpfulness are the rules of thumb here among all the friendly animal keepers. There are over 70 different species spread over the park grounds, including buffalo, cougars, pumas, lynx, antelope, African lions, kinkajous, llamas, and cota mundi, just to name a few. You can sense the great reverence for animals that seems to be everywhere in the operation of this game park. Over the years children have delighted in the friendly playfulness of the younger babies, animals like African lion cubs, timber wolves, tiger cubs, panther cubs, cougars, bears, chimps and other youngsters. The park houses a complete gift shop featuring unusual local and international items. Have a look at Oregon collector plates, myrtlewood, pottery, chime clocks, and Indian turquoise, for example. Lunch and snack foods are available. Visa and MasterCharge are accepted. The park is open year 'round. In winter, it is advised that you call ahead to check on current, specific times open. Park hours: March 1-Nov 30, open seven days a week; Jan. and Feb., open weekends. Children under two admitted free; special group rates available; call or write for details.

(See special invitation in Appendix.)

BOOKS/SCIENCE EXHIBIT

THE CONTINUUM CENTER
175 Second Street (Old Town)
Bandon, Oregon
503-347-4111

A bookstore and free exhibit of science, religion, philosophy, parapsychology, medicine, and art in a beautiful, little fishing village? The nationally acclaimed Continuum Exhibit, first seen at the California Museum of Science and Industry, invites you to a journey of interior lit pictures and colorful graphics on several fascinating themes, such as the immortality of consciousness, life after life research, and out-of-body phenomena. You can also see a prize-winning film strip in a little theater, see the amazing three-dimensional hologram, or take home a photograph showing the energy field (aura) of your own fingertip made with a newly designed camera, the kirlian machine. The Center Bookshop has a fascinating collection of books dealing with metaphysical subjects as well as literature, poetics and travel. There is also a charming and very comprehensive book section for children of all ages.

CANDY/GIFTS

CRANBERRY SWEETS COMPANY
(On the waterfront in Old Town)
280 First Street
P.O. Box 501
Bandon, Oregon 97411
503-347-2526

Hours: Mon-Sun 9-5:30

If your experience with the succulent cranberry has been limited to juice, jelly, with a turkey dinner and, perhaps, some garland strings around a Christmas tree, you are in for a surprise. Cranberry Sweets offers some of the most delectble, inspired creations of chocolate candy I've munched anywhere. There are 27 varieties of cranberry candy from which to choose. Begin with the original cranberry candy (cranberries and English walnuts) or a cranberry mint in milk chocolate, then perhaps some yummy apple-cranberry sweets or a chocolate dipped cranberry nut candy. The business has been open for 26 years and local owners, Clifford and Margaret Shaw, with their son, Clayton, have been creating sweet concoctions and sending their famous candy around the country for the past 12 years. The Shaws' emphasis is on offering the public the highest quality chocolates anywhere available. They are all handmade with the very best, fresh ingredients. The cranberries come from local Oregon cranberry bogs, harvested in October and November of each year. The assortment of offerings include the ultimate in chocolate truffles, pie candies (like lemon meringue, pumpkin or apple), jelly candies (like raspberry-cranberry or plum-cranberry dipped in white chocolate), lots of different fruits and nuts, mints, cranberry fudge, handmade granolas, and much more. They offer a large selection of chocolate gift boxes including combination samplers which will let you try a little of everything. As part of their service, the Shaws will gift wrap and mail your gift of cranberry sweets directly to recipients. While you are visiting, wander around Margaret's unique selection of gift items. They are just beautiful and are sure to delight you. There is a brochure and gift price list available. Visa and MasterCard are accepted.

CHEESE/GIFTS

BANDON'S CHEDDAR CHEESE
680 E. Second Street (Hwy 101)
Bandon, Oregon 97411
503-347-2461

Hours: 8-5 Mon-Sat, 10-4 Sun

Here's the place to see and taste some of the best locally made cheese anywhere. Mix ingredients like abundant rainfall, the mild, cool climate of the Coquille Valley, fine green pasture lands dotted with Jerseys and dairy farms, and you have the recipe for renowned, local cheesemaking. Bandon Cheese's well-deserved reputation for fine quality began way back in 1939 when local dairymen established the Coquille Valley Dairy Cooperative. The current manager, Ralph Richmond, Jr., says that today the coop is owned by 31 local farmers. They are proud to be the single largest employer in Bandon, staffed by a loyal, dedicated team who enjoy greeting visitors and showing them around the operation; people like Helen Evans who has been serving up warm smiles and great cheeses to people for some 27 years.

The cheesemaking coop in Bandon has earned the reputation as one of the very finest small cheese plants to be found on the West Coast. Meticulous care is taken to age Bandon cheddars according to customers' preference, with mild cheddars being aged for at least three months while the sharper cheddars are aged carefully for anywhere from one to five years. Up to one million pounds of cheese can be seen aging here at any one time. Besides the cheddars, Bandon Cooperative also offers scrumptious Monterey Jack, whole curd, specially flavored club cheeses, and sweet cream butter churned locally. All the cheeses here are made with homegrown, Oregon loving care, and that means old-fashioned hand stirring is still the method here to ensure the finest quality and customer satisfaction. All the cheddars are made from pure, pasturized milk. You can choose from gourmet rich whole milk cheddars or part skim, lower-fat varieties. Individual orders of Bandon cheese are shipped throughout the United States and to many foreign countries. Consumer-sized packages and a wide assortment of gift boxes are available and can be shipped via United Parcel Service or parcel post. Along with their cheesemaking, the cooperative also offers visitors a chance to view a video movie on the process. There is a full gift shop here featuring a wide selection of Oregon wines, fine crystals and pendants, local jams, jellies, smoked fish, souvenirs, and travel books, along with an information center. Free brochures on Bandon cheese and gift selection leaflets with order forms are available.

CRAFTS/GIFTS

CRAFT CREATABLES
Highway 101 and 12th
Bandon, Oregon
503-347-9325

Hours: Mon-Sat 10-5:30

Here's the place to come for all your craft needs. Owner Dolores Franks has been nursing a love affair with crafts all her life and when she had the opportunity a few years ago to move from Illinois to her other great love (the coast of Oregon, of course!), it was like a dream come true. The result is a yarn, craft and gift center tucked right in beautiful Bandon where Dolores is ready to help satisfy any and all of your craft needs. Specialties include a full line of Canadian and U.S. yarns, acrylic, and natural fiber cottons, all in a sunburst of colors. Dolores stocks needles, DMC floss for cross stitch and embroidery, doll making materials, holiday craft items, and everything you'll need for making silk flowers and latch hook rugs. Craft Creatables features hundreds of books with knitting, crocheting and craft projects, ribbons and laces, plastic canvas in an array of colors and all the accessories to create craft items you'll be proud to display. Gifts include handmade bears, dolls, soft sculptures, sweaters, afghans, jewelry and unique lace fantasy. Dolores gladly accepts commission work.
Both individual and group craft classes are available.

(See special invitation in Appendix.)

EVENTS

CRANBERRY FESTIVAL

Enjoy Bandon's granddaddy festival of them all — the Cranberry Festival held every September. The festival begins with the coronation of the Festival Queen and her court, and continues with a series of fun filled activities like a Queen's Ball, casino night, Lion's barbecue, the cranberry parade, cranberry food fare, street fair, football, and Saturday and Sunday breakfasts put on by the VFW Auxiliary. Enjoy the color and pageantry of this harvest celebration with walking human cranberries, marching bands and the smiling Bandon community.

SANDCASTLE CONTEST — SEAFOOD AND WINE FESTIVAL

Whether it's lions, otters, whales, plain old sandcastles or seafood and fine Oregon wine, you'll have a great time at this Memorial Day festival held in Bandon. On Saturday and Sunday, the Bandon Stormwatchers will host their Seafood and Wine Festival featuring the best in Oregon wines, gourmet seafood dishes, local cheeses and desserts, held at the Bandon Airport. Meanwhile, hundreds of people flock to Bandon's beach to view the fun, artistic teamwork of artists and creative people, young and old, work for cash prizes at the Bandon Sandcastle Contest. So join in on a little indoor and outdoor fun to kick off the summer season at beautiful Bandon by the sea.

FESTIVAL OF THE PHOENIX

Celebrate the coming of spring in Bandon with the birth of the Phoenix. Like the mythical phoenix, Bandon has risen from the ashes of two fires which destroyed the town in 1914 and 1936. Held the weekend following Easter, the Bandon community celebrates with a street fair, parade with colorful floats, plays, musical entertainment, storytelling and dancers. So leave the house, come to Bandon and start celebrating a new beginning.

JULY FOURTH CELEBRATION

Boat races, fiddlers, dunk tanks, fish fries, red, white and blue streamers and traditional fireworks mark Bandon's version of our nation's birthday with fun-filled activities for you and your family. Join the friendly Bandon community in celebrating the 4th Bandon style.

GIFTS

THE COUNTRY MERCHANT
Highway 101 and Elmira
(in Bandon Mercantile Building)
Bandon, Oregon
503-347-4341

Summer hours: 9:30-5:30 Mon-Sat, 12-4 Sun
Winter hours: 10-5 Mon-Sat

The atmosphere of country permeates everywhere here — handsome, carbon steel pans and casseroles, the aroma of freshly ground coffee and delicate teas, pots of local honey, and mustard. Run your fingers along the etched glass mugs, admire the local pottery and handcrafted, Oregon-made lamps, and take a wiff of homemade jams and jellies that will make your mouth water. Owners Ed and Beth Wood have created one of the largest gift shops to be found on the Oregon coast and filled it with many fantastic things by local craftspeople and specialties including a complete line of gourmet kitchenware designed to suit the needs of even the most discerning cook. All types of cooking utensils line the shelves. You'll find cast iron ware, Chicago cutlery, woks, gadgets, plain champagne and wine glasses, and even the latest in myrtlewood clocks. But the Woods didn't stop here. They also feature a wide selection of quality clothing, hats, 100% cotton sweaters, wind socks, house decor, and adorable, handcrafted teddy bears. You'll love the natural fiber, 100% cotton rugs, and be sure to check out the full line of cookbooks. Not only is there something for everyone (man, woman or child), but the prices are very, very fair.

(See special invitation in Appendix.)

SEAGULL MYRTLEWOOD
Highway 101, 3 miles south of Bandon
At Beach Loop Junction
Bandon, Oregon
503-347-2248

Hours: 8-8 Mon-Sat, 8-5 Sun

Take native Oregon, ancient myrtlewood with its intricate graining patterns and colorings, extreme hardness and exquisite beauty, handmill and tenderly season it, and it is ripe for handcrafting into articles of lasting beauty. Step into this rustic emporium and you'll see just what creative hands can make with this unique south coast wood. Make sure you ask the owners Frank and Joan Besenhofer about the myrtlewood tree growing in the yard outside their wonderful shop. There are tables, footstools, top quality clocks from table top to grandfather size, one-of-a-kind driftwood sculptures, fishes and sea creatures carved from beach wood. Run your hands along the smooth finish of wood wind racks, or rub against the texture of local pottery mugs and lamps dressed in coral shades. The myrtlewood salt and pepper mills and unique music boxes are special favorites with us. The Besenhofers offer woodcarving classes and a refinishing service for those wood bowls and collectibles you may already own. Frank and Joan accept individual orders for myrtlewood and will ship each one promptly to anywhere in the United States. A brochure is available which describes their business and highlights some of the very special qualities myrtlewood possesses.

(See special invitation in Appendix.)

MUSEUM

COQUILLE RIVER MUSEUM

Steamboats, pioneers, disastrous fires, black sand gold and the Na-so-mah — all of these and more make up the fascinating history of Bandon that you can see at the Coquille River Historical Museum. Here you can have fun searching for evidence of Bandon's past and turn up artifacts, bones, burned earth and old photographs, all from different periods of history from the day the Na- so-mah enjoyed the setting sun and the settlement of the pioneers to the economic boom of the late 19th century and the catastrophic fires that destroyed Bandon in 1914 and 1936. You can learn about the courageous people who braved the western wilderness and made Bandon the unique community that it is today.

PIZZA

RAGTIME PIZZA
Highway 101 (2 blocks north of Old Town)
Bandon, Oregon
503-347-3911

Open: 11-10 Mon-Sat, 1-10 Sun

We found the aroma streaking out from this place to be just too tempting to resist. Out-of-this-world pizza crust can be covered with a big selection of toppings from smoked oysters to sauerkraut linguica, plus mounds of grated cheese. Al and Sylvia Layne have come up with some great ideas for specialty pizzas. Try the Bandon Tiger, the Trust Me, or the Veggies (loaded with mushrooms, black olives, peppers and all the trimmings). On weekdays, Ragtime serves up a great bargain lunch — all the pizza and salad bar you can eat for one low price. This family style eatery features a full range of deli-style sandwiches served up in whole or half size with a selection of different dressings and garnishes, plus horse radish or Grand Perry sauce upon request. Ragtime offers hearty soups, soft drinks, juices, along with wines and beer by the pitcher. Here's a tip: ask about the "U-bake pizza" where the first topping comes free. Al and Sylvia provide orders to go and birthday party specials. Where else can you find a restaurant which offers to custom flavor your pizza sauce with oregano or garlic according to your personal preference. We think you'll agree that that's what good food and hospitality is all about.

(See special invitation in Appendix.)

RESTAURANTS

ANDREA'S OLD TOWN CAFE
160 Baltimore Street (Old Town
between 1st and 2nd Streets)
Bandon, Oregon
503-347-3022

Summer hours: 8am-9pm Mon-Sat;
   10-3, 5:30-9 Sun
Winter hours: 9-4 Mon-Thurs;
   9-9 Fri & Sat; 10-2:30 Sun

Words like "delicious food" aren't enough in trying to describe this neat, comfy eatery. Imagine hearty baked breads, bagels, plump muffins and pastries, all lovingly prepared fresh from scratch daily by Andrea; local oysters, cod, shrimp, tender crab entrees, succulent fresh fruits, vegetables, Bandon cheeses, and cranberries picked locally. The emphasis here is on natural, gourmet cuisine prepared meticulously for the past nine years by chef/owner Andrea Gatov. The restaurant sits snugly in the historic Old Town section of Bandon and overflows with the kind of casual ambiance and coffeehouse atmosphere that keeps locals and visitors coming back for more. Andrea serves some of the freshest, best prepared entrees you are likely to find anywhere. There are lots of options here: great chowders, lighter fare, fresh seafood, huge salads brimming with shrimp and avocados, and Andrea's specialty, lamb dishes (probably because she raises the lambs herself on her farm). For lunch, her thick, deli-style sandwich stuffed with turkey, sprouts and cranberry sauce was the best we've had anywhere. For dinner, we especially recommend ordering one of Andrea's imaginative crab dishes. They have been award winners at a number of prestigious culinary shows and it is easy to see why — they are out of this world! The wine list here is impressive too, with nearly 40 to choose from including a number of Oregon wines. By the way, be sure to save some room in the midst of this gastronomic feast, because Andrea's homemade cheesecake has to be one of the very finest on Oregon's coast. Brunch is a local Sunday tradition here, and it is not unusual to find you are relaxed and accompanied by a contemporary backdrop of featured musicians.

THE BANDON BOATWORKS RESTAURANT
(on the south jetty, across from Coquille River Lighthouse)
Bandon, Oregon
503-347-2111

Imagine sitting upstairs here, taking in a resplendent view of the Coquille River Lighthouse, the jetty, and the sun creating a glow of orange as it dips below the horizon of the Pacific Ocean. While the view here may indeed be the finest to be had anywhere along the Oregon coast in any restaurant, it is equally matched by excellent dishes prepared from only the freshest seafood. Owner Larry Stewart has been in the business of creating fine cuisine for the past 15 years and opened The Boatworks in Bandon some seven years ago. You might say Larry was raised on a gourmet palate, especially since his dad has, for many years, been the executive chef for the Hilton in exclusive Monterey, California. Lunches here feature terrific sandwiches, and hamburgers like the Elizabeth and the Flying Dutchman are yummy. We enjoyed the J.J. Loggie, a half-pound burger topped with local Oregon cheddar, Canadian bacon, and fresh, sauteed mushrooms. Another specialty is squid and chips, lightly breaded in a secret recipe batter. All the hearty breads and desserts are baked fresh right on the premises. One unusual and quite delicious item on the menu which we enjoyed is the cranberry bread. Soups and chowders are all homemade, and a full salad bar is available at lunch and dinner. At dinner, there are a number of scrumptious entrees to choose from. We liked the Cioppino, a Portuguese dish stuffed with crab, clams, fresh snapper, prawns, scallops, tomato, basil and garlic — super good! Another delectable entree is the rack of lamb (loin of lamb broiled to your liking and served with an English mint sauce). All dinners include choice of salad bar or clam chowder, rice pilaf with seafood dinners, and baked potato with steak dinners. For red meat lovers, we suggest the prime rib or veal. Every day, The Boatworks offers a specialty Mexican dish or two on the blackboard. For those of us watching calories, I suggest the poached chicken on a bed of rich with melted Jack cheese and a crisp green salad. Another feature worth mentioning — Larry prefers to use only Qualman's oysters that are from the local area, so his guests can be assured of the finest quality. The pasta, too, is top notch; fettucini and linguini handmade right here in the restaurant. The Boatworks offers a selection of wines, and imported and domestic beers. The Sunday champagne brunch here has become a renowned tradition among locals and returning visitors alike.

(See special invitation in Appendix.)

FRASER'S RESTAURANT
Highway 101 and 10th Street (uptown)
Bandon, Oregon
503-347-3141

Hours: 6am-10pm Mon-Thurs, 6am-11pm Fri, 7am-11pm Sat, 8am-10pm Sun

Here's the place to go for the best clam chowder we've had anywhere up and down the whole Oregon coast. Fraser's is a warm and cozy, family-style operation. Locals Gerry and Trudy Fraser, with the help of their sons and daughter, have been serving up fresh, homestyle cooking at super lower prices here for the past 26 years. Breakfasts are great — ham and fresh eggs with shredded hash browns, choice of toast, yummy bran muffins and juice, coffee or tea. For lunch, we like the chicken strips, all tender white meat served with baked potato or French fries and creamy cole slaw; or try the French dip, a French roll piled high with roast beef slices and a tasty au juice sauce. Dinner specialties center around seafood and prime steaks. The fresh oyster entree is one of our favorites, served with a choice of potato, and soup or salad. Fraser's offers a full service bar and selections of table wines. Now remember, even with all the menu choices, don't forget to include an order of their famous clam chowder. Their son, Pat, makes it fresh from scratch every day, and I've dubbed it the "best chowder served on the Oregon Coast". For dessert, try Fraser's homemade ice cream. You'll love this for an ending to a great family style meal.

(See special invitation in Appendix.)

SEAFOOD

BANDON FISH MARKET
Boat Basin, on the riverfront in Old Town
Bandon, Oregon
503-347-4282

Summer hours: 8-8, seven days a week
Winter hours: 10-6 Mon-Sat, 11-4 Sun

How about some succulent local crab or salmon, maybe red snapper, ling cod, sole or shrimp. It's all right here, fresh off the boats to delight you. James and Darlene Wise and daughter, Wendy, know the treasures of the sea. After all, Dad has been fishing the Oregon waters on commercial trollers for the past 15 years. Imagine strolling among the boat docks, the bite of salty sea air at your back, while your eyes wander across gleaming glass cases filled with the freshest shrimp, oysters and halibut you're likely to see anywhere. You are in for some tough choices here. Pamper your palate with smoked, locally caught salmon or seafood gently sizzling right here in the market. All the seafood is offered at bargain prices and dishes come complete with great, crispy French fries and a choice of either shrimp salad or cole slaw. For a really good sampling, we suggest their combination plate decked with deep fried prawns, scallops, oysters and ling cod. The shrimp cocktail is a real favorite, brimming with fresh Oregon shrimp with tangy sauce — it is yummy! Soft drinks, milk and coffee are available plus gift packs of canned seafood, a blissful reminder to share with friends of the culinary joys rising up from our Oregon waters.

(See special invitation in Appendix.)

WOMEN'S APPAREL

BLACK HORSE BOUTIQUE
Second and Chicago Streets (Old Town)
Bandon, Oregon
503-347-9847

Hours: Mon-Sat 9:30-5:30, Sun noon-4

Whether your taste runs to classic twill suits, comfortable night wear to lounge in, or a great swim suit for showing off on our spectacular Oregon beaches, try the Black Horse Boutique in Bandon. Virginia Weaver, with the help of her daughter, Jackie, brings 18 years of experience to the boutique which caters to women of all ages and sizes. The emphasis is on casual wear, from brand label dresses to Wrangler jeans, polar fleece casual tops, Bandon t-shirts, and assorted sweat suits. Styles are geared toward girls 7-14 years old, teens, misses, junior petites, and queen sizes up to size 46. Many of the major department store brands are here with the added attraction of Virginia's personal and very friendly touch. A full line of accessories including belts, purses and jewelry is available to coordinate with your fashion choices. Prices are moderate and often below manufacturer's suggested retail price in larger stores. By the way, don't forget to check out the sales racks, because we've seen some good bargains tucked away there.

(See special invitation in Appendix.)

YARN/GIFTS

WESTERLY WEBS
170 Second Street (Old Town)
Bandon, Oregon
503-347-3682

Step inside this handsome fiber design center with skylights filtering sunshine onto wood looms, and soak in the loving energy of textile artists busy turning natural fibers into colorful, touchable, durable creations you'll be proud to own and display. Once inside for an "experience in soft technology", you will see why owners Joyce Farr, Buzzy MacQueen, and Maggie Hart have earned a reputation for having the only working studio/shop of its kind on the Coast. The name Westerly Webs was coined by Joyce when she started the business nine years ago as the mostly westerly yarn shop in Oregon. There is a commitment here to fine quality work, artistic expression and service to the public. The full range of tools of the trade and the availability of individual instruction in weaving, knitting and spinning attest to that commitment.

More than 20 brands of commercial yarns are available as well as hand dyed, hand spun yarns in cottons, wools and silks. The book and pattern library contain hundreds of ideas for knitting and weaving. Westerly Webs is a distributor for Schacht and Harrisville looms, Loet spinning wheels and Brother knitting machines.

Recently seven fiber artists have joined the group and excitement is running high. More and more quality items are available every day, including some remarkable handmade Teddy bears. It is a rare day when you won't find one or more of the artists weaving, knitting, spinning or answering questions about fiber techniques or design. Your visit to Westerly Webs and Fiber Designers will be pleasant and informative.

BANDON TOUR

If you'd like to have a fun day of relaxed shopping, dining and breathtaking scenery, you're in the right place. Bandon's Old Town has some of the best choices in a four block area than anyplace on the Oregon Coast. A favorite place for the entire family is the West Coast Game Park. For an unforgettable day, take the Bandon tour.

TIME	PLACE	DESCRIPTION	HOW TO FIND IN BOOK
Breakfast	Fraser's Restaurant	Best breakfast	Bandon/Restaurants
A.M.	Bandon's Cheddar Cheese	Best cheese/gifts	Bandon/Cheese/Gifts
A.M.	Westerly Web	Best yarn/crafts/gifts	Bandon/Yarn/Gifts
A.M.	Black Horse Boutique	Best women's apparel	Bandon/Women's Apparel
A.M.	The Country Merchant	Best gifts/gourmet coffee	Bandon/Gifts
Lunch	Andrea's Old Town Cafe	Best lunch	Bandon/Restaurants
P.M.	Cranberry Sweets Company	Best candy/gifts	Bandon/Candy/Gifts
P.M.	West Coast Game Park	Best game park	Bandon/Attractions
P.M.	Seagull Myrtlewood	Best myrtlewood/gifts	Bandon/Gifts
Snack	Bandon Fish Market	Fresh seafood	Bandon/Seafood
Dinner	The Bandon Boatworks Restaurant	Best dinner	Bandon/Restaurants

Chapter Seven

CURRY COUNTY

PORT ORFORD

ACCOMMODATIONS

HOME BY THE SEA, BED AND BREAKFAST AND BEACH
P.O. Box 606
Port Orford, Oregon 97465
503-332-2855 for reservations and directions

Dramatic ocean and beach view includes massive off-shore sea stacks, contemporary owner-built two story homes built just a block from Port Orford's extraordinary harbor, where each day its unique "fleet on wheels" is launched via a huge hoist. Access is easy to miles of agate and driftwood-festooned beaches. During the fall, the Elk and Sixes Rivers become excellent salmon producers. Storm watchers love the warm and exciting winter storms and devote hours to beachcombing for agates, petrified wood and prized Japanese glass fishing floats. This part of the Oregon coast is also a favorite for scuba divers, surfboarders and sailboarders. Whale watching seasons runs from October to May and the Oregon Island's National Wildlife Refuge is just offshore. The hosts are long time residents, a school teacher and carpenter. Among their interests are the Apple computer and the finer arts of hand-spinning and weaving.

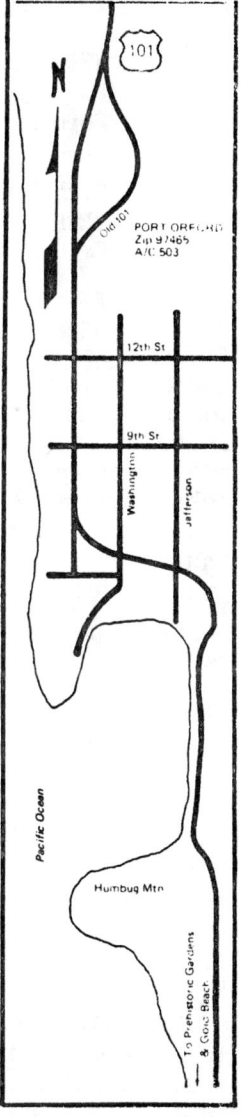

They do not smoke and ask guests to smoke outside. They serve hearty, continental breakfasts and have one cat, laundry facilities, and kitchen privileges. Rates are reasonable and reservations are highly recommended.

ART GALLERY

THE ART HATCHERY
Highway 101 near the center of Port Orford
Port Orford, Oregon
503-332-4011

Summer hours: 9-6 Mon-Sun
Winter hours: 9-3, closed Mon
Credit cards, MasterCard and Visa accepted

I really was not looking for the kind of art gallery I found when I stopped at The Art Hatchery. I wanted a mobile for the family room, and I found one as well as a very sophisticated collection of art work done by some 35 of Oregon's best artists, including the owners Robert and Vicki Courtright. One of the first things which impressed me about The Art Hatchery was the size of the place. It has five showrooms and over 4,000 square feet filled with everything from large welded sculptures to tiny sea creatures executed in perfect detail. There are oils, water colors, wood and metal sculptures and probably the largest selection of pottery in the state.

The uncanny realism becomes less surprising the more you talk with these easy-going artists who own and operate this gallery. They have spent a lifetime learning their arts, and part of Bob's lifetime has been spent as a professional marine biologist. This explains the perfect detail of some of the sculptures. Vicki and Bob are also potters and Vicki specializes in delightful highfire stoneware sculptures of birds and other critters. Although the sea and its denizens would appear at first glance to be Bob's main interest, don't be fooled. This man has developed fresh water bass fishing to an art form with the same eye for detail and attention to realism that his art shows. He also designs lures and other products for two national companies.

The Art Hatchery, showplace of this couple's lifetime devotion, offers valuable art objects for the serious collector as well as something for those of us who just want a casual gift. Prices range from a couple of dollars to several thousand dollars.

However, don't feel like you have to spend money to come in, as the Courtrights are happy to just chat and point out the best places to camp, fish, beachcomb or play to help you have a pleasant visit on the Southern Oregon Coast.

ATTRACTIONS

THE PREHISTORIC GARDENS
36848 Highway 101 South
Port Orford, Oregon
503-332-4463

Open 8am-dusk, seven days per week

Did you ever dream of walking through a rain forest and meeting a live dinosaur face-to-face? Such a meeting would be impossible, of course. Dinosaurs and the other prehistoric reptiles that once dominated the land, sea and air have been extinct for a long time, and Man has never seen a living dinosaur. Fortunately, their skeletons were sometimes covered by sand or mud which slowly hardened into solid rock, protecting the fossil bones. These fossils have been removed from the rock, assembled and displayed in many of the larger museums where we can marvel at the size and shape of these prehistoric beasts.

Working from the measurements of these assembled skeletons, and from the paintings and drawings of famous paleontologists, the sculptor, E.V. Nelson, has recreated a "Lost World" at The Prehistoric Gardens where you can see life-sized reconstructions of the dinosaurs and other prehistoric animals, displayed in Oregon's rain forest among the primitive plants that flourished during the days when monster reptiles ruled the earth.

Nelson's interest in dinosaurs began in grade school when he read about them in the *National Geographic* magazine, and he decided that someday he would build some dinosaurs in a natural setting. Many years later, he started seriously looking for the proper site for his Prehistoric Gardens and after months of searching, he found the ideal setting. In the fall of 1953, the Nelsons sold their business and home in Eugene, Oregon, and moved to their new property just 14 miles north of Gold Beach on the Oregon Coast Highway 101 where they had found the perfect background for their project: a dense growth of towering trees, huge ferns, mosses, lichens, and many other native plants that make The Prehistoric Gardens a "Land of Long Ago" where you are seemingly transported back through time to the days of the dinosaurs.

The Gardens have been operating for over 30 years, and have been featured in many national magazines such as *Life*, *Better Homes and Gardens*, *Popular Mechanics*, *Sunset*, and *National Geographic*, and in dozens of newspapers. It is recommended by most travel directories, and a trip through The Prehistoric Gardens will be one of the highlights of your visit to the Oregon Coast.

GIFTS

FROM OREGON WITH LOVE
½ block north of Battle Rock Beach
on Highway 101
Port Orford, Oregon
503-332-7325

Summer hours: 10am-closing, seven days a week
Winter hours: 11-6, six days a week
   12 noon-5pm Sun

As the name suggests, this is an intimate little shop filled with Oregon products that reflect both the unique and the common aspects of our state. Tim and Becky Flake have stocked their store with handmade items such as dolls, wall hangings and wood carvings, as well as quality machine-made goods such as the complete line of Gerber knives from Portland. They also carry Oregon honeys and jams, hummingbird feeders from Salem, cranberry sweets candy from Bandon, and books and cards about Oregon. Tim and Becky also carry their own handcrafted work, animal carvings by Tim and cutting boards by Becky. This is the best little gift shop in Port Orford. Every item has been personally selected From Oregon With Love.

(See special invitation in Appendix.)

THE WOODEN NICKEL
Highway 101, in the middle of Port Orford
Across from the grade school
Port Orford, Oregon
503-332-5201

Winter hours: 9-5, seven days a week
Summer hours: 8-7, seven days a week

The Wooden Nickel myrtlewood factory is place of pleasant smells. When you open the door, you are immediately gathered in like an old friend by the smell of carved wood and several kinds of oils and waxes, and by the easy-going manner of the owners, Tracy and Glenda Hasset. Tracy has a lot in common with the rugged but beautiful Oregon coast where he lives —a man of nature that takes raw Oregon myrtlewood and turns it into a beautiful, smooth piece of art. In their shop and factory, Tracy and Glenda have a storehouse of wood-carved treasures, 75% of which is made in the factory. Their pieces are of their own top quality design (rejects go into the firewood pile). Many of the myrtlewood products you see for sale in other places are crafted right here in this factory by Tracey or his able assistant. The Wooden Nickel is the only place in Oregon that makes myrtlewood bells, cups and saucers. They also manufacture and sell cutting boards, wall hangings, salt and pepper shakers, and many other items. A catalog of all items is available upon request. The Hassets offer free, year 'round gift wrapping and they ship anywhere. They also offer a complete line of coastal gifts, including kites and wind socks. The Wooden Nickel is famous for quality and you will find many of their items featured in gift shops up and down the Oregon Coast.

(See special invitation in Appendix.)

RESTAURANTS

TRUCULENT OYSTER
Downtown Port Orford on Hwy 101
Port Orford, Oregon
503-332-9461

Open: 11-9 Mon-Sat, 12-9 Sun
MasterCard, Visa and American Express accepted.

The most striking feature of the Truculent Oyster is the aroma. It greets me like an old friend whenever I pass through town and either reminds me of what I'm missing if I don't stop or what gastronomic pleasures are in store for me when I do stop. For four years now, these pleasant and intriguing smells have been drifting up and down the streets of Port Orford and shanghaiing helpless but hungry bystanders. Once inside, it is not hard to see why people keep coming back. The helpings are large even by Oregon standards, and the quality of the food is superb. Bill and Cindy Grier have been in the restaurant business for 16 years. The smooth, well- organized and rapid service, as well as the attractive, tasty dishes reveal their expertise and the efforts to which they and their nephew, Todd Cavanaugh, go. The fare is from the best of local products and is prepared fresh from scratch every day. They offer seafood, steak and the services of a full bar. For those who want to eat but are less than hungry, they have excellent "deli-style" sandwiches. Although everything in the house is well prepared and worth trying, I generally have a platter full of steamer clams if they are in season, or chicken teriyaki when they are not. The dinners include a crisp green salad and special rice. For lunch, try a plate of pan-fried oysters. The chowder is highly satisfactory, and with salad and bread, makes a very nice, light lunch. To avoid waiting too long without satisfaction in the presence of that teasing smell, it is probably best to make reservations, especially during the summer.

GOLD BEACH

ABOUT GOLD BEACH

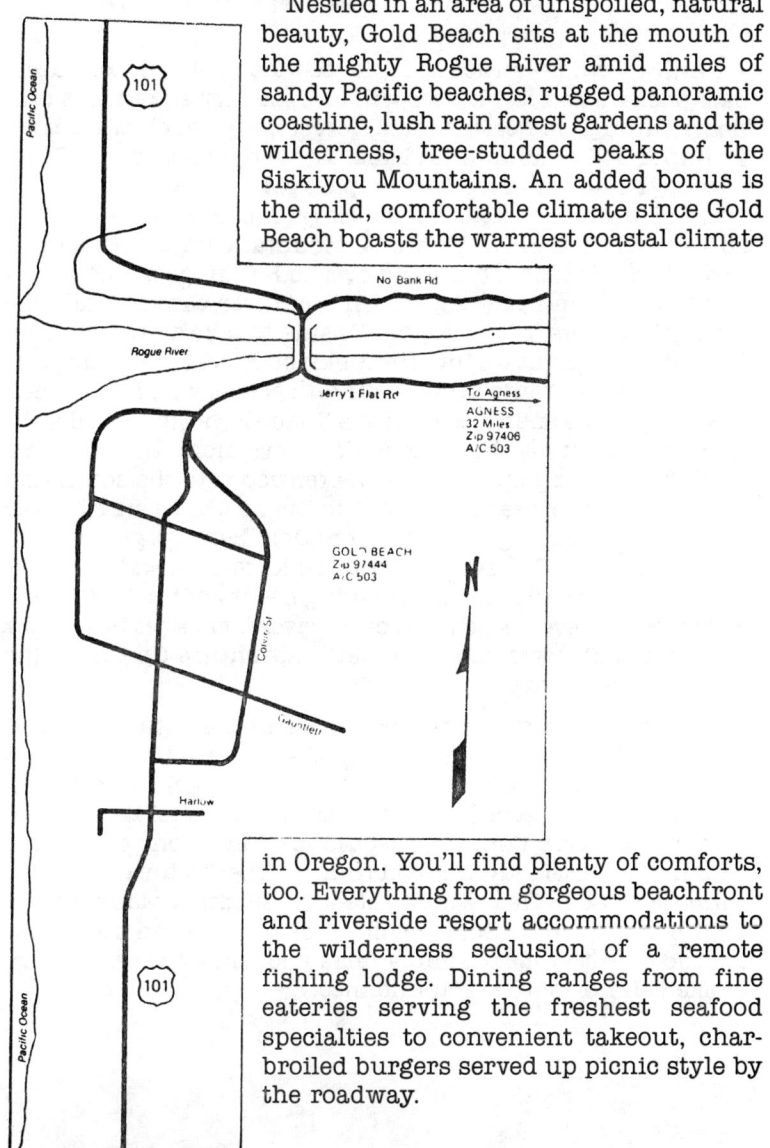

Nestled in an area of unspoiled, natural beauty, Gold Beach sits at the mouth of the mighty Rogue River amid miles of sandy Pacific beaches, rugged panoramic coastline, lush rain forest gardens and the wilderness, tree-studded peaks of the Siskiyou Mountains. An added bonus is the mild, comfortable climate since Gold Beach boasts the warmest coastal climate in Oregon. You'll find plenty of comforts, too. Everything from gorgeous beachfront and riverside resort accommodations to the wilderness seclusion of a remote fishing lodge. Dining ranges from fine eateries serving the freshest seafood specialties to convenient takeout, char-broiled burgers served up picnic style by the roadway.

Fishing is a real passion in the Gold Beach area. You can fly fish for trout in a wilderness creek in the morning, ocean fish for salmon or bottom fish by noon, and then cast for migratory steelhead before the sun goes down. Dig for clams, pluck mussels, try your hand at pulling in some scrumptious Dungeness crab, or lease a charter boat and fishing guide for an afternoon.

Natural wilds entice people to the Gold Beach area. Backpackers and day hikers will love the myriad of trails that weave through majestic coastal forests, crystal clear streams and up to lofty mountain vistas. Try the trail that winds its way up the Rogue River Canyon past pioneer ranches and the cabin of western novelist, Zane Grey. You can hike the trails on Cape Sebastian or Humbug Mountain for endless open views of the Pacific. Then head over to Kalmiopsis Wilderness where you'll find the rugged Illinois River canyon and rare plant life unique to this region. Be sure to take a car trek from Hunter Creek right up into the Siskiyou Forest, winding your way through unforgettable mountain scenery and then back down along the south bank of the Rogue River to Gold Beach. Another favorite is the spectacular drive along Highway 101 with the towering splendor of the redwoods to the south and the breathtaking seascape vistas to the north. Be sure to take advantage of the Rogue River. From Gold Beach it gushes into the heart of the Siskiyou Mountains forming a water spewn nature trail. Experience the thrilling beauty of the Rogue, one of America's seven wild and scenic rivers, via a jet passenger boat trip that takes you on a water adventure up the Rogue Canyon Wilderness.

Once your energy winds down from all the nature exploration, take time to relax and enjoy the historic flavor of Gold Beach itself. Stroll around the antique landmarks like Skookumhouse Butte, Devils Backbone, Battle Bar, Pistol River. Head over to the Curry County Museum for collections of pioneer and Indian artifacts, and then on to the historic *Mary D. Hume*, a wood hulled whaling steamer originally launched at Gold Beach in 1881. Gold Beach — lots of vacation options to see and do with time to simply relax and while away the hours in the calm of nature's abundance.

CHAMBER OF COMMERCE

If you would like information on lodging, dining establishments, attractions, maps and special events, contact Gold Beach Chamber of Commerce, P.O. Box 55, Gold Beach, Oregon 97444, of phone 503-247-7526.

ACCOMMODATIONS

IRELAND'S RUSTIC LODGES
Located on the south end of Highway 101
Gold Beach, Oregon
503-247-7718 for reservations

For a unique stay on the Oregon coast and just 200 yards from the beach, try Ireland's Rustic Lodges. They are only rustic on the outside. Inside are spacious and comfortable rooms, each with fireplaces, all the firewood you need, and furnished with color TV, tubs with showers, plush lamb's wool mattress pads for a luxious night's rest, printed linens, and pillows so soft it's like putting your head on a cloud. Ralph and Wilma Richmond take pride in their rooms as well as their landscaping with beautiful flowers in a natural setting of trees and shrubs. If you feel like having a picnic, there is a barbecue area with picnic tables for you to enjoy with easy access to the beach. Ralph and Wilma, and their managers Bill and Joyce Roth, welcome you to Ireland's Rustic Lodges for a memorable vacation by the sea. New non-smoking units and real log cabins are the best choice for rustic comfort on the Oregon Coast.

TuTuTum LODGE
Located seven miles upriver on the Rogue
Gold Beach, Oregon

A river so beautiful that it attracts people from all over the world, a special lodge located on the banks of such a river. This is TuTuTum Lodge, a rustic but tasteful place located in a remote, breathtaking setting. The river is Oregon's famous Rogue and TuTuTum Lodge seems to reflect that beauty in its architecture. People from around the world have enjoyed the renowned accommodations and the meals served splendidly at this special place. Dick and Laurie VanZante are the expert hosts that see to every detail for a comfortable visit. The main lodge features a massive stone fireplace, lounge, library and the world-famous gourmet dining room. There is a heated pool, pitch and putt golf course, an antique pool table, and player piano. The lodge has its own boat dock and hiking trails that lead to beautiful scenery. For remote elegance, try this best choice — TuTuTum Lodge, seven miles upriver on the Rogue from Gold Beach.

ATTRACTIONS

JERRY'S ROGUE JETS
Located at the Port of Gold Beach
Gold Beach, Oregon
503-247-7601 or 247-7601

Write: P.O. Box 1011
Gold Beach, Oregon 97444

Open daily: May 1-Oct 30, seven days a week
Reservations recommended

Can a person have one of the most exciting and enjoyable days of their life learning about history, geology, ecology, and stream flow? I did, sitting comfortably and safely in a jet — a jet boat, that is — Jerry's Rogue Jets, the jet boats that make a ride on the Rogue all of the above plus much more. Jerry's originated the jet boats on the Rogue and their popularity keeps growing season after season. It should with all they offer. Narrative pilots have carried people up the river since 1960. The pilots have all been on the river for years and know where you'll see deer, bald eagles, historic spots, lodges and restaurants. The guided trip is fun and safe. You don't need to worry about anything. All your needs are cared for, including lunch on the river. Before you leave, Jerry's offers a nice gift shop with warm weather clothes if need be, and lots of gifts to help you remember this great adventure. Bill McNair, owner and manager, is, as of this writing, president of Gold Beach Chamber of Commerce. So if you need information about Gold Beach, this could be the next best place to stop after the Chamber office. A best choice for history, geology, and ecology — Jerry's Rogue Jets, the jet boat trip of a lifetime.

(See special invitation in Appendix.)

LODGE TO LODGE HIKING
On the Rogue River Trail

Imagine hiking for days along the 40 mile Rogue River Trail with only the bare minimums to haul in your day pack; perhaps a swim suit, change of clothes, rain jacket, first aid kit, water and an energizing snack or two. While it's not only possible but delightful since seven rustic riverside lodges stand ready to serve your overnight needs with six lodges in a span of 16 miles, spend a weekend of five days to cover the whole trail. Lined with yellow Siskiyou iris and fragrant, wild azaleas, the lodges provide bed, dinner, breakfast and a sack lunch for the trail. On the western half of the trail upstream, they are no more than six miles apart in an easy day's hike from one another. The western trail is about 35 miles north of Gold Beach and ½ mile from Foster Bar, a popular boat landing. Park there and walk east and north on the paved road until you see signs on the left marking the Rogue River Trail.

The first lodge you come to, just one mile from the west trailhead, is Illahe Lodge which is open year 'round. Two miles further in is Wild River Lodge. Although this lodge is not accessible to hikers, the proprietor will be happy to boat you in from the trail for a weekend stay. Six miles from the start of the trailhead sits Clay Hill Lodge, a nice spot for day hikers and picnickers, sporting swimming and panoramic downriver view. Another 5.7 miles along is the lodge at Half Moon Bar, a lovely, quiet, remote spot where guests are ferried in across the river by jet boats. A bit further at the upriver end of the Rogue River Jet Boat Tour, you'll find Paradise Lodge. Stay overnight or stop in for food and camp supplies. Four miles further east is the site of a century old homestead now operated as Marial Lodge. The last of the lodges, Black Bear Lodge, is found another 14.7 miles east on the trail. Here the atmosphere is rustic and cozy. Make arrangements ahead of time for owner Bill Hull to ferry you across the river. From Black Bear Lodge, continue hiking 9.6 miles and you'll arrive at the eastern trailhead at Grave Creek Bridge, 27 miles north of Grants Pass. The entire Rogue River Trail follows a gently rolling grade from the eastern end with a 650 foot elevation to a western trailhead elevation of 250 feet. You'll almost always be hiking the trail with the river in view and there are frequent side paths to allow access. Live oak, fragrant myrtle trees casting shadows across canyon walls, stands of Douglas fir, hemlock, hand-built bridges across tumbling creeks and the majesty of the great outdoors wait to welcome you in your trail adventure.

PACIFIC AIR SERVICE
Located at the port of Gold Beach airport
Gold Beach, Oregon
503-247-2414 (day) or 247-7853 (night)

Have you ever flown over a growling sea lion or a famous river low enough to see the fish jumping? These scenes of the coast and of rugged wilderness areas such as the Rogue, Illinois and Pistol Rivers, will meet your every expectation when you take a scenic flight with Pacific Air Service. You'll fly down the coast with Bill Riley, an experienced pilot, who narrates the tours to Mack Arch that stands 325 feet high, then out to sea to view the largest sea lion and bird rookery on the west coast. Quite often you'll see whales offshore and fishing boats which dot the ocean. Next are breathtaking panoramic views of the coast wilderness range, the Pistol River with its big craggy wilderness area with a birdseye view of the rugged Illinois River and then on to where it meets the wild and beautiful Rogue River. Pacific Air Service also has pickup and delivery service in air freight. Their prices are very reasonable. In fact, as of this writing, it was well under $25 per person for a 45 minute tour (with three people minimum). A best choice for unforgettable scenery — fly with Bill Riley's Pacific Air in Gold Beach.

ROGUE RIVER MAIL BOATS
Turn east off Hwy 101 on north side of
Rogue River Bridge; go ¼ mile
P.O. Box 1165
Gold Beach, Oregon 97444
503-247-7033 for reservations

The Rogue River is famous for its beauty and an unusual boat trip. Just one-quarter mile up the north side of the Rogue River off Highway 101 at Gold Beach you'll find the famous "mail boats" and they really do deliver the mail. In fact, during the summer, the city of Agness, Oregon, gets all its mail from the boats. They also deliver milk, bread and other perishables for stores and lodges along the way. In 1895, the first mail trip was made up river by Noble Price in an 18 foot boat. For the 40 mile trip it took four days, using poles, oars and sails to navigate the swift currents of the Rogue. The Rogue Mail Boat Service, owned by Ed and Sue Kammer, is one of the few remaining water mail routes in the United States and has been written up in numerous magazines and newspapers nationwide. The Rogue is still a wild, roaring river with some of the most beautiful scenery in the world, teeming with wildlife in their natural habitat, and the river is still a salmon and steelhead fishermen's paradise. Reservations are recommended and they are open May 1 to October 31, seven days a week. All trips are narrated and you'll find they will be a real educational experience for all ages. Call or write for a full color brochure. For a beautiful adventure, enjoy this best choice — the Mail Boats of the Rogue River at Gold Beach.

(See special invitation in Appendix.)

BAKERY

TOBEY'S BAKERY
965 S. Ellensberg (Hwy 101)
Gold Beach, Oregon
503-247-6418

Wild blackberry pie made with berries picked along the Rogue River's lush banks is one of the specialties at Tobey's Bakery located at the south end of Gold Beach, easy to get to right on Highway 101. Everything is fresh every day and you'll find such delectable items as muffins, apple fritters, raised and cake doughnuts, maple bars, cinnamon rolls, turnovers, cookies, wedding and birthday cakes, and all types of bread. Carla Simon, with the help of Juanita and Wayne (her mom and dad), takes pleasure in helping you with your choices from their tasty assortment. Try one of Carla's scrumptious macaroon cookies with your favorite beverage. Many items in the bakery are made from Oregon ingredients, such as their famous Rogue River Wild Blackberry Pie. A best choice for good taste — Tobey's Bakery in Gold Beach.

(See special invitation in Appendix.)

GIFTS

ROGUE RIVER MYRTLEWOOD
710 North Ellensburg (Hwy 101)
Gold Beach, Oregon
503-247-2332

There is a special shop in Gold Beach where you can see local craftsmen at work making items from wood that is over 100 years old — bowls, plaques, lamps, clocks, and many other beautiful items. The only wood used is Oregon's famous myrtlewood. For a myrtle tree to mature for commercial use, it takes 100-150 years. The characteristic of this harder-than-oak wood is that after being crafted into a piece, it grows darker with age. Dave and Denise Middleton are the craftsmen at Rogue River Myrtlewood, and they invite their customers in for a full tour of how myrtlewood is shaped into all those useful items. Over 70% of the inventory is crafted by the Middletons. The shop is bright and cheerful, and there is something offered for everyone. Prices are very reasonable and quality is at its best. A best choice for beautiful Oregon crafts, visit Rogue River Myrtlewood, just ½ mile south of the Rogue River Bridge in Gold Beach.

(See special invitation in Appendix.)

RESORT

JOT'S RESORT/RESTAURANT
Located on the north side of the
Rogue River Bridge on the banks of the
Rogue River off Highway 101
P. O. Box J
Gold Beach, Oregon
503-247-6676

The true beauty of Oregon is found in its many rivers and lush forests that end up on the sandy beaches of the rugged Pacific coastline. To experience this beauty at its best, one only needs to find the famous Rogue River and its most luxurious hideaway, Jot's Resort. Jot's is located on the north bank of the Rogue just across the bridge from Gold Beach, Oregon. Here you'll find accommodations at their best with condominium units with fireplaces, luxurious furnishings, spiral staircases, and a breathtaking view of the Rogue and the Pacific Ocean. Jot's offers a gift and tackle shop that is filled to the brim with the things you need, from sweatshirts and hats to fishing gear to finer gifts. There are also rental boats for pleasure or fishing and rental bicycles for enjoyment, along with all the other things you'll need for a day of fun on the river. The jet boats that are a famous part of the Rogue actually use Jot's Resort as a pickup and drop off point for their guests and others hoping for a ride on this magnificant river. Room service is offered from the **Rod N' Reel Restaurant** located at Jot's, known for high quality and fresh seafood and steak. The Rogue River epitomizes the beauty of Oregon and the best choice, Jot's

Resort, helps us discover what makes Oregon so great. During July and August, you should call 30-60 days in advance for reservations.

(See special invitation in Appendix.)

RESTAURANTS

ROD N' REEL RESTAURANT
Located on the north side of the
Rogue River Bridge on the banks of the
Rogue River off Highway 101
Gold Beach, Oregon
503-247-6676

Located on the banks of the Rogue River just across from Jot's Resort, the Rod N' Reel Restaurant has stood for 35 years serving some of the best food on the Oregon coast. The restaurant has been transformed recently into a new building that matches the environment of its surroundings with a waterfall cascading down a high cliff. The formal dining room sits at the bottom of this beautiful scene. It's a come-as-you-are place along with a "dressy" place; you can sit in a formal area, casual area, or pick the lounge. The restaurant is open for breakfast, lunch and dinner seven days a week with something for everyone including light entrees for light eaters and a special child's menu. Fresh Oregon seafoods are featured, along with steak. With full dinners, you receive homemade soup, relish tray, breadsticks, and a choice of salad and dressings. For 35 years the Rod N' Reel has been a best choice for dining — see you there!

GOLD BEACH TOUR

A wild ride up the famous Rogue River, a lunch at one of the most unique resorts in Oregon, and a scenic flight over land and sea. You won't have a more memorable day anywhere on the coast and you won't end up spending a fortune either. Having fun — that's what this tour is all about!

TIME	PLACE	DESCRIPTION	HOW TO FIND IN BOOK
Breakfast	Tobey's Bakery	Best breakfast and coffee	Gold Beach/Bakery
A.M.	Jerry's Rogue Jets or Rogue River Mail Boats	Best cruise	Gold Beach/Attractions
Lunch	TuTuTum Lodge	Best lunch and resort	Gold Beach/Accommodations
P.M.	Pacific Air Service	Best scenic flight	Gold Beach/Attractions
P.M.	Rogue River Myrtlewood	Best gifts	Gold Beach/Gifts
Dinner	Jot's Resort and Restaurant	Best resort and restaurant	Gold Beach/Resort

BROOKINGS / HARBOR

ABOUT BROOKINGS / HARBOR

When you visit Brookings and Harbor, you can immediately see why these small, friendly communities are called the Southern Gateway to Beautiful Oregon. Here in the extreme southwestern tip of the state, you can see some of the most rugged and beautiful coastal scenery in the world. Quietly nestled in a picturesque coastal plain with the deep blue Pacific Ocean to the west and high coastal range to the east, and the mouth of the Chetco River linking the two worlds, Brookings and Harbor offer a little bit of everything for everyone.

Visiting Brookings and Harbor in Curry County, you will enjoy the unusual mild climate with temperatures averaging between 50 to 70 degrees the year 'round. Cool sea breezes in the summer and mild, frostfree winters. The climate and soil are perfect for some of the most beautiful varieties of flowers and shrubs that bloom throughout the year. You can see as many as 50 or more flowers blooming in the heart of winter, such as Acacia, broom, camellias, callalilies, fuchsias, geraniums, heather, roses, primroses, and pansies. There are also edible wild berries that grow in abundance. In fact, 90% of all Easter lilies in the United States come from this area. The lily crop alone produces around $4,000,000 annually and provides work for many people. The Easter lily blooms in June and July, and the bulbs are sent to florists who pot them for Easter blooming.

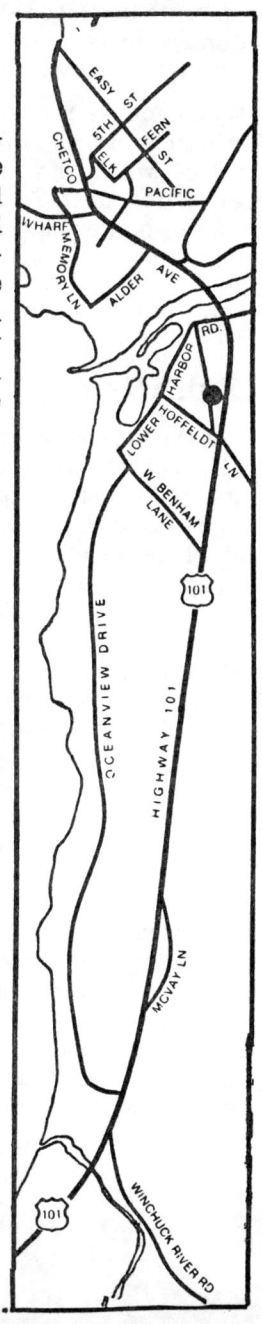

Dotting the nearby fields and hills, cattle and sheep are a great part of the agriculture in the area. You'll find more sheep than cows because 90% of all wool sold to the papermaking industry for felt comes from Curry County's sheep because of the wool's special felting quality.

When you want to spend your time in town, the Brookings/Harbor community offers you a great wealth of fun, gifts and services, whether you need a special birthday present, lodging or a fine meal. You'll find locals who are very friendly and who will make that extra effort to make your stay, meal or finding that gift more enjoyable. The saying goes in these parts that the locals are truly friends whether you live next door or not.

ATTRACTIONS

For the recreation enthusiast, Brookings and Harbor are virtually a nature lover's paradise. You can enjoy ocean or fresh water fishing, boating from the calmest, safest bar along the Oregon Coast, surfing, skin diving, beachcoming, picnicking and whale watching. The fishing enthusiasts will find excellent streams just a short distance from Brookings/Harbor. The Chetco, Winchuck, Smith, Rogue, Pistol, Elk and Sixes Rivers offer the sportsman trout in the spring and steelhead and salmon during the fall runs. For posterity or when you get hungry, there are also facilities where you can have what you catch custom canned or smoked. On the other hand, ocean fishermen can explore the challenge of the Pacific by surf casting or rock fishing right along the coast. If you choose, you can launch your own boat from a launching ramp provided by the Port of Brookings or charter a boat in season for salmon and year 'round bottom fishing. All the boating supplies you need are there near the ramp at the small boat basin at the mouth of the Chetco River. Again, this is the calmest, safest bar on the Oregon Coast — from this bar, charter and sports boats rarely miss a trip. For the beachcomber, the clean sandy beaches offer unlimited treasures from the deep — shells, driftwood, small marine life, and sometimes semi-precious stones. You can also enjoy the larger marine life by watching whales roll and spout off the coast.

BED AND BREAKFAST

HOLMES SEACOVE BED AND BREAKFAST
17350 Holmes Drive
Brookings, Oregon 97415
503-469-3025 for reservations

If you enjoy comfort like that of your own home, then just two miles north of Brookings turn left on Dawson Road and enjoy the scenic beauty of the Oregon coast as well. Among fir trees stunted from the winter winds you'll see an abundance of wild blackberries, azaleas, myrtle and violets as you meander to Holmes Drive and the seclusion and friendliness of your hosts Jack and Lorene at Holmes Seacove with its spectacular view of the mighty Pacific. For accommodations, they have a separate and new guest cottage or two beautiful suites on the lower level below their home. All rooms have fantastic, breathtaking views of the ocean and each suite has a queen sized bed, bath, refrigerator, color TV and enough room in which to kick back and enjoy the comfort. A delicious continental breakfast will be served in your room between the hours of 7-9:30am. The Holmes have found the ideal place to live and they share it with many visitors. You can stroll through the trees down the winding trail for a walk on the beach or to the private picnic area complete with tables by a small, bubbling stream. For the comfort of your own home along with one of the best views in the world, try this best choice — Holmes Seacove Bed and Breakfast in Brookings.

(See special invitation in Appendix.)

SEADREAMER INN
(Bed and Breakfast)
15167 McVay Lane
Brookings, Oregon 97415
(4 miles south of Brookings,
off Highway 101 onto McVay Lane)
For reservations, phone 503-469-6629

You can relax in luxury at the Seadreamer Inn in a large brass bed fitted with a lamb's wool mattress pad and plush comforter for the ultimate in restful sleep, and tastefully decorated with antique furnishings. Your hosts, Bob and Judy Blair, will serve you complimentary sherry and appetizers of homesmoked salmon that they catch and smoke themselves.

Sea Dreamer Inn was named for Bob and Judy's sailboat, the Seadreamer, a 30 foot Bahama Islander docked in the port of Brookings. The inn was built of redwood in 1912 and the Blair's have made application to be included in the national register of historical places. Situated among pines, fruit trees and year 'round blooming flowers, you have a panoramic view of Oregon's famous lily fields and the sea. Breakfast is a hearty, gourmet delight and served in the inn's formal dining room. On a lucky morning, you may be served aebleskiver, a Danish pancake in the shape of a ball that is unusually good, or a large German apple pancake that takes up two giant plates. Rates are very reasonable, perfect for many conferences or family reunions. Call or write for a brochure. A best choice for relaxing luxury — the Seadreamer Inn in Brookings.

(See special invitation in Appendix.)

THE WARD HOUSE
516 Redwood Street
P.O. Box 86
Brookings, Oregon 97415
503-469-5557 for reservations

If you enjoy friendly people and old-world charm, this vintage home overlooking the ocean in downtown Brookings is just what you are looking for. It was built in 1917 by a wealthy lumberman and restored by your hosts Shell and Gro Lent. You see, Gro is a very modern lady that has that special European style in cooking and comfort. The house is available for the guests with spacious living room, dining room, protected sun deck, newly installed hot tub and sauna, TVs and VCR. The bedrooms are upstairs, furnished with queen size beds and a comfortable sitting area. Shell and Gro, along with their daughter, Lisa, have created a homelike atmosphere to make your stay very restful and relaxing in their tastefully furnished house. As tradition has it, on a normal morning you can expect such things as Eggs Benedict, heart-shaped Norwegian waffles, and freshly baked breads. All their sauces and jams are homemade and Gro goes to extremes to make sure you love the food she serves. Just one block from Highway 101, The Ward House is conveniently located within walking distance of parks, the Chetco River, the ocean, stores and restaurants. Gro has a creative side and spends time making many handcrafted items which are unique and wonderful ways to remember your stay in such a beautiful place. A best choice for old-world charm and a warm, friendly, family-like atmosphere — The Ward House bed and breakfast in Brookings.

(See special invitation in Appendix.)

BOAT AND FISHING OUTFITTERS

LEO'S SPORTHAVEN MARINA AND SPORTHAVEN ANNEX
Located in the heart of the Brookings port
Harbor Drive
Harbor, Oregon (Brookings)
503-469-3301

If you are wishin' to go fishin', Leo's Sporthaven Marina is a must. Leo and Maxine Shurtleff have been in the same location for 26 years. They know the area and can give you expert advice on where to make your catch. Leo's Marina has everything you need for year 'round fishing in fishing supplies, bait, tackle, rods, outdoor wear and raingear. Their son, Dee, manages the business and is an artist as well. Oil paintings of Pacific Ocean fish are his specialty and many of his paintings are hanging in the store. Maxine is also an artist. Contact Leo's Sporthaven Marina for guided trips for ocean fishing, salmon or bottom fish, or for trips on any of the many rivers in the area. You can also rent ocean tackle, nets and crab rings.

The Sporthaven Annex is run by son Larry Shurtleff. The Annex handles a wide range of marine supplies and accessories. Sports Haven Annex is an authorized dealer for Evinrud and OMC Stearn Drive and has factory trained mechanics. They also repair any inboard/outboard motors. They carry just about everything pertaining to boats, compasses, all kinds of boat hardware, electronics and life jackets. Visit the Sporthaven Marina and the Sporthaven Annex and meet the fishing family and best choices for your wishes to come true — Leo, Maxine, Dee and Larry.

EVENTS

Nearly all year long you'll be able to enjoy the warmth and spirit of several community festivals hosted by the citizens of Brookings and Harbor.

STEELHEAD DERBY

The fun starts in January with the Steelhead Derby at Smith River. Contests and fishy fun are in order at this festival.

BEACHCOMBER'S FESTIVAL

Every year in mid-March, beautiful exhibits, demonstrations, displays, slide shows and contests of various categories of art created from driftwood or other beachcombing material makes Brookings/Harbor the charming pilgrimmage for beachcombers and artists of all ages.

AZALEA FESTIVAL

This festival is held every May on Memorial Day weekend. Parades, seafood, beef barbecues, flower and art shows, and square dancing are but a few of the fun activities of this festival. The Azalea Festival Queen and her court reign over festivities, most of which take place among the beautiful blooms at Azalea State Park.

FOURTH OF JULY CELEBRATION

This festival for our nation's birthday centers most of its events at the Port of Brookings. Festivities vary from year to year and there is always a spectacular fireworks display.

FISHERMAN'S CLINIC AND SPORTS SHOW

A fisherman's dream come true, this is definitely a show for fishermen of all ages. Held annually during late summer and early fall, classes feature ocean and river techniques for fishing salmon and steelhead for the old pro and novice. There are also interesting factory and dealer displays and booths as well as door prizes, raffles, fishing derbies, precision casting contests and fish fries.

FISHING GUIDE SERVICE

PERRY'S CHETCO RIVER LODGE
97666 North Bank Chetco River Road
Brookings, Oregon
For reservations, phone 503-469-4773

An experience of a lifetime — fishing with record holding professional guides on the many great rivers located just minutes from one of the best full service fishing lodges anywhere. Perry's Chetco River Lodge has a setting that is perfect, with tall firs and lush greenery like none other in the world. This area of southern Oregon coast is called the "banana belt" by the locals because of the mild climate with temperatures ranging around 60 degrees all winter. When I visited the lodge, it was early December and the temperature outside was 65 degrees and sunny. The lodge is full service, and that is an understatement, with lodging, gourmet meals prepared by a certified chef and all the tackle needed, with a top guide to get you on the river to catch your choice of steelhead, salmon or trout. The lodge is open year 'round because something is always biting and the guides pick the choicest river offering the best results. And what a choice! With the Chetco, the famous Rogue, Smith, Elk and Sixes Rivers all within minutes of the lodge, your guides have some of the best choices in the world. The owners of this unique lodge are Val Perry and Corky Iwalsaki, both avid sportsmen and knowledgeable hosts. The dinner meal is a gourmet's delight — six courses altogether. All the food is exceptional and you won't forget the fishing or the food for many years once you've tried the lodge. For a best choice, call Perry's Chetco River Lodge — it is an adventure of a lifetime.

GIFTS

COUNTRY ORIGINALS
Brookings Harbor Shopping Center
(off Hwy 101, Harbor)
Brookings, Oregon
503-469-6231

Open: 9:30-5:30 Mon thru Sat

A gift shop that is more than fun to browse through, Country Originals has some of the friendliest people you'll meet in Brookings. They are Jim and Joyce Milner, with their daughter, Teri. They have been operating Country Originals for six years and have hundreds of unique items in their shop. In fact, the Milner's say there is not one practical item — they are all for fun and for the joy of giving. With special care, Joyce or Teri would love to help you choose a doll, toy, stuffed animal, mechanical toy, collectible or something special to decorate your home. Or you can just browse through the many ceramics, candles, collectible dolls and bears, kitchen items, and decorative items for all rooms in the house. For the visitors wanting a souvenir, they have just what you are looking for. The shop specializes in a large inventory of infant and children's clothes with something for everyone, even newborns. So, if you are looking for a friendly, fun place to shop for unique gift items, try this best choice — Country Originals in the Brookings Harbor Shopping Center, Brookings, Oreogn.

(See special invitation in Appendix.)

DRIFTWOOD, ETC.
15850 Highway 101
(In the Treasure Harbor Village,
look for large landlocked ship)
Brookings, Oregon
503-469-4801

Open: 10-5 Mon thru Sat

Offering beauty and humor from the sea with an eye for the creative, Ray and Patsy Short are the "crafty folks" at Driftwood, Etc. Specialists in beachcombing, they craft clocks, tables, paintings, and many unique items from the driftwood and shells that they gather, clean and polish. They are always happy to share their beachbcoming spots with you as well as helping you with your do-it-yourself projects. Along with the many craft and gift items, Ray and Patsy handle all necessary supplies to create your own ideas, including a complete selection of quartz clock works and weather instruments, polish and finishes, tools and glue. While you are there, be sure to see their display of unique items they have collected from the beach. Their prices are fair and they will ship anywhere. They have been located for three years in the Treasure Harbor Village, 1½ miles south of the bridge over the Chetco River at Brookings. Look for the landlocked boat that looks just like a giant ark. A best choice for humor, beauty and fun from the sea — Driftwood, Etc.

(See special invitation in Appendix.)

GULLEY'S MYRTLEWOOD PRODUCTS
16039 Highway 101 South
(Just off Hwy 101, next to Bimore Gas,
One mile south of Brookings)
P.O. Box 312
Harbor (Brookings), Oregon
503-469-2012

Ross and Helen Gulley specialize in myrtlewood. They have hundreds of items that are all nicely displayed in their store. Custom-designed myrtlewood rockers, patterned from a rocker Abe Lincoln used, made larger and beautifully upholstered, is part of their unique handiwork. There are bowls, salt and pepper shakers, trays, mirrors, natural-finish wall mounted clocks, mantel clocks and even clocks shaped like Oregon. You will also find plaques of all sizes, hand-painted with coastal and country scenes, cutting boards, refrigerator magnets, table boxes, carvings, jewelry, and something for everyone. Everything is made of myrtlewood and prices are very reasonable. The Gulleys have lived in Brookings for 30 years and are very respected by the local people for their volunteer work. Ross was a volunteer fireman for 25 years and taught elementary school in Brookings for 16 years. Helen taught elementary and primary school for over 26 years in Brookings. Both Ross and Helen helped reorganize the first ambulance service on the Southern Oregon Coast and were involved in that service for 13 years. The Gulleys are special people, both craftsmen and volunteers for services that are much needed. Stop in, give them a friendly "hi" and check their low, low prices. They accept Visa and Mastercharge for your convenience. A best choice for a huge selection in handcrafted myrtlewood — Gulley's Myrtlewood Products in Brookings.

STATELINE MYRTLEWOOD
14377 Highway 101A South
(just 25 feet across the
southern Oregon border)
Brookings, Oregon
503-469-2307

Open: 8:30-5:30 seven days a week

As you drive along scenic Highway 101 in northern California, you abruptly see the big green sign welcoming you to Oregon. Slow down, not because the speed limit is different but because just 25 feet across the border a welcoming committee is ready to greet you to our beautiful state. The unofficial committee is the staff and management of Stateline Myrtlewood. This store is one of the best Oregon has to offer. As noted in its name, it carries one of the most beautiful products our state is famous for — myrtlewood. Inside the store, along with friendly information and directions, you'll find a beautiful array of hand-turned myrtlewood bowls, clocks, tables, carved items and more. Along with myrtlewood, there is a fantastic selection of finer gifts, gifts from and about Oregon in wonderful displays that keep the whole family interested. Tours of the factory are happily given by the staff and many tour groups enjoy this exciting stop. The owners, John and Tricia Shreck, are always there to help you and wish you well on your journey ahead along Oregon's rugged coastline. A welcoming committee and a best choice — Stateline Myrtlewood, just 25 feet across the southern border on Highway 101 in Oregon.

(See special invitation in Appendix.)

PARKS

AZALEA STATE PARK

This is one of the loveliest parks you'll ever see. On this 76 acre natural park, you can enjoy not only the peace and serenity of nature, but also its dazzling scents and colors. Wild azaleas abound and are hundreds of years old. There are also the rare weeping spruce trees in the park. Modern picnic facilities, electric stoves and sinks are available.

BOARDMAN STATE PARK

Twelve miles north of Brookings along breathtaking views of the Pacific, the park has three picnic areas as well as many view points where visitors can park their cars and take pictures or just enjoy the salt air of the coast. There are also many trails that lead from the highway down to the beach all along the park.

HARRIS BEACH STATE PARK

This park's 141 acres are composed of two sections. One is an overnight camp with a total of 150 spaces, 33 of which have complete trailor hookups, running water, public bath houses and sanitary facilties. The other section is on the shore where sandy beaches, rocky outcroppings, driftwood and trickling streams fill the senses. A shower for bathers, picnic tables, running water, wood fireplaces and sanitary facilities are also provided and the park is open all year 'round.

LOEB STATE PARK

Located eight miles east on the Chetco River, there are 320 acres of beautiful stands of virgin myrtle trees with swimming, fishing, camping and picnic facilities. Huge old myrtle trees, secluded beaches and unpolluted water make Loeb State Park a delightful place to visit for you and your family.

LONE RANCH STATE PARK

A lonely ranch used to stand on this beautiful spot overlooking a beach that is especially breathtaking in early morning or at sunset. You'll wonder why the rancher ever left. The park has plenty of parking and bathroom facilities, but it is for day use only, with picnic tables and barbecue pits provided.

RESTAURANTS

SANDY'S COUNTRY KITCHEN
(Brookings Harbor Shopping Center)
Brookings, Oregon
503-469-3355

Winter hours: 6am-7pm Mon thru Sat, 6-6 Sun
Summer hours: 6am-8pm, seven days a week

For family style dining at its best and friendly service, come in and meet native Oregonians and owners Sandy and Keith Hislop at Sandy's Country Kitchen. They feature daily specials for breakfast, lunch and dinner made with the freshest and highest quality ingredients. For breakfast, try their famous omelettes and for a special treat, try the kitchen omelette which has everything in it but the kitchen sink, with real cheeses, ham, mushrooms, and green pepper along with your choice of freshly made hashbrowns, toast or pancakes. For a quick breakfast, try a freshly baked, gooey cinnamon roll with coffee — you'll love it! For lunch, a suggestion would be to start out with a delicious bowl of clam chowder, freshly made everyday, and full of clams. Then have fish and chips made with red snapper lightly breaded and a large order of golden fries. Or you might choose one of the large varieties of sandwiches featured. As a suggestion for dinner, you can choose a steak freshly cut in Sandy's kitchen or your favorite seafoods. A best choice for family fare and something for everyone with high quality and low prices — Sandy's Country Kitchen, located in Brookings Harbor Shopping Center.

(See special invitation in Appendix.)

SHARON'S PELICAN BAY RESTAURANT AND SEAFOODS
(Located on the harbor)
16403 Lower Harbor Road
Brookings, Oregon
503-469-7971

If you are looking for a restaurant where locals eat for "downhome cooking" at bargain prices, try Sharon's Pelican Bay Restaurant. The owner, Sharon Scritchfield, opens at 5 am each day except Sunday, with hearty breakfasts such as a large serving of homemade biscuits and gravy for just $1 (as of this writing), omelettes or huge hotcakes served on a platter. A suggestion for lunch may be fish and chips made with fresh snapper and a bountiful side of curly fries. All sauces are homemade and all fish is fresh daily. For dessert, there is always fresh homemade pies, either fruit or creams. Come in and meet Sharon and her daughter, Sherry, and rub shoulders with the local fishermen and loggers having real country cooking.

Adjoining the restaurant is a fresh fish market open 9 am to 6 pm Monday through Saturday, where you can buy fresh snapper, sole, cod, salmon, oysters, shrimp, batter mixes, and sauces. Local Dungennes crab is cooked on the premises. You'll also find the best shrimp cocktail you've ever had at a very reasonable price, and soft drinks to go. For a best choice for homecooked food, fresh seafood and low prices — come share a bench at Sharon's Pelican Bay Restaurant, on the harbor in Brookings.

THE TEA ROOM CAFE
434 Redwood Street
(The Abbey Mall)
Brookings, Oregon
503-469-7240

Summer hours: 7am-5pm Mon-Sat
Winter hours: 7am-4pm Mon-Sat

While you are in downtown Brookings, dine at The Tea Room Cafe and you'll go back many times for the superb food and service. Ron and France Alden and daughter, Kim, are beaming with personality and delight in preparing one of their Ginger Chicken salads made from a secret recipe, or one of Ron's supreme sandwiches which are built not made, using cracked wheat bread made exclusively for them by the Whirling Pin Bakery in Brookings. The sandwich includes ham, turkey, lettuce, tomatoes, Swiss cheese, avocado and bacon. You'll find your favorite beverages, including gourmet coffees, expresso, capuccino and cafe mocha; a long list of specialties in herbal teas; Palmasan wines, Chablis, rose and burgundy; and beer. As a suggestion, try a Smoothy, a blend of fruit juice and yogurt, or one of the many exotic juices they carry like papaya and guava. Of course, you can order your favorite and they'll have it, too. Along with the variety of great sandwiches, you can enjoy a bowl of homemade soup or chili made fresh daily, and a delicious dessert. Ron and France also serve a variety of breakfast items like Belgium waffles, fresh cinnamon rolls, croissants, homemade biscuits, or bacon, eggs and hashbrowns. The Tea Room is a best choice. Even the seagulls will attest to that. They feed on all the bread left over at the end of the day.

(See special invitation in Appendix.)

RESTAURANT/BAKERY

TROVAA/TEN'S
Off Highway 101, north end of Brookings
Across from Spindrift Motel
Brookings, Oregon
503-469-7020

Bill and Evelyn Davies believe in providing homemade, wholesome bakery breakfast and lunch foods at prices everyone can afford. Everything here is made fresh from scratch, daily: hearty breads like wheat, rye and white; great cinnamon rolls; banana nut loaves; puffy banana and raisin muffins using secret family recipes. There are lots of different types of cookies, doughnuts, maple bars and croissants. For breakfast, have some coffee, juice and a helping of their hearty potato pancakes or waffles. For lunch, enjoy one the sandwiches featuring a choice of top grade deli meats served on fresh slabs of homemade bread. There are hearty, homemade soups like clam chowder, navy bean or vegetable to choose from, plus a selection of lighter salad offerings. The cabbage rolls are great, a super blend of ground beef and rice rolled into tender cabbage leaves. Coffee, tea, hot cocoa and soft drinks are available, plus be sure to check on the daily lunch specials; Monday and Wednesday, the bakery serves family style portions of chicken and dumplings. So when you want homestyle, yummy bakery goods, or you just want to enjoy a relaxing breakfast or lunch at reasonable prices, this is the place to head for in Brookings.

(See special invitation in Appendix.)

SPORTING GOODS

BROOKINGS SPORTS UNLIMITED
625 Chetco Avenue
Brookings, Oregon
503-469-4012

Open: 9-6 Mon-Sat, 10-5 Sun

In the heart of downtown Brookings is Sports Unlimited, the store that has everything for the sportsman and men's clothing. Lew and Dolores Sapp, the owners, have imported thick wool coats from Sweden and sell them at fantastic prices. They also have wool shirts and jackets, chamois shirts, Levis, gloves, men's and women's outdoor rain clothing, hip boots, work boots and hiking boots, and athletic shoes. You will also find Army surplus from both the United States and Scandinavian countries, military surplus and all kinds of camping gear. A complete line of fishing and hunting supplies includes license and tags, guns such as Weatherby, Ruger, Browning and others, ammo, a large variety of knives and your every fishing need — rods, reels, bait, crabbing supplies and rain accessories. For team sports, you'll find all sorts of athletic items including clothing and shoes for football, basketball, and baseball. They also have beach and outdoor wear. Brookings Sports Unlimited is a large store and truly has everything for any sport. Lew and Dolores and their friendly staff know the area and can help you find the best spots for fishing or hunting. They are very happy to give you that kind of information. For a best choice for all your sporting needs in Brookings, try Brookings Sports Unlimited.

(See special invitation in Appendix.)

BROOKINGS TOUR

Tour a myrtlewood factory, stroll on a lonely beach, enjoy a delicious meal or just see the flowers blooming all year. Brookings has something for everyone. Some of the best fishing rivers in the world are within minutes of here. Your whole family is sure to have fun in Brookings.

TIME	PLACE	DESCRIPTION	HOW TO FIND IN BOOK
Breakfast	The Tea Room Cafe	Best breakfast	Brookings/Restaurants
A.M.	Brookings Sports Unlimited	Best sporting goods	Brookings/Sporting Goods
A.M.	Driftwood, Etc.	Best gifts from the sea	Brookings/Gifts
A.M.	Stateline Myrtlewood	Best myrtlewood factory & gifts	Brookings/Gifts
A.M.	Gulley's Myrtlewood	Best myrtlewood	Brookings/Gifts
Lunch	Sandy's Country Kitchen	Best lunch	Brookings/Restaurants
P.M.	Country Originals	Best gifts	Brookings/Gifts
P.M.	Leo's Sporthaven Marine & Sporthaven Annex	Best fishing information	Brookings/Boat and Fishing Outfitters
Snack	Sharon's Pelican Bay Restaurant & Seafood	Best fresh seafood	Brookings/Restaurants
P.M.	Beach at Lone Ranch State Park	Best sunsets	Brookings/Parks

APPENDIX

You are cordially invited to
Lindstrom's Danish Maid Bakery
1132 Commercial St., Astoria, Oregon
Buy two loaves of our fresh bread and receive one loaf free.
Offer good thru 1988.

--- ✂ --- *CUT HERE*

You are cordially invited to Young World
1144 Commercial St., Astoria, Oregon
Receive $2 off any $20 purchase or more.
Not valid on sale priced merchandise.
Offer good thru 1988.

--- ✂ --- *CUT HERE*

You are cordially invited to Nordic Butik
211 12th Street, Astoria, Oregon
Receive a free pattern with any $5 purchase or more.
Offer good thru 1988.

--- ✂ --- *CUT HERE*

You are cordially invited to
Captain Fox's Marketplace Restaurant and General Store
146 11th Street, Astoria, Oregon
Seniors receive 10% off any lunch or dinner purchased.
Offer good thru 1988.

You are cordially invited to Josephson's Smokehouse and Dock
106 Marine Drive, Astoria, Oregon
Receive 10% off any purchase of Josephson's products.
Offer good thru 1988.

---- CUT HERE ----

You are cordially invited to Anita's Corner
416 Broadway, Seaside, Oregon
Receive 10% off on any purchase.
Not valid with any other discount.
Offer good thru 1988.

---- CUT HERE ----

You are cordially invited to Lynn's Art Studio
317 S. Columbia, Seaside, Oregon
50% off frames on any commissioned art sale.
Offer good thru 1988.

---- CUT HERE ----

You are cordially invited to Phillips Candies
217 Broadway, Seaside, Oregon
Receive ½ pound of taffy free with any one pound purchase.
Offer good thru 1988.

---- CUT HERE ----

You are cordially invited to Columbia Chocolates by Mordens
Seaside, Oregon
Receive a free, hand-dipped chocolate candy of your choice.
One per customer, please. No purchase necessary.
Offer good thru 1988.

You are cordially invited to Mrs. Claus' Emporium
8 North Downing Street, Seaside, Oregon
Present this invitation to receive a gift
with any $20 purchase or more.
Offer good thru 1988.

---- ✂ ---- CUT HERE

You are cordially invited to Oregon Only
3111 Highway 101 North Gearhart, Seaside, Oregon
Receive 10% off on any $25.00 purchase or more.
Offer good thru 1988.

---- ✂ ---- CUT HERE

You are cordially invited to Seaside Agate Shop
408 Broadway, Seaside, Oregon
Receive 10% off any purchase of $20.00 or more.
Offer good thru 1988.

---- ✂ ---- CUT HERE

You are cordially invited to Royale Motel
531 Avenue A, Seaside, Oregon
Free! One night with any two nights or more paid stay.
Valid October thru March excluding weekends and holidays.
Not valid with commercial rates. Offer good thru 1988.

---- ✂ ---- CUT HERE

You are cordially invited to The Light House Restaurant
220 Avenue U, Seaside, Oregon
Receive a free dish of ice cream with
Each dinner when ordering two or more dinners.
Valid winter and summer. Offer good thru 1988.

You are cordially invited to Lumpy's Fishworks Restaurant
104 Broadway, Seaside, Oregon
Receive 10% off on two meals or more.
Not valid May thru September. Offer good thru 1988.

--- ✂ --- *CUT HERE*

You are cordially invited to Tolovana Inn, Cannon Beach, Oregon
Receive your second night's lodging free
on purchase of first night's lodging.
Valid Oct. 1-May 30 only; not valid school spring vacation,
all holidays or three day holiday weekends.
On available space only. Offer good thru 1988.

--- ✂ --- *CUT HERE*

You are cordially invited to Lillie's Antiques
179 Chisana Street,, Cannon Beach, Oregon
Receive 10% off any purchase of $10 or more.
Not valid with any other discounts.
Offer good thru 1988.

--- ✂ --- *CUT HERE*

You are cordially invited to Bruce's Candy Kitchen
256 N. Hemlock, Cannon Beach, Oregon
Receive ¼ pound salt water taffy free
With any $10 purchase. Offer good thru 1988.

--- ✂ --- *CUT HERE*

You are cordially invited to Grandma Lee's Chowder House
1235 S. Hemlock, Cannon Beach, Oregon
Receive a free cup of our clam chowder
With any two or more dinners purchased.
Offer good thru 1988.

You are cordially invited to The Whaler Restaurant
200 Hemlock, Cannon Beach, Oregon
Receive free dessert with full dinner purchase.
Good up to a party of four.
Offer good thru 1988.

------------------ ✂ ------------------ CUT HERE

You are cordially invited to Geppetto's Toy Shoppe
247 N. Hemlock, Cannon Beach, Oregon
Receive 10% off on any purchase.
Offer good thru 1988.

------------------ ✂ ------------------ CUT HERE

You are cordially invited to Nehalem Antiques
Highway 101, Nehalem, Oregon
Receive 10% off on any purchase of $10 or more.
Not valid with any other discount.
Offer good thru 1988.

------------------ ✂ ------------------ CUT HERE

You are cordially invited to The Captain's Lady Bed and Breakfast
Rockaway Beach, Oregon
Receive $5 off with any two night's stay or more
Offer good thru 1988.

------------------ ✂ ------------------ CUT HERE

You are cordially invited to Shellay Gift Shop
Rockaway Beach, Oregon
Receive a free shell necklace dipped in real gold
With $5 purchase or more. Not valid with any other offer.
Offer good thru 1988.

Appendix—Invitations   271

You are cordially invited to The Clothes Hanger
Rockaway Beach, Oregon
Receive 10% off with any $10 purchase.
Not valid with any other discount.
Offer good thru 1988.

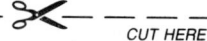

You are cordially invited to Bay Front Bakery and Deli
Highway 101, Garibaldi, Oregon
Receive a free cup of coffee with a $5 purchase or more.
Up to two free cups per invitation.
Not valid with any other offer. Good thru 1988.

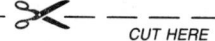

You are cordially invited to Virginia's Gifts
Highway 101, Garibaldi, Oregon
Receive a gift with any $10 purchase or more.
Offer good thru 1988.

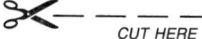

You are cordially invited to Blue Heron French Cheese Factory
Highway 101, one mile north of Tillamook, Oregon
Receive free a small box of flavored popcorn
With any purchase of our famous Brie cheese.
Offer good thru 1988.

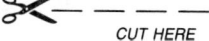

You are cordially invited to Tillamook County Creamery Association
Highway 101, just two miles north of Tillamook, Oregon
Present this invitation for a free taste of cheese.
Offer good thru 1988.

You are cordially invited to Kitch-N-Ideas
113 Main, Tillamook, Oregon
Present this invitation for a free cup of gourmet coffee.
With any $10 purchase or more, receive 5% off.
Not valid with any other discount. Offer good thru 1988.

---- CUT HERE ----

You are cordially invited to Hadley House Restaurant
2203 Third Street, Tillamook, Oregon
Receive 10% off one dinner meal
Listed under seafood or steak portion of the menu.
Not valid on specials or with any other discount.
Offer good thru 1988.

---- CUT HERE ----

You are cordially invited to House on the Hill Motel
Oceanside, Oregon
Receive $5 off on any two nights' stay or more.
Not valid with any other offer.
Offer good thru 1988.

---- CUT HERE ----

You are cordially invited to Sea Gypsy Motel
145 N.W. Inlet, Lincoln City, Oregon
Receive 30% off on room rate during midweek winter stays.
Holidays excluded. Call for more details.
Offer good thru 1988.

---- CUT HERE ----

You are cordially invited to Ocean Lake Studio Gallery
Lincoln City, Oregon
Become a registered collectible customer with your
First purchase & receive 10% discount on future purchases.
Offer good thru 1988.

You are cordially invited to The Christmas Cottage
3305 S.W. Highway 101, Lincoln City, Oregon
Receive a free Christmas ornament
with any $10.00 purchase or more.
Offer good thru 1988.

---- ✂ CUT HERE ----

You are cordially invited to Parlor Bears
1423 N.W. Highway 101, Lincoln City, Oregon
Receive a gift with any $5 purchase or more.
Offer good thru 1988.

---- ✂ CUT HERE ----

You are cordially invited to Seagull Factory
1020 S.E. Third Street, Lincoln City, Oregon
Receive 10% off on any concrete purchase.
Not valid with any other discount.
Offer good thru 1988.

---- ✂ CUT HERE ----

You are cordially invited to Lacey's Doll Museum
3400 N.E. Highway 101, Lincoln City, Oregon
Receive one free child's admission
with any two paid adult admissions.
Offer good thru 1988.

---- ✂ CUT HERE ----

You are cordially invited to Gallucci's Pizzeria
2845 N.W. Highway 101, Lincoln City, Oregon
Receive a free, large pitcher of soft drink
With any 15" or 19" pizza ordered.
Not valid with any other offer.
Offer good thru 1988.

Appendix—Invitations

You are cordially invited to Lil' Sambo Restaurant
3262 N.E. Highway 101, Lincoln City, Oregon
Receive a free gift with any two meals purchased.
Offer good thru 1988.

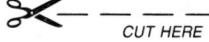
CUT HERE

You are cordially invited to The Shipwreck Cellars
3521 S.W. Highway 101
Present this invitation for a free taste of wine.
No purchase necessary. Must be 21 years or older.
Offer good thru 1988.

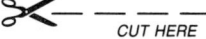
CUT HERE

You are cordially invited to Coast Roast Coffee Company
Gleneden Beach, Oregon
Receive a free cup of coffee with any purchase.
Offer good thru 1988.

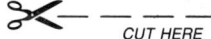
CUT HERE

You are cordially invited to Hot Pots Cookware
Gleneden Beach, Oregon
Receive 20% off any $25 purchase or more at regular price.
Offer good thru 1988.

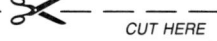
CUT HERE

You are cordially invited to Neptune's Reserve
South of Depoe Bay bridge, Depoe Bay, Oregon
Receive free packaging and shipping
with any canned fish gift pack purchase.
Offer good thru 1988.

You are cordially invited to Whale Cove Inn Restaurant and Motel
Depoe Bay, Oregon
Receive one free breakfast with one paid night's stay at the Inn.
Good up to four in each party.
Offer good thru 1988.

------------------------------ ✂ ------------------------------
CUT HERE

You are cordially invited to Embarcadero Dock
Newport, Oregon
Receive $5 off rental of bay boat.
Minimum 3 hours. Good year 'round except holidays.
Offer good thru 1988.

------------------------------ ✂ ------------------------------
CUT HERE

You are cordially invited to Ripley's Believe It or Not
Mariner Square, Newport, Oregon
Receive a free child's admission
With the purchase of two adult admissions or more.
Offer good thru 1988.

------------------------------ ✂ ------------------------------
CUT HERE

You are cordially invited to Undersea Gardens
Newport, Oregon
Receive one free child's admission
With the purchase of two or more adult admissions.
Offer good thru 1988.

------------------------------ ✂ ------------------------------
CUT HERE

You are cordially invited to The Wax Works
Mariner Square, Newport, Oregon
Receive one free child's admission
With the purchase of two or more adult admissions.
Offer good thru 1988.

Appendix—Invitations 281

You are cordially invited to Bridge Bakery
1006 S. Coast Highway, Newport, Oregon
Receive a free cup of coffee with any purchase.
Offer good thru 1988.

CUT HERE

You are cordially invited to Land's End Gifts
1610 N. Coast Hwy, Newport, Oregon
Receive 10% off any purchase at regular price.
Offer good thru 1988.

CUT HERE

You are cordially invited to The Whale's Tale
Bay Blvd. & Hubert, Newport, Oregon
Receive a free cup of our special coffee of the week
With any lunch or dinner purchased.
Valid up to a party of four. Good thru 1988.

CUT HERE

You are cordially invited to Cathy's Apparel
716 N.W. Beach Drive, Newport, Oregon
Receive 10% off any purchase.
Not valid on sale items. Offer good thru 1988.

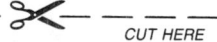
CUT HERE

You are cordially invited to Pacific Stitch
1620 N. Coast Highway, Newport, Oregon
Receive a free gift with any $10 purchase or more.
Offer good thru 1987.

You are cordially invited to Trident Antiques and Country Store
Downtown, Waldport, Oregon
Receive 10% off any brass or baskets.
Not valid with any other discount.
Offer good thru 1988.

--- ✂ CUT HERE ---

You are cordially invited to The Fireside Motel
Yachats, Oregon
Receive 10% off any stay Oct. 15 thru May.
Not valid holidays. Offer good thru 1988.

--- ✂ CUT HERE ---

You are cordially invited to Shamrock Lodgettes
Yachats, Oregon
Receive $5 off each nights' stay.
Valid Oct. 15-May 15; not valid on holidays.
Offer good thru 1988.

--- ✂ CUT HERE ---

You are cordially invited to The Tole Tree
Yachats, Oregon
Receive a free gift with any $10 purchase or more.
Not valid with any other offer. Good thru 1988.

--- ✂ CUT HERE ---

You are cordially invited to The Myrtletree Factory
Yachats, Oregon
Receive a gift with any $20 purchase or more.
Offer good thru 1988.

You are cordially invited to Driftwood Shores Surfside Resort
88416 First Avenue, Florence, Oregon
Receive 25% off normal room rate.
Valid October 1-May 1, excluding holidays and spring break.
Offer good thru 1988.

--------------------------- ✂ ---------------------------
CUT HERE

You are cordially invited to Sand Dunes Frontier
Receive a free round of Miniature Golf with the purchase of one round.
Not valid with any other offer.
Offer good thru 1988.

--------------------------- ✂ ---------------------------
CUT HERE

You are cordially invited to Incredible-Edible Oregon
1336 Bay Street, Florence, Oregon
Receive a free gift with any $20 purchase or more.
Offer good thru 1988.

--------------------------- ✂ ---------------------------
CUT HERE

You are cordially invited to The Quest for Gifts
1383 Bay Street, Florence, Oregon
Receive 10% off any purchase at regular price of $20 or more.
Offer good thru 1988.

--------------------------- ✂ ---------------------------
CUT HERE

You are cordially invited to Florence Golf Club
Highway 101, Florence, Oregon
Receive one free greens fee with purchase of one round at full rate.
Valid October 1-March 31.
Offer good thru 1988.

Appendix—Invitations

You are cordially invited to B.J.'s Ice Cream Parlour
2930 Hwy 101 North, Florence, Oregon
Receive 10 cents off any size cone.
Not valid with any other special
Offer good thru 1988.

--- ✂ CUT HERE ---

You are cordially invited to The Sportsman
Highway 101, Florence, Oregon
Receive 10% off any $20 purchase or more.
Not valid with any other discount.
Offer good thru 1988.

--- ✂ CUT HERE ---

You are cordially invited to J.R.'s For Gifts
417 Fir Avenue, Reedsport, Oregon
Receive a gift with any $20 purchase or more.
Offer good thru 1988.

--- ✂ CUT HERE ---

You are cordially invited to Pizza Ray's and Suzy's
2165 Winchester Avenue, Reedsport, Oregon
Receive a free small pitcher of soft drink
With any giant pizza ordered. Valid at all three locations.
Not valid with any other offer. Good thru 1988.

--- ✂ CUT HERE ---

You are cordially invited to Seafood Grotto Restaurant
8th & Broadway, Winchester Bay, Oregon
Purchase two meals or more and receive a free,
non-alcoholic beverage for each member of your party.
Offer good thru 1988.

Appendix—Invitations 289

You are cordially invited to Spinreel Dune Buggy Rentals
9122 Wildwood Drive, North Bend, Oregon
Receive 10% off rental price of total time out.
Valid October 15-March 15 only.
Offer good thru 1988.

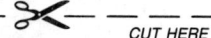

You are cordially invited to Myrtlewood Chalet
North Bend, Oregon
Receive 10% off with any purchase of $20 or more.
Not valid with any other discount.
Offer good thru 1988.

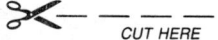

You are cordially invited to Kentuck Golf Course
475 Golf Course Lane, North Bend, Oregon
Receive 41 off on two greens' fees or more.
Offer good thru 1988.

You are cordially invited to Englewood Clock and Gift Shop
355 Anderson, Coos Bay, Oregon
Receive 10% off any purchase.
Not valid with any other discount.
Offer good thru 1988.

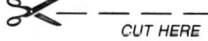

You are cordially invited to Hurry Back
Downtown, Charleston and Broadway, Coos Bay, Oregon
Receive 5% off any purchase of $2 or more.
Not valid with any other offer.
Offer good thru 1988.

Appendix—Invitations 291

You are cordially invited to Northwest Divers Supply
Highway 101, Coos Bay, Oregon
Receive $1 off any T-shirt in stock.
Not valid with any other offer.
Offer good thru 1988.

--- ✂ CUT HERE ---

You are cordially invited to Ocean Boulevard Seafoods
12855 Ocean Boulevard, Coos Bay, Oregon
Receive a free taste of our own smoked seafood.
Offer good thru 1988.

--- ✂ CUT HERE ---

You are cordially invited to Fiddlesticks Toys and Joys
Downtown, Coos Bay, Oregon
Receive a gift with any $10 purchase or more.
Offer good thru 1988.

--- ✂ CUT HERE ---

You are cordially invited to Portside Restaurant
Charleston, Oregon
Receive a free, nonalcoholic beverage with
Any two dinners or more. Up to a party of four.
Offer good thru 1988.

--- ✂ CUT HERE ---

You are cordially invited to The Inn at Face Rock
3225 Beach Loop Drive, Bandon, Oregon
Receive $5 off two nights' stay or more.
Not valid with any other offer.
Offer good thru 1988.

You are cordially invited to Prosper Village
Route 2, Box 1080, Bandon, Oregon 97411
Present this invitation to receive a free gift
with any one week stay or more.
Offer good thru 1988.

--- ✂ CUT HERE ---

You are cordially invited to
Wagon Wheel Antiques and Collectibles
1984 Sherman Ave., North Bend, Oregon
Receive a 10% discount on purchases over $10.
Offer good thru 1988.

--- ✂ CUT HERE ---

You are cordially invited to Frank's Flight Service
Highway 101, Bandon, Oregon
Receive $5 off the total cost of one hour's scenic flight or more.
Offer good thru 1988.

--- ✂ CUT HERE ---

You are cordially invited to West Coast Game Park
Route 1 Box 1330, Bandon, Oregon
Receive $1.00 off on any two adult admissions.
Not valid with any other offer.
Offer good thru 1988.

--- ✂ CUT HFRE ---

You are cordially invited to Craft Creatables
Highway 101 and 12th, Bandon, Oregon
Receive 10% off any purchase at regular price.
Offer good thru 1988.

You are cordially invited to The Country Merchant
Hwy 101 and Elmira, Bandon, Oregon
Present this invitation to receive a free cup of gourmet coffee.
No purchase necessary. Offer good thru 1988.

--- CUT HERE ---

You are cordially invited to Seagull Myrtlewood
Highway 101, Bandon, Oregon
Receive 5% off on any bowl purchased.
Offer good thru 1988.

--- CUT HERE ---

You are cordially invited to Ragtime Pizza
Bandon, Oregon
Receive a free small pitcher of soft drink with any
Family-sized pizza order. Not valid on take-outs.
Offer good thru 1988.

--- CUT HERE ---

You are cordially invited to The Bandon Boatworks Restaurant
275 Lincoln, Bandon, Oregon
Receive $1 off two meals or more.
Offer good thru 1988.

--- CUT HERE ---

You are cordially invited to Fraser's Restaurant
Highway 101 and 10th Street, Bandon, Oregon
Receive a free cup of coffee with any meal purchased.
Good for up to four members in a party.
Offer good thru 1988.

You are cordially invited to Bandon Fish Market
Boat Basin, Bandon, Oregon
Receive a free shrimp cocktail with any $15 purchase or more.
Offer good thru 1988.

---- ✂ CUT HERE ----

You are cordially invited to Black Horse Boutique
Second and Chicago Streets, Bandon, Oregon
Receive 20% off on any purchase.
Not valid on discounted or sale merchandise.
Offer good thru 1988.

---- ✂ CUT HERE ----

You are cordially invited to From Oregon With Love
Port Orford, Oregon
Receive 10% off any purchase.
Offer good thru 1988.

---- ✂ CUT HERE ----

You are cordially invited to The Wooden Nickel
Port Orford, Oregon
Receive a free, $3 retail gift with any $20 purchase or more.
Valid at Lincoln City store and Port Orford.
Offer good thru 1988.

---- ✂ CUT HERE ----

You are cordially invited to Jerry's Rogue Jets
Gold Beach, Oregon
Receive 10% off entire party. Not valid with any other discount.
Offer good thru 1988.

You are cordially invited to Rogue River Mail Boats
Gold Beach, Oregon
Receive a 10% discount on the whole party.
Not valid with any other discount.
Offer good thru 1988.

------------------------------ ✂ ------------------------------
CUT HERE

You are cordially invited to Tobey's Bakery
965 S. Ellensberg, Gold Beach, Oregon
Receive free beverage (coffee, tea or milk)
With this invitation. Valid up to
A party of four. Offer good thru 1988.

------------------------------ ✂ ------------------------------
CUT HERE

You are cordially invited to Rogue River Myrtlewood
710 N. Ellensburg, Gold Beach, Oregon
Receive 10% off on any purchase of $5 or more.
Not valid with any other discount.
Offer good thru 1988.

------------------------------ ✂ ------------------------------
CUT HERE

You are cordially invited to Jot's Resort
Gold Beach, Oregon
Receive one night's stay free with the purchase of two nights.
Valid November thru April. (Not valid any other time.)
Offer good thru 1988.

------------------------------ ✂ ------------------------------
CUT HERE

You are cordially invited to Holmes Seacove Bed and Breakfast
17350 Holmes Drive, Brookings, Oregon
Receive $5.00 off any two nights' stay or more.
Offer good thru 1988.

You are cordially invited to *Seadreamer Inn*
15167 McVay Lane, Brookings, Oregon
Receive $5.00 off any two night stay or more.
Offer good thru 1988.

--- ✂ CUT HERE ---

You are cordially invited to *The Ward House*
516 Redwood Street, Brookings, Oregon
Receive $5 off any two consecutive night stays.
Not valid in the month of August.
Offer good thru 1988.

--- ✂ CUT HERE ---

You are cordially invited to *Country Originals*
Brookings Harbor Shopping Center, Brookings, OR
Receive $2.00 off any $20.00 purchase or more.
Not valid on sale priced items.
Offer good thru 1988.

--- ✂ CUT HERE ---

You are cordially invited to *Driftwood, Etc.*
15850 Highway 101, Brookings, Oregon
Receive a free gift with any $10 purchase or more.
Offer good thru 1988.

--- ✂ CUT HERE ---

You are cordially invited to *Stateline Myrtlewood*
14377 Highway 101A South, Brookings, Oregon
Receive a free gift with any $10 purchase or more.
Offer good thru 1988.

You are cordially invited to Sandy's Country Kitchen
Brookings Harbor Shopping Center, Brookings, OR
Receive free large beverage with any two or more meals purchased.
Offer good thru 1988.

------------------------------ ✂ ------------------------------
CUT HERE

You are cordially invited to The Tea Room Cafe
434 Redwood Street, Brookings, Oregon
Receive a free cup of regular coffee with Any meal purchased.
Up to three in any party. Offer good thru 1988.

------------------------------ ✂ ------------------------------
CUT HERE

You are cordially invited to Trovaa/Ten's
Brookings, Oregon
Receive a free cup of coffee with any $2 purchase or more.
Up to four people in any party.
Offer good thru 1988.

------------------------------ ✂ ------------------------------
CUT HERE

You are cordially invited to Brookings Sports Unlimited
625 Chetco Avenue, Brookings, Oregon
Receive a free updated tide table book and fishing guide.
No purchase necessary. Offer good thru 1988.